LOCAL STUDIES
COLLECTION
MANAGEMENT

LOCAL STUDIES COLLECTION MANAGEMENT

Edited by
Michael Dewe

ASHGATE

Published by
Ashgate Publishing Limited
Gower House
Croft Road
Aldershot
Hants GU11 3HR
England

Ashgate Publishing Company
131 Main Street
Burlington, VT 05401-5600 USA

Ashgate website: http://www.ashgate.com

British Library Cataloguing in Publication Data
Local studies collection management
   1. Libraries - Great Britain -Special collections -
History, Local
I. Dewe, Michael, 1940-
026.9'41

Library of Congress Cataloging-in-Publication Data
Local studies collection management / edited by Michael Dewe.
      p. cm.
   Includes bibliographical references and index.
   ISBN 0-566-08365-5
     1. Libraries--Great Britain--Special collections--Local history materials. 2. Great Britain--History, Local--Bibliography--Methodology. 3. Libraries--Special collections--Local history materials. 4. Local history--Bibliography--Methodology. I. Dewe, Michael.

Z688.L8 L625 2001
026'.941--dc21

2001046269

ISBN 0 566 08365 5

Typeset in Century Old Style by IML Typographers, Birkenhead, Merseyside and printed and bound in Great Britain by TJ International Ltd., Padstow, Cornwall.

Contents

List of contributors

Jill Barber has been Education and Publications Officer, Westminster City Archives, since 1995. Prior to that she was Local Studies Librarian, London Borough of Barnet, and Open Learning Manager at the Department of Information and Library Studies, University of Wales, Aberystwyth. She has also researched sources for local and family history in Wales, trained to teach history at secondary level, and has been a school librarian and an assistant librarian in an education library.

Michael Dewe worked in a number of London public libraries from 1956 and from 1975 to 1996 he was a lecturer in the Department of Information and Library Studies, University of Wales, Aberystwyth. Amongst other topics, he taught a course on local studies librarianship, on which subject he has written widely. He has also written on the local history of Fulham and on popular music of the 1950s. He is a committee member of the Local Studies Group of the Library Association and its Welsh Branch, of which he was a founder member and chairman. He received the Dorothy McCulla Award for contributions to local studies librarianship in 1988.

Diana Dixon has worked at the College of Librarianship, Wales and the Department of Library and Information Studies at Loughborough University. Her particular research interest is access to English provincial newspapers and she has been involved with NEWSPLAN projects both in the East Midlands and in London and the South East. She is currently preparing an international bibliography of local studies librarianship.

Eileen Hume has been Local Studies and Archives Librarian, Knowsley MBC since 1997, having previously been with Liverpool John Moores University Learning Services and Wirral Library Services. Before a career change to librarianship in 1988, she was a schoolteacher. Winner of the Dorothy McCulla Award in 1999, she is a committee member of the Local Studies Group, North West Branch, and a member of the Earl Local Studies Task Group and the Society of Archivists. The digitization of local studies collections is a major interest and she has made many presentations on the subject at UK meetings and seminars.

Alice Lock is Local Studies Librarian at Tameside MBC. She has worked in Tameside Local Studies Library since 1976, occupying the post of librarian since 1980. She is a committee member of the North West Branch of the Local Studies Group and vice-chair of the national committee. She has published books and articles on various aspects of local history in Tameside and received the Dorothy McCulla Award in 2000.

Elizabeth A. Melrose has been Information Services Adviser, North Yorkshire County Library Service, since 1996. She has been consistently involved in information and local studies librarianship in public libraries over many years, as reference librarian for Lincolnshire County Library Service and principal librarian, Information Services, for North Yorkshire. She has the certificate in Regional and Local History, University of Hull, and was awarded the Library Association Centenary Medal. She is currently chairman of the LINC-NEWSPLAN and of the Local Studies Group of the Library Association.

Nicola Smith is Senior Lecturer, School of Information Management, University of Brighton. She has worked in government, academic and public libraries, spending seven years as local studies librarian in the London Borough of Southwark, and is currently researching the growth of local history collections in public libraries.

Acknowledgments

The editor wishes to acknowledge the persistence and hard work of the book's contributors, sometimes under difficult professional and personal circumstances, and also to thank local studies librarians for the information and assistance given to the book's various authors. The editor is also grateful for the support of Suzie Duke, commissioning editor at Ashgate, and for the facilities provided by the Department of Information and Library Studies, University of Wales, Aberystwyth to enable this publication to be brought to completion.

Preface

Modelled to some extent on J.L. Hobbs, *Local history and the library* (second edition, 1973), *Local studies collections: a manual* was published by Gower in 1987.[1] Following its appreciative reception, a complementary second volume was published in 1991 which covered topics not dealt with in the first volume, such as reminiscence work and the bibliography of local history, and extended the coverage of other subjects treated earlier: information technology, and preservation and conservation, for example. The two volumes also provided an introduction to various types of local material – books, pamphlets, maps, plans, newspapers, periodicals, prints and visual materials, including drawings and watercolours.

Taken together, the two volumes offered a comprehensive *vade mecum* for all those who work with local studies collections and much of the content of both volumes still remains useful. This new book, while to some extent consolidating the content of the earlier two volumes, does not attempt the same range of subject coverage or the same depth of treatment in every instance. Indeed, following the experience gained with Jill Barber in 1994 from the production of a distance learning module, *Local studies: sources and services*, for the Department of Information and Library Studies, University of Wales, Aberystwyth, the present work endeavours to present the subject field within a somewhat different framework and in a more concise fashion. Consequently, in this new work a small number of themes, such as management, information retrieval, marketing and enquiry work, are used as the basis for a description and discussion of the whole area of work with local studies collections at the start of this new millennium.

The aims of the earlier work, however, remain largely unchanged in this new version: to provide an overview account of local studies librarianship, to offer practical guidance on various aspects of local studies work, such as collection management, and to report on developing areas of local study activity – family history, the World Wide Web, and the digitization of local materials, for example.

While the editor has been largely responsible for the concept of this new version of *Local studies collections*, and for some of its content, the body of the book results from six other contributors who, with two exceptions, are working with local studies and archival collections in a variety of public library services in England. Because of this, and given the new constitutional arrangements in the UK, contributors have been asked to ensure that appropriate developments in Northern Ireland, Scotland and Wales are given every consideration. Chapter 2 also provides some basic information on resources for local studies in the Republic of Ireland.

Where information is available, contributors have also been asked to include reports on developments in local studies abroad, thus reflecting the international dimension of the earlier work. A final chapter provides a short general overview of the international local studies scene, as part of the background to a consideration of the future of local studies libraries and librarianship in the UK.

Local studies collections are usually seen as a public library specialism and this library context is reflected in the content of this book. However, in many instances local studies materials are increasingly housed alongside local archival collections and this situation has required some attention. Also given due weight is the relevance and relationship of the public library and its local collection to other libraries – national, academic and special – museums, and other relevant institutions and organizations, such as schools and local history societies. And such bodies should also find the contents of this publication of interest and value.

The 1987 and 1991 volumes of *Local studies collections* have been used by practising librarians, library school students and others for over a decade now, both in the UK and overseas. As a result, it is believed, they have been influential in fostering the professional development of local collection provision in many places both at home and abroad. The publisher, the editor and the contributors fully expect that the present volume will have a like professional impact and value and thus fulfil a similar role in the coming decade.

Of special importance also have been the UK Library Association's guidelines for local studies provision in public libraries, published in 1990.[2] A number of references to a new edition of the guidelines, to be published in 2002, are made in this book.

NOTES

1   Originally issued in 1987 as *A manual of local studies librarianship*, edited by M. Dewe, Aldershot: Gower.

2   Library Association Local Studies Group (1990), *Local studies libraries: Library Association guidelines for local studies provision in public libraries*, London: Library Association.

1 Local studies and libraries

Michael Dewe

In the UK, the term 'local studies' seems to have come into general currency in the library and information profession in the 1970s. Prior to this, the local studies collections in public libraries were known as local collections or as local history collections, the latter term reflecting a particular view as to their purpose in the provision of information about a given locality or community. The nature of the study of individual localities, however, has changed considerably in the last 50 or so years, as have the needs of the more varied group of people who now undertake it and, with the increasing range and availability of information and communications technology, the tools that they are able to utilize. These changes have to some extent been reflected in the professional terminology – 'local studies' rather than 'local history' – although this may not now be a sufficient response to the opportunities presented by the demand for sources and services to enable the study of the many aspects of a community.

LOCAL STUDIES AND LOCAL HISTORY

In education, 'local studies' is used to describe pupils acquiring and processing information about aspects of their area: for example, its people, industries and local authority; its services and public utilities; its animals and plants; its sport and recreational facilities. While these investigations, often involving fieldwork, may have a historical dimension to them, this local approach to learning may be used with other subjects, such as geography and science.[1]

In education 'local studies' shares subject matter and enquiry skills with 'local history', but the latter has a much clearer historical focus. 'Local studies', then, while not neglecting the past, seems more concerned with the current nature of a community; 'local history', as the term implies, is more often focused on the past than on present-day conditions. For librarians, and possibly teachers too, 'local studies' is seen as inclusive of local history and so the local collection should

1

support studies that look at the historical past, both distant and recent, or at current concerns in the community, such as local environmental issues, or plans for the future development of a locality – matters of interest to a wide audience.

Although librarians have adopted the term 'local studies', it has to be said that, in terms of both subject emphasis and the attitude of librarians, such collections continue to be seen largely as providing historical information about a community. Some continue to be designated local history collections, and this is still the term used in the USA, for example, for this type of library provision in public and other libraries.[2]

In the UK, this continuing historical emphasis in the public library local studies collection is increasingly encouraging an alliance with archival collections (and, to a lesser extent, museums), rather than with reference service and community and tourist information provision. Libraries, archives and museums in the same local authority department, especially in Wales, for example, and Re:source, the new Council for Museums, Libraries and Archives in England, may encourage further cooperation or integration. Ideally, local studies provision should perhaps encompass all of the above elements but in reality a variety of alliances and service mixes operate, there being no uniform pattern of UK provision. Given that local history is such a dominant aspect of local studies, this chapter briefly outlines the development of local history writing, the proposed outcome of much research activity.

DEVELOPMENT OF LOCAL HISTORY WRITING

There is a long record of local history research and writing in Britain, which is generally seen to have begun in the 15th century, although the contribution made in the mediaeval period, especially by church and monasteries, should not be overlooked.[3] However, the work of the Tudor topographers, such as John Leland and William Camden, and cartographers like Christopher Saxton and John Speed, intent on describing and mapping Britain, is usually viewed as the genesis of the subject.

Alongside this generalist approach to British topography there developed the individual county history, the province of gentry and clergy, starting with William Lambarde's *Kent* in 1576. As well as county history, however, local historians have written urban, parish and village histories in an attempt to chronicle the varied communities of Britain.[4]

The county history movement culminated in the Victoria County History (VCH) project, which, begun in 1899, with the aim of writing an outline history for the whole of England, remains incomplete 100 years later, although much has been accomplished in spite of funding difficulties.[5] Over its existence, however, the

VCH has changed its subject coverage to reflect the changing way in which local history is viewed.

Wales too had its 16th-century cartographer, Humphrey Llwyd, and an 18th-century topographer, Thomas Pennant, but has no equivalent to the VCH, although there are a number of 20th-century county histories. Scotland also has nothing like the VCH but the *Statistical accounts* of its parishes in the 18th, 19th and 20th centuries are an important local information source. In Ireland, county history, inspired by the VCH, developed at the end of the 19th and early 20th century and these and other publications assumed particular importance after the destruction of the Irish Record Office in 1922. In the late 20th century, Geography Publication, Dublin, began issuing a history for each county in Ireland; published volumes include those for Down, Londonderry, Kilkenny and Waterford.[6]

In the UK, the 20th century was characterized by a flood of local history writing (including county histories), commissioned by local authorities, publishers, local history societies and other organizations, and this writing activity continues. Many such local publications are the work of amateur local historians, continuing the tradition of earlier writers, but deal not only with places but also with local people, events and activities.[7]

LOCAL HISTORY, COMMUNITY HISTORY AND LOCAL STUDIES

Much early local history research and writing can be characterized as being topographical or antiquarian in approach: concerned with the description of places and the collection of facts. These works remain important for precisely those attributes, but they do not constitute local history as viewed today. As the authors were usually gentry or professional men, they were concerned with topics such as the descent of the manor, pedigrees, ancient monuments and the church and its fabric, although this, and other information, might be presented in a way which was detrimental to a clear historical narrative and did not provide a balanced approach to subject content.

In criticizing the works of earlier local historians, however, it should be remembered that the resources modern local historians take for granted – libraries, archives, etc. – were not easily available to them, if at all, nor were the benefits of modern methods of communication. Their publications remain particularly valuable, therefore, for their recording of lost documents, sites, monuments, etc., and for the information that their contemporary description of localities provides.

Local history as an accepted field of academic study can be said to date from the founding of the Department of English Local History at Leicester University in 1948.[8] The pioneering work of Hoskins[9] and Finberg encouraged the use of the landscape as historical evidence, and evangelized the need for local history to explain as well as describe, to have a developing narrative rather than be a collection of interesting information, and to treat subjects that involved the common people and their day-to-day lives and communal endeavours:[10] a people's history, rather than one limited to the powerful and privileged and their particular concerns.

The increasing recognition of the value of local history, however, did not depend solely on a changed approach to its subject content and presentation but on the realization of the contribution that it can make towards an understanding and interpretation of regional and national history. Local history has also come to be seen as having social values for individuals and groups in that it gives people a pride in their locality, a sense of belonging, an understanding of their personal origins and a stake in the future.[11] A shared sense of local history, and an involvement with it, can also be seen as a way of strengthening communities and helping towards the goal of social inclusion.

One result of this popular interest in the past is the boom in family history research, triggered by a desire to trace one's ancestors and to understand the places and times in which they lived, and the corresponding growth of related societies and publications, along with a greater use of local studies libraries and archives, to cater for the boom.

'Community history' is a newer term that is being used alongside or even to replace 'local history'. It recognizes that much local history is constricted by administrative boundaries – county, town, city or parish – that have often changed significantly in recent times, and that there are natural communities (within and across such boundaries) that have continuity and a particular community identity and should be the concern of both the historian and the local studies librarian.[12] Community history can also be seen as one in which everyone is encouraged to participate by lending materials, writing or taping their memories; local studies librarians have been particularly active in these matters in recent years.[13]

While it has been suggested that antiquarianism has been replaced by a more constructive attitude to local history, not all view this as being the case. The heritage approach, with its romantic view of the past, has been deplored as antiquarian and a warning has been given about 'the narrow obsessions of the conservation movement, which themselves threaten to usurp history'.[14] Even with this warning in mind, however, local studies librarians cannot ignore the 'heritage' or 'nostalgia' dimension to local history.[15]

While most topics can be looked at with a local focus, those broad subject areas that the local studies librarian needs to be particularly aware of, in addition to family history, are archaeology, landscape history, industrial archaeology, oral history, population studies, and agrarian, transport and economic history. However, it must be emphasized that local studies librarians, as their designation implies, must encourage and support types of local study other than the purely historical.[16]

POPULARIZATION OF LOCAL AND FAMILY HISTORY

Not only has the nature of local history changed in recent decades, but there has been an enormous increase in the number of people involved with it. This democratization can be put down broadly to:

● better access to historical sources,
● the general acceptance of the subject,
● its active promotion,
● changes in society.

Improved access to historical resources is the result of better and more accessible local studies libraries and record offices and the use of microfilm and, more recently, computers to provide access to records in a fragile condition or held elsewhere.

The greater acceptance of local history is evidenced by the variety of Workers' Educational Association and other courses provided locally, and the certificate, diploma and degree courses available in the subject at various universities, including the Open University course on family and community history.[17] Also the National Curriculum requires or encourages the use of local enquiry in its history syllabi and schools are being encouraged to build up their own local studies collections in their libraries.

For some years now local and family history have been actively promoted by radio and television programmes, such as *The century speaks* and those featured in the BBC's *Historyzone* or *History hour*. The BBC's history output, through its History 2000 campaign, points viewers to museums, local history collections and heritage centres via its history website. More locally the subject is promoted by societies for local and family history, who often have a publications programme, as indeed might the local studies library. General and specialist publishers too contribute to the number of publications on individual places or about the subject itself.[18]

Localities may also actively promote the historical dimension of their area as a tourist asset through its association with an author, a particular industry, television programme or distinctive architecture, and organizations like the National Trust welcome visitors in increasing numbers to historic houses and sites.

Lastly, in addition to students of all ages engaged in local historical study of some kind, there is now a group of active, retired, older people who, through social change, have the leisure, interest and means to pursue such work. This is a relatively new phenomenon that could itself be altered by future demographic change and the structure of employment. All in all, local studies and local and family history have become outstanding vehicles for the modern concept of lifelong learning, promoted by government, educationalists and the library and information profession. Local authorities now have to prepare Lifelong Learning Plans, in which libraries play a key part. In a reorganization at Westminster, libraries have been put under a newly created Lifelong Learning Directorate placed within the Education Department and no longer linked to leisure. This was also partly in preparation for the government's requirement for Local Cultural Plans.

THE LOCAL STUDIES COLLECTION

The public library local studies collection, especially where large, may be housed separately within a library building (or in purpose-built or adapted accommodation elsewhere) and may have its own staff and budget. Its significance to local historians and others is emphasized by the publication in 1998 of a handbook to the contents and use of such collections.[19] Whatever its size, the local collection is likely to have its own distinctive service role, policies, practices, procedures and clientele. Given these characteristics, it might be argued that it forms a special collection that does not fit easily into the loan-oriented ethos of the public library service.[20] Indeed, the current trend, of bringing together archives and local studies collections, may be in part a recognition of this. Whatever the future of the local studies service within public libraries, however, there is much to celebrate in the achievements of the last 150 years.

It is clear from the debate surrounding the passing of the Public Libraries and Museums Act, 1850 for England and Wales that the provision of 'topographical libraries' was seen as a potential feature of the proposed municipal institutions.[21] By 1878, when W.H.K. Wright, the librarian of Plymouth, gave a paper on local collections at the first annual meeting of the Library Association, they were already an established feature of some libraries, such as Manchester, Bristol and Cambridge. In the years following Wright's advocacy of the local collection, they were founded in towns and cities such as Norwich, Swansea and Dundee. Characteristics of these early local municipal collections included:

- the collection of material about areas beyond their own administrative boundaries.
- the donation or purchase of the collection of a local antiquary or historian.
- the inclusion of local records and manuscripts.
- being housed as part of the reference library.

The Public Libraries and Museums Act, 1919, which saw the creation of the county library service, meant that counties too began collecting local material but could not rival the well established municipal collections. Edinburgh under Ernest Savage is credited with being the first public library to make the local collection a subject department (the Edinburgh Room) in its own right in 1932, and the major library buildings of the 1930s, such as that at Sheffield, provided better accommodation for the local collection.

The first specialist text, *Library local collections*, also appeared at the end of that decade,[22] and the McColvin Report of 1942 noted that most urban libraries had excellent local collections.[23] The post-war period saw the publication of *Libraries and the material of local history* by J.L. Hobbs in 1948. This, and his subsequent *Local history and the library*, did much to promote the public library local collection. The growing importance of local studies is shown by the appearance in 1973 of a second edition of the last-named work, as well as other texts.[24]

The 1960s and 1970s were notable for local government reorganization in the UK, with changes in local authority boundaries and structures that inevitably impinged on local studies services and patterns of provision. In general terms this reorganization, although not consistent in its application throughout the UK, created larger library authorities and was considered beneficial for public libraries in general and for local studies in particular. Specific benefits included the greater recognition of the importance of local studies provision, the employment of specialist local studies staff, central support services, and the better housing of local collections and improved service provision. Better accommodation for such collections, such as that to be found in the larger libraries of the period at Calderdale and Birmingham, had been a feature of the post-war new library buildings boom. Later large buildings, including extensions, refurbishments and adaptations, such as those at Cardiff and Southampton, also offer examples of separate local studies departments.[25]

By the late 1980s, it was felt that local studies – often a deprived and neglected aspect of library service – had improved greatly in the previous 30 years or so.[26] However, while recent decades demonstrated the concern of local studies librarians for such matters as publications programmes, the development of oral history, and the use of government schemes to do work that might not otherwise be carried out (e.g. retrospective indexing of local newspapers), it might be argued that librarians were not concerned enough about the preservation of the materials in their care and were slow to take up the opportunities offered by information and communications technology. Improvement in local studies provision continued into the 1990s, but unless the general health of public libraries in the UK is improved, local studies provision (given the challenges that face it) will suffer setbacks, even though the importance of public libraries and local studies to society's well-being has come to be recognized through social audit techniques.[27]

LOCAL STUDIES LIBRARIANSHIP: EDUCATION AND TRAINING

It has been contended that librarians do not offer the best possible service to family and local historians because of inadequate training. This is thought to be due to a lack of appreciation of the importance of the local studies collection and to the demands made by users on the staff, who are consulted, often without prior warning, about sources on all aspects and periods of local and family history.[28]

A training policy and programme, it is suggested, at a general level and in relation to a given place, are required to meet the needs of demanding users who look for a depth of subject knowledge and require a high standard of help. Such a programme is necessary because, on the whole, a professional education in library and information work does not equip individuals sufficiently well to work with local collections. Few UK library schools now offer a course on local studies librarianship, which, in any case, has always been optional, although the Department of Information and Library Studies at the University of Wales Aberystwyth has offered an optional local studies module since 1995, as part of a distance learning undergraduate programme, which has proved popular.

What such courses, whether full- or part-time, are unlikely to be able to teach, however, is the detailed familiarity with source material, whatever its format, that comes with the experience of handling and exploiting the material itself. The practising local studies librarian can accelerate this process and broaden their knowledge by undertaking research within the local collection, perhaps with a view to a publication, or as part of the preparation for an exhibition, or in connection with a higher degree in local history or an associated discipline. It has been suggested that staff be expected and, where possible, encouraged in a practical fashion, to take an appropriate further qualification, if they do not already have one. A case is made for a strong commitment to this specialist area by all sides, so that 'Candidates coming for interview could be asked to explain how their plans might be integrated with the library's [training] programme'.[29] However, all public library staff, whether professionally qualified or not, are likely to field local studies enquiries from time to time and in-house training programmes should equip them to respond appropriately. Four categories of staff and the nature of their training, from visits to other collections, record office and museum to the care of equipment and clerical procedures, have been identified:

- professional staff who work full-time with a main local studies collection,
- professional staff who work with other local studies collections within the library service,
- professional staff not specializing in local studies,
- non-professional staff, whether working as local studies support staff or elsewhere in the library service.[30]

Nor should the use and training of volunteers be overlooked.

Although the Library Association's guidelines indicate the educational and other requirements of local studies librarians, emphasizing the completion of a course on local studies work,[31] in practice employers seemingly ignore this, emphasizing experience and interest (and perhaps not even the former). A recent examination of over 30 advertisements for local studies staff in public libraries, excluding archives-only posts, suggests that public libraries are requiring too little of their local studies staff as regards the possession of appropriate formal qualifications.[32] In-service training, while very important, must involve much more than learning on the job.

LOCAL STUDIES GROUP OF THE LIBRARY ASSOCIATION AND THE SCHOOL LIBRARY ASSOCIATION

Local studies may now be largely absent from professional education but it has a strong professional presence at both national and international level (see the later section on 'The international dimension') in the shape of the Local Studies Group of the Library Association. Originally a sub-group of what is now the Information Services Group, it became an independent group in 1982 and now has a membership of nearly 1,800. While bringing together librarians with an interest in local studies and providing a channel of communication between them, it also aims

- to ensure best professional practice in local studies librarianship,
- to act as a focus for comment and to campaign on all issues affecting local studies.[33]

It achieves these objectives through:

- publication of the twice-yearly *Local studies librarian*,
- publication of guidelines for local studies libraries,
- a regional branch structure,
- the annual Dorothy McCulla award, presented in recognition of services to local studies librarianship,
- the encouragement of continuing professional development through weekend schools, contributions to conferences, etc.

A major achievement of the group was the publication of *Local studies libraries: Library Association guidelines for local studies provision in public libraries* in 1990. Endorsed by the Library Association, the new edition (in process of publication) is, like the first, the result of extensive consultation with colleagues.[34]

The School Library Association has also published guidance on the provision of local studies collections in schools. *A sense of place*, while providing practical guidance on the acquisition and organization of material, also raises the question of a local studies policy and responsibility for a school's archives.[35] A later publication, *Setting the scene*, covers all pre-tertiary education groups and draws attention to the value of a local studies collection to support work across a number of subject disciplines, as well as the leisure interests and personal development of pupils.[36]

LOCAL STUDIES LIBRARIES: POLITICAL AND FINANCIAL INFLUENCES

For the United Kingdom, the 1990s saw significant political, constitutional and administrative change at national, regional and local levels. With the coming to power of New Labour in 1997, librarians were faced with a government, and a newly named department of Culture, Media and Sport, whose ministers were much more sympathetic to and appreciative of public libraries than the former Conservative administration. While the present government is making money available for particular library projects, such as the People's Network,[37] there is no doubt that public libraries and their local studies collections can only flourish in the future with a more modern legislative and secure financial base: one that allows for the proper day-to-day running of the service as well as well-funded one-off projects.

Devolved political power in Scotland, Wales and Northern Ireland, with their respective parliament and assemblies, will mean that cultural matters, including libraries, archives and museums, will be subject to both central and regional influences, but it remains to be seen whether the latter influence will improve matters fundamentally. As well as devolving political power, the government has indicated the importance of a regional strategy, the bringing together of several authorities within the English regions to facilitate the delivery of government policy, such as that for cultural services.

Under a Conservative government, local government was reorganized once more in 1996–7, with the result that in England a number of new unitary authorities, in which county and district level functions (including that for libraries) were merged, have been created alongside existing library authorities. In Wales and Scotland libraries are the responsibility of the 22 and 32 single-tier councils, respectively. In Northern Ireland, libraries continue, for the time being, to be the responsibility of the five area education boards. As with the earlier local government reorganization of London and elsewhere from 1965 to 1975, such local authority changes have impinged upon the work of public libraries generally and local studies collections in particular, as in the new unitary authority, Telford and Wrekin, for example.[38]

Under both Conservative and New Labour administrations, local authorities and their public libraries have been beset with buzz words, inspirational reports and fashionable obsessions, such as contracting out,[39] best value, standards (from April 2001), annual plans and inclusivity, the latter surely a public library strength for many years. While financial resources for public libraries may not have shown much of a gain, nevertheless attitudes have changed and the profession is a much more accountable, self-critical, evaluative and consumer-oriented one, and that is no bad thing.

Public libraries, like other institutions, have been encouraged to look for sources of extra funding. Local studies libraries have generated income internally from publication sales and research services, for example, and, where possible, externally. This can be from European Union-funded initiatives for digital heritage and cultural content and from the money generated by the National Lottery, established in 1994 with the objectives of providing money for good causes, as well as prizes. Whether from the Heritage, Millennium Festival or New Opportunities Fund, lottery money has been allocated to a variety of library initiatives. Those relating to local studies include:

- the conservation of 3,500 local and regional newspapers published between 1800 and 1950,[40]
- building projects, such as the Surrey History Centre[41] and the new home for the Cornish Studies Collection in a listed building at Redruth,
- a cataloguing project at Redbridge,[42]
- digitization projects in Powys[43] and for Information North, the north-east libraries consortium.[44]

While the opportunities that lottery funding creates are to be welcomed, this is not the way, as the earlier Carnegie experience demonstrated, to fund sound, long-term development of a library service. It is generally accepted that levels of funding, staffing (including specialists), the number of service points and the hours of opening of public libraries have all declined in the UK in the last 25 years. This service erosion has affected local studies provision, a service where public demand has increased. Describing precisely the extent of that decline and its effect on local studies libraries, however, is difficult, because, as the results of a 1990 survey have shown, many authorities 'do not know how much money is spent on local studies books, and even more have only a general conception of how much time is spent by staff on local studies work'.[45]

Hard evidence as to how the cuts have affected local studies provision are thus not easy to come by, but a small 1995 survey of various local authorities in the north-west of England provides some indication.[46] As well as asking about staffing levels and changes as regards geographical or format coverage, the survey tried to establish whether respondents:

- felt the service was acceptable,
- could keep up with demand and develop the service,
- could identify specific reductions that had taken place.

Only three out of 12 respondents felt local studies had a high priority in their organization and only one felt that staff morale had not suffered because of the cuts. The results of reduced staffing in a labour-intensive service meant that enquiry, stock and promotional work had all suffered in the region and it was noted that there was an emphasis on libraries as a leisure rather than an educational service. The survey concluded that, although there was a high level of commitment amongst local studies staff, there was cause for concern.

SOME PROFESSIONAL CONCERNS

USERS AND THEIR NEEDS

Users and their needs continue to be at the heart of the concerns of local studies librarians and so, for example, the use of local materials for reminiscence and therapy work with those perhaps unable to visit the library should not be overlooked.[47] For the local studies *Guidelines* recognize that 'Users of local studies come from all areas of society' and lists the various categories of user, noting their special local studies requirements.[48] A day school organized in 1999 looked at the special problems of particular client groups – ethnic minorities, the housebound, children, students and the visually and physically impaired – in gaining access to local studies materials. As well as identifying barriers, solutions were considered in respect of each group, such as training, consultation, provision of special equipment and organizing library visits.[49]

There is, however, a great deal of anecdotal evidence about users: their numerical increase, who they are, where they come from and their predominant fields of interest. As with many aspects of local studies work, however, published information is hard to come by. Two surveys from the 1990s, one of which relates solely to visitors to archives, gives some indication of trends.

Bolton's Archives and Local Studies Unit conducted a survey of all customers, except those with quick reference enquiries, in February 1994 and results showed that

- 50 per cent of respondents consisted of retired people and full-time students,
- 69 per cent lived in Bolton,
- 39·61 per cent were interested in family history and genealogy,
- 18·08 per cent were undertaking research for a first or higher degree,
- 30 per cent were 'first-timers'.

The authors of the survey report noted with some alarm that over 15 per cent had learned of the unit's existence 'by accident'.[50]

A survey of 11,000 visitors to more than 100 British archives in June 1998 found that

- 37 per cent were retired,
- 61 per cent were researching family history,
- 12 per cent were overseas visitors and thus providing benefits to the UK economy,
- 33 per cent had travelled over 20 miles,
- apparently, 70 per cent of all visits are accounted for by regulars (monthly or more frequent visits).

'Younger people, women and ethnic minorities are under represented in the archive user population [and] archives must address this through finding new methods of service delivery and new ways of delivering content.'[51] Nearly ten years earlier, a study of the relevance and existing practices of local studies provision, etc. in a multi-ethnic society acknowledged the potential relevance and advantages of such a service.[52]

In both user surveys, staff were commented on favourably, but improvements suggested by respondents included longer opening hours and better user facilities. Bolton considered that the survey had not resulted in any great revelations but that it did provide information to support managerial strategies and deciding on priorities – a programme of equipment updating was an immediate result.

Another survey of local studies users, carried out in 1999 in Derby and Derbyshire, offers some further statistical information for comparison with the above and useful insights, such as those into varied attitudes to new methods of service delivery: 'the dreaded computer' to some.

ACCESSIBILITY

Access to local studies materials might be seen as:

- physical access – through the provision of appropriate space to house the collection or collections, staff, users and equipment,
- information access – through shelf organization, catalogues, indexes and the World Wide Web,
- guided access – through enquiry and research services and publications about the contents of the collection.

Physical access to local collections has been assisted by better local studies accommodation, by branch library collections, the compilation of village packs, cooperation with local history societies and by, for example, recent outreach initiatives. Birmingham's History Van was set up to take historical materials to those who might not think to or, like the elderly and the physically disabled, are unable to visit the library, although the service is now focusing on community libraries and established community groups. Funding came from the Inner City Partnership and the van has visited a wide range of locations and organizations, including schools, carnivals and summer events in parks.[53]

In 1998 the Public Record Office of Northern Ireland (PRONI) proposed to set up a number of regional study centres (now called outreach centres), in order to raise awareness regionally and locally of its work and of the source material in its custody, and to help overcome space limitations in its own building. The centres, of which four have been opened so far, are also there to help prepare researchers for visits to PRONI's headquarters building. Accommodation, etc. for each centre is to be provided by the host organization, PRONI supplying the electronic and hard copy media appropriate to each outreach centre.[54]

Access to local studies materials, as the PRONI example indicates, may also be enhanced by electronic means, notably a website, a recent, well publicized example being that of Knowsley. Its avowed intention was 'to reach a far bigger audience than would have been possible by traditional methods'. In its first four months, it fielded 125,000 hits, mainly from the UK but also from around the world – America to New Zealand.[55]

Improvements in library building provision in recent years usually mean that local studies material is more visible and accessible, bearing in mind questions of security and conservation. Increasingly, perhaps, and starting with the local collection catalogue, the contents of a local collection – text, pictures, sound – will be available on-line. As this becomes a nationwide phenomenon, each local studies collection will create a major resource for all kinds of local and comparative studies.

COLLECTIONS

The 1990 local studies statistical survey showed that determining levels of bookfund allocated to local collections is difficult, as, even if there was a separate purchasing fund for the main collection, smaller collections at other service points were sometimes maintained out of other bookfund allocations.[56] The professional *Guidelines* argue for a separate budget of sufficient purchasing power and for 'adequate contingency funding ... to purchase items of local interest that appear on the market from time to time'.[57]

Leaving aside questions of funding, it has been pointed out that, as the time for acquiring material decreases, librarians 'must not be guilty of censorship by selection' and should see that their collection covers the whole community, including the black and travelling communities and women.[58] It has also been suggested that librarians should show more concern for local popular culture, such as sport and music, and in particular not ignore the cultural activities of young people.[59] A project that goes some way to fulfilling these criteria is the York Oral History of Popular Music 1930–1970. It is important not only to obtain the documentary record for such activities but, where appropriate, to cover their sounds and images.

Cooperation with other libraries and institutions over the acquisition of material is also important, because it affects policies related to collection building. It suffices to state here the need for local studies librarians to be fully involved in formal schemes to create a more structured approach to ensuring the satisfactory collection and preservation of local material throughout the UK.

INFORMATION AND COMMUNICATIONS TECHNOLOGY

Community history (seen as inclusive) and identity were together considered one of the principal strands of a report to transform Britain's public libraries through a people's network. Part of the vision for local studies included the digitization of older formats to make them more widely accessible, the national networking of local collections and the availability of local history catalogues from across the world. The availability of electronic formats and library records of local studies material, as well as those for archives and museums, will help blur the supposed differences between the three institutions.[60]

As part of the plan, a People's Network team has been set up and a number of digitization projects have been embarked upon. Local studies librarians have expressed concerns about the priority that will be given to this strand of the vision and, more practically, the questions of replacing hardware, of training staff, providing guidance to users and the continuing problem of the preservation of existing materials.[61] A potential danger also is that routine activities – acquisition work, cataloguing, indexing etc. – will be relegated in favour of showy interactive web sites and high-profile 'events', thus possibly jeopardizing the future of local studies collections.

ACCOMMODATION

Whatever the future influence of networked local studies information might be, there still seems to be a desire to provide better physical accommodation for local studies collections,[62] often in conjunction with a record office. Better accommodation will usually mean a substantial increase in visitors, 70 per cent having been experienced by the then new Leicestershire Record Office, which includes the county's local collection, when it opened in 1993 in a converted and extended Victorian school.[63]

The present author has attempted the search for a standard space allocation for local studies departments related to the size of the population served, the number of volumes housed and the overall size of the library building housing the department. An analysis of 40 buildings, described as containing space for 'local studies/archives', and for which a separate space allocation was indicated, demonstrated an apparent erratic relationship between these elements. However, it was possible to suggest that 5–6 per cent of the total space in a public library building might be needed for local studies but that this tentative conclusion requires further investigation.[64]

MANAGERIAL ISSUES

It has been suggested that local studies librarians need to be both subject specialists and good managers of the resources and services under their control, and that this demanded a planned systematic approach.[65] There is a requirement to be not only a good manager, with an interest in marketing, etc., but also one that is able to function effectively within the prevailing national and local government and financial cultures noted earlier, and to be able to assess and address issues, such as best value, in terms of their implications for local studies provision. The introduction to the new local studies *Guidelines* suggest that local studies librarians will therefore need to be able to build on their existing ability to manage change.

INTEGRATION AND COOPERATION

Increasingly, it would seem, certain aspects of local authority provision – local studies libraries, archives, museums and archaeology – are being brought together in various combinations. This integration, often under the title of 'local studies centre', or similar description, is not universally accepted by members of the constituent professions involved. Where no such integrated situation obtains, the local studies *Guidelines* make clear the necessity to develop cooperation and good working relationships locally, not only with archivists and museum staff, but also with community groups, teachers and lecturers, other library and local authority staff and the media.[66]

While integration may not be to everyone's liking, cooperation, which may include strategic planning, is essential, whether within a local authority area or on a regional or national level. Such cooperation may operate through informal or formal networks and may include a variety of institutions, community groups and individuals. In Cambridgeshire, for example, there was at one time a Heritage Officers Group which consisted of representatives from the archives, libraries, museums, building conservation and education,[67] but the group was made defunct by restructuring that brought specialists together and thus allowed for less formal cooperation. In West Sussex there is a Special Events Group with key input from archive and library departments which also cooperate formally on matters like enquiries, training and outreach.[68]

STRATEGIC PLANNING

Library and information plans (LIPs) are part of a strategic planning process involving information providers in the public, private and voluntary sectors set up with the aim of maximizing awareness, access and availability of information in a given area or region. England and Scotland have a number of separate LIPs, such as those for Wiltshire, Bradford and the Highlands and Islands. Northern Ireland and Wales have single LIPs.[69] An early stage in the planning process involved an audit of existing resources in a given region, county or area to include local studies. The LIP for the combined counties of Gloucestershire, Hereford and Worcester has a section headed 'Local history and studies, including public archives'. This reviews the responsibilities, holdings and services of the public libraries, record offices, cathedral and related libraries, museums (including the Archaeological Section at Worcester), the libraries of local archaeological and natural history societies, the art gallery and bodies devoted to the preservation and conservation of wildlife.[70]

Shropshire described its more specialized heritage strategy in part as 'to identify institutions, societies and organisations with an interest or active involvement in Shropshire's heritage and to identify local heritage aspirations'. Telford and Wrekin carried out a similar audit, as have some other authorities, the aim of such plans being, for example, to identify the significance of local history societies to local heritage activity, especially those who have their own collections, and how they might be helped.[71] Staffordshire, on the other hand, is in the process of creating a specific local studies strategy as a means of taking the service forward.

The Cambridgeshire regional heritage strategy was produced by three local authorities and based on a 1997 survey of museums, archives, libraries and other providers of local history in the southern half of Cambridgeshire and parts of Essex and Hertfordshire. While the strategy document examines the aforementioned institutions and the role of databases, the involvement of local history societies is apparently not covered. In distinguishing the requirements of family history researchers from those of local history, it was noted that the former are more numerous and tend to use a small range of documents, but may go on to become local historians. As noted earlier, as more people take part in local studies for either leisure or academic reasons, the demand for greater access and expert guidance is likely to rise and so branch libraries and village colleges were seen as possible sites for secondary facilities. Although a regional strategy document and an umbrella group for discussion and monitoring is thus in place in Cambridgeshire, its financial implications were not addressed at this stage.[72]

COOPERATIVE PRESERVATION

Research published into the cooperative preservation activities of libraries, archives and other organizations, including museums and commercial bodies, showed that there was cooperation on microfilming and digitization projects, over sharing facilities and technical expertise, and in competing for external funding. It was found that 17 public libraries and 24 archives and record offices (non-national) were involved in cooperative preservation activities. The National Preservation Office encourages and coordinates cooperative preservation activities as part of its national strategic plan, but it is recognized that preservation can no longer be the sole responsibility of individual institutions, including those at the national level.[73]

NEWSPLAN

NEWSPLAN, established in 1985, and operating under the aegis of the British Library in ten NEWSPLAN regions, was an ambitious project to list every local and regional paper published in the UK and Ireland. Supported by the newspaper industry, NEWSPLAN is seen as a major example of cooperation between public, academic and national libraries. The NEWSPLAN reports paid considerable attention to the physical condition of local titles, identifying those that needed conservation microfilming on a cooperative basis.[74]

NATIONAL PUBLISHED ARCHIVE

In an article noting the concepts of a National Published Archive (NPA) and a National Bibliographic Resource, it was stated that currently there was little formal cooperation in the acquisition coverage of local publications between the British Library and other libraries and that there was a need to build better cooperation and notification between the national library and public libraries especially. The writer acknowledged: 'the financial and legal underpinning of the work of public libraries is insufficient in so many cases to fulfil the moral responsibility for coverage of local collections, which so many of these libraries would (and do) consider a prime obligation.'[75] However, it was thought that understandings and expectations might be built into the annual library plans but that all that is possible at present seems to be 'a cross-sectoral group to keep arrangements for local publications within the national published archive under review'.[76]

The need to create a truly distributed National Published Archive, where local publications are generally held locally or regionally for the nation, is, however, a situation that is unlikely to be resolved without changes to copyright, library legislation and appropriate funding.[77]

PARTNERSHIP

On a more positive note, it was observed that a valuable aspect of the creation of Knowsley website was the collaboration with Connect (part of Liverpool University Computer Science Department), Prescot Museum and the Lancashire Record Office, and that there was potential for developing and building on such partnerships.[78]

THE INTERNATIONAL DIMENSION: CONTACTS AND COMPARISONS

The international dimension to local studies can be considered firstly from a professional point of view: the nature of this specialist field of librarianship in other countries and how it compares with (and what can be learnt by) UK practice. Allied to this are questions of international contact and cooperation and the worldwide furtherance of the concept of local studies librarianship.

Secondly, as regards the subject itself, there is the comparative aspect of local studies, carried out within a country, and technological developments make this much easier than in the past. Comparative studies, however, can be cross-border (the comparison of communities in different countries) and regional studies may also be carried out across national boundaries: the south-west of England could be seen as part of the 'Trans-Manche' region.[79]

In 1993 the Local Studies Group of the Library Association adopted an international policy whose aims were 'to spread the benefits of the strong tradition of local studies to colleagues in other parts of the world, via individual and group contact' and 'to learn from colleagues overseas'.[80] In practical fulfilment of these ideals the group developed a programme that included contact with specific countries.

Even before the adoption of this statement, however, the Local Studies Group (LSG) had hosted a visitor from Spain, who spoke at a weekend school in 1991. Assumpta Bailac represented Spain's Local Studies Group, founded in 1987, and one of the boards of the Public Library Group. Her comments largely concerned the situation in Catalonia, where a survey had been conducted to assist in the preparation of guidelines similar to those in the UK.[81]

In the following years the LSG established contact with local studies librarians in Romania, Hungary and Latvia, the last two countries having local studies groups within their professional associations.[82] In Romania, the LSG was able to make a contribution to the cost of a county periodicals bibliography, while in Hungary the group has taken over responsibility for its own journal exchange and in 1998 partly subsidized and made arrangements for ten Hungarian librarians to visit London for a six-day study tour. The participants agreed to disseminate their experiences to colleagues at their local studies conference. This association with Hungary is the one that has flourished most and there is a regular exchange of speakers and visitors between that country and the UK.[83] The existence of formal groups of local studies librarians in Hungary and elsewhere, Australia for example, make further international contact and cooperation a real possibility.

The twinning and other arrangements between British and, for example, European cities and counties can provide a basis on which such studies, as well as mutual understanding, can be facilitated. Two examples of this are provided by the twinning arrangements between Portsmouth and Caen and Devon and Calvados. In both cases local history exhibitions were held, there was an exchange of deposit collections (e.g. Hampshire–Normandie collections) and a leaflet on comparative local studies work provided, as it was thought important to encourage such research.[84] Subsequent experience shows that a variety of factors – the contribution of individuals, local government reorganization and the changing local library situation – can all affect the effective continuance of such endeavours.

CONCLUSION

The study of local communities, in all their facets, and of the people who live in them, is long-standing and, over the years, the approach to that study has been a changing one. Public libraries, through their local studies collections, have, from their early days, taken the responsibility for collecting the printed and other materials that constitute the local people's memory and make such studies possible. The popularization of local studies in the last 50 years, particularly local and family history, and the arrival of new forms of information and communications technology, have led to new demands on local studies librarians as regards their skills, role and the services to be offered to those they serve.

Local collections, as part of the UK's public library service, exist within a local authority framework that also provides complementary services to students, enquirers and researchers through record offices and museums. Both they and local studies libraries have been affected by recent local government reorganization, and by devolution within the UK, as well as by the government's financial regime within which cultural, arts and leisure facilities are provided and overseen.

As shown in this chapter, and demonstrated more fully in the next, the public library local collection does not exist in isolation – and cooperation, convergence or integration of the local collection, record office and museum are increasingly coming about. The seeker after local information may use the local studies library as part of a network of resources providers at local, regional and national – and even international – level. Access to and the use of resources in other countries will also create the potential for 'international local studies', if that is not seen as a contradiction in terms.

NOTES

1 This historical dimension to local studies may, however, be emphasized. See Copeland, T. (1998), *The teacher's handbook for local studies*, Swindon: Royal Commission on the Historical Monuments of England.
2 Phillips, F. (1995), *Local history collections in libraries*, Englewood, Colorado: Libraries Unlimited.
3 Davies, S.J. (1991), 'The development of local history writing', in *Local studies collections: a manual*, vol 2, edited by M. Dewe, Aldershot: Gower, 28–54.
4 Paul, D. (1991), 'The bibliography of local history', in *Local studies collections: a manual*, vol 2, edited by M. Dewe, Aldershot: Gower, 102–10.
5 For a recent assessment of the VCH's achievements, see Currie, C.R.J. (1997), 'The Victoria County History', *Local history magazine* (59) January/February, 18–20.
6 Outlines of the local historiography of Scotland, Wales and Ireland can be found in the *Oxford companion to local and family history* (1996), edited by D. Hey, Oxford: OUP, 240–47, 406–12, 483–91.
7 For recent publications see the reviews and listings in *Local historian* and *Local history magazine*.
8 For a description of the work of the department, see *English local history: the Leicester approach: a departmental bibliography and history 1948–1998* (1999), edited by M. Tranter, Leicester: Friends of the Department of Local History, University of Leicester.
9 Phythian-Adams, C. (1992), 'Hoskin's England: a local historian of genius and the realisation of his theme', *Local historian* 22 (4), 170–83.
10 Hoskins, W.G. (1955), *The making of the English landscape*, London: Hodder and Stoughton; Hoskins, W.G. (1959), *Local history in England*, London: Longmans; Finberg, H.P.R. and Skipp, V.H.T. (1967), *Local history: objective and pursuit*, Newton Abbot: David & Charles.
11 Archibald, R. (1999), *A place to remember: using history to build community*, London: Altamira.
12 Chandler, J. (1998), 'A sense of belonging', *Local history magazine* (68) July/August, 20–21.
13 Chinn, C. (1993), 'Community history in Birmingham', *Local studies librarian* 12 (1), 8–10; 'Library report gives community history a high profile' (1997), *Local history magazine* (63) September/October, 4–5. For a discussion and description of taping memories, see Llwyd, R. and Evans, G. (1987), 'Oral history recordings', in *Local studies collections: a manual*, vol 1, edited by M. Dewe, Aldershot: Gower, 309–44.
14 Marshall, J. (1997), *The tyranny of the discrete: a discussion of the problems of local history in England*, Aldershot: Scolar Press.
15 Drew, P. (1993), 'Local history and heritage: the BALH annual conference, York, 1993', *Local studies librarian* 12 (2), 14–19.
16 Library Association Local Studies Group (2002), *Local studies libraries: Library Association guidelines for local studies provision in public libraries*, 2nd edition, London: Library Association, para A1.1.

17 For details of courses and student participation, see 'Local history courses: who decides?' (1999), *Local history magazine* (76) November/December, 9; 'Local history students – universities target the "oldies"?' (1996), *Local history magazine* (56) July/August, 14–15; Drake, M. (1995), 'Doing local studies: a new course from the Open University', *Local studies librarian* 14 (1), 6–10.

18 For example: Iredale, D. and Barrett, J. (1999), *Discovering local history*, Princes Risborough: Shire.

19 Winterbotham, D. and Crosby, A. (1998), *The local studies library: a handbook for local historians*, Salisbury: BALH.

20 Maxted, I. (1998), 'Local studies libraries as rare book collections', *Local studies librarian* 17 (1), 2–7.

21 Ansell, R. (1987), 'The historical development and the present structure of public library local studies provision in the United Kingdom', in *Local studies collections: a manual*, vol 1, edited by M. Dewe, Aldershot: Gower, 27–51. A case study of the Leicestershire Collection is included in Dixon, D. (1996), 'Civic pride and posterity', *Local studies librarian* 15 (1), 6–10.

22 Sayers, W.C.B. (1939), *Library local collections*, London: Allen and Unwin.

23 McColvin, L.R. (1942), *The public library system of Great Britain*, London: Library Association.

24 Hobbs, J.L. (1948) *Libraries and the materials of local history*, London: Grafton; Hobbs, J.L. (1962), *Local history and the library*, London: Deutsch; Hobbs, J.L. (1973), *Local history and the library*, revised and partly rewritten by G.A. Carter, London: Deutsch; Lynes, A. (1974), *How to organise a local collection*, London: Deutsch; Nichols, H. (1979) *Local studies librarianship*, London: Bingley.

25 Other buildings of the post-war period with local studies accommodation include those in Holborn, Portsmouth, Reading, Glasgow, Croydon and Taunton.

26 Dewe, M. (1987), 'Introduction', in *Local studies collections: a manual*, vol 1, edited by M. Dewe, Aldershot: Gower, 5.

27 Usherwood, B. (1999), 'The social impact of local studies services', *Local studies librarian* 18 (1), 2–6.

28 Paul, D. (1995), 'Training 2000? Local and family history in libraries', *Librarian career development* 3 (4), 4.

29 Paul (1995), 'Training 2000?', 8.

30 Dansie, J. and Dewe, M. (1987), 'Staffing', in *Local studies collections: a manual*, vol 1, edited by M. Dewe, Aldershot: Gower, 118–20; Lock, A. (1993), 'National Vocational Qualifications', *Local studies librarian* 12 (1), 17–18. Training is also endorsed in Library Association Local Studies Group (2002), *Local studies libraries: Library Association guidelines . . .*, para B7.3.

31 Library Association Local Studies Group (2002), *Local studies libraries: Library Association guidelines . . .*, para B7.1.

32 Garratt, M. (1999), 'Vacancies and the prospective candidate: some personal observations', *Local studies librarian* 18 (1), 15–17.

33 Library Association Local Studies Group (1995), 'Mission statement', *Local studies librarian* 14 (2), 23–4.

34 Martin, D. (1996), 'Getting the guidelines right', *Scottish libraries* (56) March/April, 17.

35 Blizzard, A.(1991), *A sense of place: local studies and the school library*, Swindon: School Library Association.

36 Southcombe, D. (1999), *Setting the scene: local studies resources in the school library*, Swindon: School Library Association.

37 *New library: the people's network* (1997), London: Library and Information Commission; 'Library report gives community history a high profile' (1997), *Local history magazine* (63) September/October, 4–5.

38 Higson, M. (1999), 'Local studies in Telford and Wrekin libraries', *Local history magazine* (72) March/April, 7.

39 For example, Southwark Education and Leisure (1995), *Southwark libraries: a specification for Southwark local studies library*, London: Southwark Council.

40 'Lottery cash to save local newspapers' (1999), *Information management report*, May, 8–9.

41 'Lottery coup for Surrey historical centre' (1996), *Library Association record* 98 (2), 64.

42 '£100m plus for local history' (1999), *Local history magazine* (74) July/August, 4–5.

43 'Bidding is open for digitisation fund' (1999), *Library Association record* 101 (10), 555.

44 'Local history lives on' (2000), *Library Association record* 102 (2), 74.

45 Winterbotham, D. (1990), 'The local studies statistical survey', *Local studies librarian* 9 (1) 6.

46 Lock, A. (1995), 'Spending cuts in local studies libraries: a survey in the North West', *Local studies librarian* 14 (2), 18–21.

47 Armstrong, N. (1991), 'Reminiscence work with local studies material', in *Local studies collections: a manual*, vol 2, edited by M. Dewe, Aldershot: Gower, 194–224.

48 Library Association Local Studies Group (2002), *Local studies libraries: Library Association guidelines...*, para A2.1.

49 Bray, J. (2000), 'Equal opportunities and local studies', *Local studies librarian* 19 (1), 6–9.

50 Campbell, K. and Mills, B. (1995), 'Bolton Archives and Local Studies: a customer survey', *Local studies librarian* 14 (1), 10–12.

51 'Who uses archives? Survey provides answer' (1999), *Local history magazine* (71) January/February, 9.

52 Sharp, D. (1989), 'Public library provision of a local studies service in a multiethnic society', Leeds Polytechnic, Department of Library and Information Studies (thesis).

53 Baird, P. and Albutt, R. (1994), 'The Birmingham history van', *Local studies librarian* 13 (1), 32–4.

54 Lammey, D. (1998), 'Regional studies centres: the Public Record Office of Northern Ireland's latest outreach venture', *Local studies librarian* 17 (2), 5–7. For addresses, see Bardon, J. (2000), *A guide to local history sources in the Public Record Office of Northern Ireland*, Belfast: Blackstaff, x.

55 Wilson, S. (1998), '"Knowsley local history": using the Internet to enhance access', *Journal of the Society of Archivists* 19 (2) October, 199–209.

56 Winterbotham (1990), 'The local studies statistical survey', 3.

57 Library Association Local Studies Group (2001), *Local studies libraries: Library Association guidelines...*, para B5.1.

58 Cooke, S. (1992), 'Local studies and the multicultural community', *Local studies librarian* 11 (1), 18–24; Sherwood, M. (1999), 'Ethnic minority archives: report on the national conference', *Local studies librarian* 18 (1), 13–14.

59 Dewe, M. (1999), 'Don't you rock me daddy-o: popular culture, local studies – and skiffle!', *Local studies librarian* 18 (2), 6–10.

60 Rayward, W.B. (1993), 'Electronic information and the functional integration of libraries, museums and archives', in *Proceedings of the workshop: Electronic information resources and historians: European perspective*, London: British Library, 227–43.

61 'The people's network and local studies' (1997), *Local studies librarian* 16 (2), 1–17; 'Library report gives community history a high profile' (1997), *Local history magazine* (63) September/October, 4–5.

62 Herbert, A.J. (1991), 'The new Centre for Local Studies, Darlington Branch Library', *Local studies librarian* 10 (1), 12–14; Lawrence, M. (1991), 'North Devon Local Studies Centre', *Local studies librarian* 10 (2), 3–7; Martin, D. (1994), 'Local studies at the new Kirkintilloch Library', *Local studies librarian* 13 (2), 2–4.

63 Harrison, C. (1995), 'Moving a record office: the Leicestershire experience', *Local studies librarian* 14 (1), 1–5.

64 Dewe, M. (1991), 'Local studies accommodation in the public library buildings of 1984–1989', *Local studies librarian* 10 (1), 5–7; Dewe, M. (1988), 'Local studies accommodation in recent public library buildings', *Local studies librarian* 7 (1), 4–5.

65 Dewe, M. (1987), 'Management: objectives, policies and finance', in *Local studies collections: a manual*, vol 1, edited by M. Dewe, Aldershot: Gower, 97–107. Management skills are also seen as one of the attributes of a good local studies librarian in Library Association Local Studies Group (2002) *Local studies libraries: Library Association guidelines...*, paras A1.3 and A1.4.

66 Library Association Local Studies Group (2002), *Local studies libraries: Library Association guidelines...*, para A3.

67 Petty, M. (1996), 'Networking local studies', *Local studies librarian* 15 (1), 2–5.

68 Hayes, M. (1997), 'Sleeping with the enemy: cooperation between archivists and librarians in West Sussex', *Local studies librarian* 16 (1), 2–5.
69 Library and Information Services Council (1990), *Library and information plan for Northern Ireland*, [Belfast]: LISC (NI); Cymru LiP Wales Management Group (1993), *Library and information plan for Wales*, Aberystwyth: National Library of Wales.
70 Brenda White Associates (c.1989), *Library and information plan for the counties of Gloucestershire, and Hereford and Worcester*, Hereford and Worcester County Council Libraries Department.
71 'Local heritage strategies and local history societies – why 30 November 1998 really matters' (1998), *Local history magazine* (69) September/October, 5.
72 'Cambridge strategy applies "five principles" to local heritage' (1998), *Local history magazine* (69) September/October, 5–6.
73 Eden, P. and Gadd, E. (1999), *Co-operative preservation activities in libraries and archives: project report and guidelines*, London: British Library.
74 For information about NEWSPLAN, see *NEWSPLAN news* (1995–). As an example of a report, see *NEWSPLAN: report of the Newsplan project in the London and South Eastern Library Region (LASER)* (1996), London: British Library.
75 Phillips, A. (1998), 'Preserving the nation's collection of rare local materials: towards a coalition', *Local studies librarian* 17 (1), 11–12.
76 Phillips (1998), 'Preserving the nation's collection', 14.
77 Bloomfield, B. (1994), 'A special case? Preserving and funding heritage collections in research libraries: the British example', *Alexandria* 6 (3), 205–14.
78 Wilson (1998), 'Knowsley local history'.
79 Maxted, I. (1994), 'Remember Waterloo: how to sabotage your library's twinning programme', *Local studies librarian* 13 (1), 10–16.
80 Library Association Local Studies Group (1993), 'An international policy for the Local Studies Group', *Local studies librarian* 12 (2), 23–4.
81 Bailac, A. (1992), 'Local studies in Catalonia, Spain', *Local studies librarian* 11 (1), 18–24.
82 Melrose, E. (1995), 'Co-operation with Romania', *Local studies librarian* 14 (2), 22–3; Melrose, E. (1996), 'Local studies in Latvia: the Public Libraries of Latvia Local Studies Conference, August 1996', *Local studies librarian* 15 (2), 13–14.
83 Melrose, E. (1994), 'Koszonom a meghivast: and the bus was very comfortable', *Local studies librarian* 13 (2), 4–6; Melrose, E. (1998), 'Hungarian local studies librarians visit London', *Local studies librarian* 17 (1), 22.
84 Stevens, P. (1991), 'Entente cordiale in Hampshire', *Local studies librarian* 10 (1), 8–10; Stevens, P. (1993), 'Entente cordiale in Hampshire – Mark II', *Local studies librarian* 12(1), 16; Maxted (1994), 'Remember Waterloo'.

2 Resource providers

Michael Dewe

DIVERSITY AND COMPLEXITY

The local institutions in the UK housing resources for those interested in local history and local studies are diverse, complex in their interrelationships and sometimes scattered geographically. The elements of such resource provision are libraries, record offices and museums, but the list could be extended to include, for example, historic houses and art galleries. Some of these resources are in private hands and access to them may well be restricted. Factors leading to such local diversity and complexity include the structure of local government, independent library and museum initiatives, and the emergence of three distinct institutional types – library, museum and archive – and professions in the last 150 years.

It is difficult to imagine another area of study, research or enquiry where the source materials are so varied and so dispersed over a variety of resource providers at local level.[1] The situation is further complicated by the potential relevance to the local studies enquirer of the material held in national, regional, academic and specialist institutions, both public and private.

The local historian will, of course, make use of other resources, such as the landscape itself, both rural and urban. Field boundaries, local vernacular architecture, ancient monuments and sites, and the gravestones in a cemetery may all provide information as significant as that found in record office, library or museum. It is important for the librarian, as it is for the archivist and museum curator, to have some understanding of this varied and complex situation, and of the potential main avenues of further enquiry outside their own collection and locality. The chosen avenues will reflect the particular history of a given area: its people, industry and associations, for example. For not every non-local institution will necessarily have something of relevance to the student of a given community.

With this broader understanding and awareness, the librarian is able to advise enquirers of further relevant resources held locally or elsewhere in the United

Kingdom and sometimes beyond. For example, information on lead mining in the vicinity of Aberystwyth could be sought from the local public library; Ceredigion Archives; the National Monuments Record for Wales; Ceredigion Museum, and the National Library of Wales, all located in Aberystwyth itself. Outside the town, the Mid-Wales Mining Museum (Llywernog Silver–Lead Mine, Ponterwyd) and the Institute of Geological Sciences, London, would also be potential sources, as would the National Museum of Wales, Cardiff.

Information on George Stephenson, the British engineer, is held at the Local Studies Department, Chesterfield Library, the National Railway Museum (York), and at the Science Museum and the library of the Institution of Mechanical Engineers, both in London. Materials relating to D.H. Lawrence are held at the library of the University of Liverpool and the D.H. Lawrence Birthplace Museum, Eastwood, in addition to the better known sources at Nottingham University and Nottingham Public Library. Sometimes such awareness must operate at the international level, for, in addition to the Conan Doyle/Sherlock Holmes collections in Edinburgh and Westminster public libraries, there are collections in the public library of Metropolitan Toronto, Canada (and elsewhere in North America), as well as Switzerland.

At a less exalted level, those advising family historians with probable relatives in the English-speaking world, such as the USA, Australia, Canada or New Zealand, will need to be aware of relevant institutions and resources in those countries, or elsewhere in the world.[2]

This greater awareness of other institutions, in particular local ones, and their resources can also lead to agreement over collecting policies and cooperation on publications, educational activities and exhibitions, for example.

While the local studies collection is usually associated with the public library, this chapter also describes the relevance of national, academic and special libraries for local studies. This is followed by a description of the other two main resource providers – archives and museums – at the national, regional and local level (including some references to the Republic of Ireland), and a somewhat briefer consideration of art galleries and historic houses. The picture is not a straightforward one, for at the national level in particular, many libraries house significant archival collections and some museums have large libraries. In some instances printed guides are available to the collections of individual libraries and archives, and reference works will note their availability. Increasingly, however, library and other catalogues are becoming available on-line and institutional groups and many institutions have their own website (which may allow electronic access to some materials held), as well as providing guidance to the individual library, museum or archive, its services and collections.[3]

Published works on carrying out local history/studies in England, and in Wales, Scotland, Northern Ireland and the Republic of Ireland, are probably still the best way of initially acquiring an overview of resource provision in a particular country and will usually offer fuller guidance to that given below.[4]

LIBRARIES[5]

PUBLIC LIBRARIES

Given the sometimes conflicting objectives of providing individual communities with access to the resources for learning about their locality and that, for example, of satisfactorily preserving local studies material for posterity, UK public libraries have responded to the provision of local studies services in a variety of ways. While the types of provision basically involve the question of the centralization or decentralization of collections and services, it is clear that the choice of one of such diametrically opposed alternatives is not likely to be entirely satisfactory in many cases. Whichever of these two main approaches has been taken will have been affected by past government reports, local government reorganization, the type of area (urban or rural), local circumstances (such as the history of local studies provision in an area) and the association of libraries with, for example, archives and museums, within a local authority department or directorate. An indication that more might be done by public libraries and other institutions for smaller communities can be seen in local initiatives, independent of (or working with) local authorities, to provide libraries and museums of local history; the examples of Market Harborough and Horley are noted below.

Centralized collections

The centralization of local studies provision is a way of dealing with the dilemma of access and the satisfactory preservation of materials, perhaps to the disadvantage sometimes of the former. At the same time, however, it provides an opportunity to enhance services and facilities through the provision of specialist staff for conservation and educational activities, often in purpose-built library accommodation. Centralization is perhaps particularly appropriate in urban authorities, where distance may not be a great problem and public transport is readily available. A late-1990s London example of centralization is that of the Merton Local Studies Centre where collections at Mitcham, Wimbledon and Morden libraries have been brought together. Nevertheless, centralization occurs to some extent in county areas, Cornwall, Flintshire (which includes a family history centre) and Cheshire, for example, and the trend towards local studies centres (discussed below) may increase this approach.

Decentralized collections

In contrast to the centralization of provision, other library services may have a number of sizeable area or district collections, usually reflecting former independent urban library authorities who had maintained their own collections. Examples include Derbyshire, Staffordshire, the North Eastern Library Board and North Yorkshire.

With the most recent local government reorganization, some of these collections, e.g. at Southampton, Derby, Portsmouth, Bristol and Swansea, re-emerge as major collections for new unitary authorities, or a new collection is developed for such new library authorities, as at Telford and Wrekin. As with some centralized collections, area or district collections may be operated in association with reference provision and one such collection may have the responsibility of holding some material on an authority-wide basis.

Branch and mobile library collections

To make up for the collection of local materials being held either centrally or decentrally in what are usually the larger service points of a public library system, it has been usual to provide some local material (at least books and pamphlets) in branch and mobile libraries. For some time now, however, it has been recognized that the scope of such collections may not fully satisfy the needs of people in smaller communities for more detailed historical and other information about their locality. As a consequence, branch and mobile libraries in some library services have been furnished with copies of newspaper cuttings, directory entries, ephemera, maps and other documents – drawn from its major collection – as an information resource which focuses more precisely on the community in question. This information may be made up into a booklet, such as the township packs produced by Cheshire Archives and Local Studies, or some other format.

Resources acquired locally by the branch library can also be copied for inclusion in its collection, after being passed to the appropriate major collection for cataloguing, etc.[6] Branch libraries can also put together programmes of local history events and activities geared specifically towards their community, as at Dronfield, Derbyshire.[7] In some instances efforts might be made to take local studies resources more directly to some community groups and mention has already been made of Birmingham's History Van in Chapter 1.

Although the location of local studies material within a library service may matter administratively and to some groups of users, for others the location of material may become increasingly unimportant, given its probable future electronic availability.

LOCAL HISTORY SOCIETY COLLECTIONS

Local studies provision in smaller libraries may be influenced by the work of local history societies (a largely 20th-century phenomenon), whose numbers are regularly increasing. A few have set up their own library and/or museum and in some instances may look to find a place for them in local branch libraries. Saddleworth Historical Society has its own website providing information about activities, publications, library and archives and offers e-mail facilities. A Saddleworth bibliography is included and there are links to other Saddleworth websites.[8]

On the evidence of the archaeological societies and their libraries (described below), local studies librarians might advance a number of reasons for not encouraging local history societies to form a library (limited availability, lack of continuity and security of collections, for example) yet societies continue to do so. This may be because public library local studies provision geared towards smaller but identifiable communities requires further development.

Clearly, one way to bring this about is to cooperate with and support a local society's endeavours in this direction, particularly by providing accommodation in the local library. This may not be the perfect solution but it overcomes some of the professional objections to local society libraries.[9] An example of such a partnership is the Horley Local History Centre, winner of the 1997 Library Association/Holt Jackson Community Initiative Award.[10] Another is the RH7 History Group in Surrey, which is a support organization for the New Lingfield Guest House Local History Centre, a mediaeval hall which also houses the county library.[11]

LIBRARIES OF LOCAL ARCHAEOLOGICAL SOCIETIES

A feature of mainly 19th-century cultural life was the founding of a number of local societies throughout the country in counties and in towns. While many such societies commonly styled themselves 'archaeological', a wide variety of terms (sometimes in combination) were used to indicate the interests of any one society, e.g. architectural, historical, antiquarian, natural history and field club. A main objective of such societies was the publication of transactions recording the results of local investigation and research. The setting up of a library was often incidental to the formation and publishing activity of the society, although at their height there were around 100 such societies, about two-thirds of which maintained a library.

The size of such collections, which tended to attract irrelevant donations, was small and an important element was the journals received on exchange from other societies. In spite of the problems associated with maintaining a library by these societies, many of the collections still exist and some are still added to. A large number, however, have passed into the keeping of public libraries, record offices and museums, where they are usually kept as a distinct reference collection, sometimes only available tomembers. The collection of Chester Archaeological Society is housed in the Chester Record Office, that of the Somerset Archaeological and Natural History Society at Taunton Library.

Of those collections which continue as working collections in their own society's hands, some, such as those maintained by the archaeological societies of Yorkshire (which has a family history section), Sussex and Surrey are regularly available and may have large collections and a professional librarian. Pinhorn has published a handy list, arranged geographically, of historical, archaeological, family history and kindred UK societies, as well as a list of local history/studies libraries.[12]

FAMILY HISTORY SOCIETIES

The growth of family history in the last three decades has seen the development of numerous family history societies, such as those in Cornwall, Glamorgan, Orkney, Bradford, Hillingdon, Wexford and the Northern Ireland Family History Society. The societies, such as Hertfordshire Family History Society, which works closely with the archives and local studies library,[13] often involve themselves in publication activity, including a journal, database, index and transcription work (memorials and documents, for example). Some societies may maintain a local and family history library and the North Cheshire, Glamorgan and Sussex family history societies are examples of this.[14]

The Church of Jesus Christ of Latter Day Saints operates a number of family history centres run by volunteers mainly in England and the larger Scottish towns. There are fewer elsewhere in the UK and Ireland.[15]

LOCAL STUDIES CENTRES

The complexity of resource provision, even at the local level, described in this chapter poses problems for the local historian and enquirer, as well as for the librarian, curator and archivist. For the latter three, problems arise over competition for and duplicate storage of some material, because there is no agreement as to what precisely constitutes the collection responsibilities of museums, libraries and archives. Obviously, close collaboration and liaison between such institutions will be of help in sharing expertise and mounting joint exhibitions, for example, but the user will still have to visit a variety of institutions in order to pursue their research or enquiry, and those institutions may not always be proximate to one another or conveniently located.

These difficulties could be overcome in many ways by the establishment of local studies centres which would represent a coming together of local material and information, regardless of its form. It would recognize that, whatever the differences in the type of materials that local libraries, archives and museums traditionally take responsibility for, these institutions have much in common as to purpose and services, and their staff make use of many similar professional skills and techniques.

Staff at such a centre could include qualified archivists, librarians and curators, with the centre head coming from one of these, or some other appropriate profession. The centre would provide the opportunity to employ specialist staff, on behalf of all, and thus to undertake information technology, educational and conservation work, for example. Such a situation would enable the sharing of technical resources, such as computer, photographic, reprographic, repair and conservation facilities.

While some small-scale research would seem to endorse the local studies centre approach as 'a viable and worthwhile alternative to the more familiar independent service provision',[16] its validity has been questioned in terms of service, the values of an open and democratic society and administrative convenience.[17] It is clear that a number of factors militate against the setting up of a such a centre: responsibility for the three services within a given locality can be varied; the current investment in separate buildings, equipment etc.; the independence (and possible mutual suspicion and even mistrust) of the three professions. Such centres would appear to be most useful and feasible in large cities where local authorities are responsible for all three types of services, although the bringing together of archives and local studies collections is the most usual outcome. Examples of the fairly long-standing convergence of a local collection and archives are to be found in the London boroughs of Brent, Camden, Enfield and Tower Hamlets, and in the metropolitan districts of Wakefield, St Helens, Dudley, Rotherham and Sandwell. Newer examples include those of the Hammersmith and Fulham Archives and Local History Centre, Croydon Local Studies Library and Archives Service, Westminster Archives Centre and county examples in Kent, North Devon, Buckinghamshire, Shropshire, Oxfordshire and Surrey.[18]

NATIONAL LIBRARIES

Librarians and researchers may not always think of national libraries in terms of resources for local history/studies but, as copyright libraries acquiring a vast range of printed material over the years, including local newspapers and periodicals, much will be of local or regional interest and may not be available locally. The origins of a national library usually mean also that a great deal of old, rare and unique material is held and that there are map, print and drawing collections, as well as collections of manuscript and archival material, much of which may refer to individual localities. Collections of non-print material, such as a sound archive, are also increasingly associated with national library provision. As well as responding to enquiries, services to readers usually include photography and reprography, as well as printed and electronic information on the use of the library for genealogy and family history, and about materials of particular interest to local studies, such as newspapers, maps and ephemera.

The British Library, founded in 1973, was originally the library of the British Museum, dating from 1753, and today is a large and complex institution operating from sites in London and elsewhere, including the major new building in the Euston Road. Of chief interest to those concerned with local history is the material available through the Humanities Reading Room, which includes printed books, official publications and the special collections of western manuscripts and maps.

The manuscripts collection contains the foundation collections of Sloane, Cotton and Harley and, as well as some manuscript maps, there is also a collection of non-manuscript material, for example seals and photographs. The map library includes topographical views in both manuscript and printed form, in addition to an Ordnance Survey collection for Britain and a number of special collections, for example maps and plans of London. The British Library Newspaper Library at Colindale, which collects UK, Irish and overseas newspapers and popular UK periodicals, is particularly important for its work in making accessible, preserving, microfilming and recording local newspapers. The British Library also houses the National Preservation Office, the focus for debate and information on preservation, conservation and security in libraries and archives, and the National Sound Archive, described below.[19]

Founded in 1907, the National Library of Wales has a special interest in materials of all kinds relating to Wales and other Celtic countries. The Department of Printed Books includes books, periodicals and music, as well as material in microform and electronic formats, of Welsh interest. Manuscript and archival material relating to Wales is held in the Department of Manuscripts and Records, and this includes archives of Welsh estates, families, institutions, politicians (the Welsh Political Archive) and writers. The library is also a Diocesan Record Office of the Church in Wales and has many ecclesiastical records; there are, in addition, substantial holdings for non-conformist denominations. The collection of the Department of Pictures and Maps includes topographical prints and drawings, photographs, portraits (the Welsh Portrait Archive), paintings and Ordnance Survey and tithe maps. The department is also responsible for the Sound and Moving Image Collection, which covers the range of recording media from wax cylinders and compact discs to film and television broadcasts. The national library's on-line catalogue allows access to a database on which the Bibliography of Wales is available.

The National Library of Scotland, established in 1925 and based on the Advocates' Library founded in 1682, provides through its reading rooms extensive coverage of printed materials, including newspapers of Scottish relevance, whether printed in Scotland or of Scottish interest or association. Scottish printed ephemera is being collected selectively and the map library includes historic maps of Scotland as well as an Ordnance Survey collection. The special, manuscript and archival collections have material relating to Scottish history, culture and literature, and the activities of Scots throughout the world. The national library published the annual *Bibliography of Scotland* from 1976 to 1987, which is now available via the Internet or CD-ROM.[20]

Much relevant information covering Northern Ireland prior to 1922 is to be found in the National Archives and the National Library of Ireland, both in Dublin.[21] The national library, founded in 1877, has extensive coverage of the humanities, with the emphasis on material relating to Ireland and the Irish people. Its collection includes printed books and pamphlets, periodicals, newspapers, maps, ephemera, drawings, topographical prints and photographs of places, and manuscripts. The Genealogical Office, part of the national library, is housed separately in Dublin and is the state authority for heraldry, genealogy and family history. There is no national library collection in Northern Ireland.

ACADEMIC LIBRARIES

Alongside public library local studies collections and those in schools are a number of local collections in the libraries of universities and colleges, the manuscript and special collections at Nottingham University, for example. Local history collections, like that of the Northern College of Education begun in the 1970s, are built up in the main as working collections for the support of teaching, project work and research in the academic institutions which they serve.[22] It is not their purpose to duplicate collections and services to be found in public libraries. However, their special and archival collections can provide important supplements to them.[23] For reasons of comparative study, a few institutions may collect material from outside clearly defined geographical and administrative boundaries.

A survey in 1984, answered by 66 academic libraries, still provides the only detailed source of information about local studies provision by this library group.[24] The survey, which looked at such matters as the scope, use and staffing of collections, as well as publications and cooperation, concluded:

- a significant number of academic libraries did not have a local collection;
- their existence depended on the requirements to serve the interests and needs in the parent institution which cannot be met in other ways, i.e. by other local libraries and record offices;

- departments with specialized interests may develop their own collections: for example, the Rural History Centre and the Ephemera Collection, both at Reading University, and the English Local History Collection, Leicester University;
- a few local societies have placed their libraries in the care of a university library: the Manchester Geographical Society in the John Rylands University Library of Manchester, and the Hertfordshire Natural History and Field Club in University College Library, University of London, for example.

Deserving of special note are the university libraries of Oxford, Cambridge and Trinity College, Dublin which, as copyright libraries, have a number of collecting strengths similar to those of national libraries, as well as housing material relating to their more immediate vicinity.

The Bodleian Library, refounded in 1602 by Sir Thomas Bodley, is the main library of the University of Oxford, and is chiefly devoted to the humanities and social sciences. Its Department of Western Manuscripts has collections of family papers and those of individuals, including politicians, university and literary figures. There are also topographical, local history, deeds and rolls, and music manuscript collections, as well as archives of various societies, including that of the Conservative Party. The library also holds the John Johnson collection of printed ephemera.

Cambridge University Library has a history dating back to the 14th century and its collections are particularly strong in the humanities and social sciences. There are specialist departments for maps, music, manuscripts, periodicals and official publications. Its manuscript holdings date largely from 1574 and have been continuously enlarged since. They include records of the Diocese and Dean and Chapter of Ely, East Anglian family and estate papers, private papers of Cambridge men, and commercial records.

The collections of Trinity College, Dublin have been built up from the 16th century and, as it enjoys legal deposit for material published in Ireland and the UK, it is now its country's largest library. It has map, music and other special collections (e.g. Anglo-Irish literature). Its manuscripts include special collections on Irish folk music, contemporary literature, and family and private papers.

SPECIAL LIBRARIES

Special libraries are 'special' for reasons that include the limited subject scope of their collections and some such libraries have a long-standing importance for local studies/history. The Society of Antiquaries (founded in the early 18th century), for example, has, in addition to its book stock, a large collection of topographical prints and drawings, archives, a number of important local collections (on Worcestershire, for example), broadsides and seals. The library of the Society of

Genealogists (founded in 1911) has a topographical collection arranged by county (including directories and poll books), family histories, genealogical periodicals, as well as a document collection covering several thousand surnames, transcripts of parish and other registers, and other manuscript material and indexes.[25] The Scottish Genealogy Society, Edinburgh, has a library and family history centre. A more recent body is the Federation of Family History Societies (1974), founded to coordinate the activities of family history societies and represent the views of family historians to official bodies It publishes a magazine and guides to records, holds meetings, undertakes transcriptions and indexing work, and provides a reference library – not open to the public, however.

Other special libraries of national standing, focusing on more precise subject fields, may also be of use for local studies: the Women's Library (formerly the Fawcett Library),[26] the St Bride Printing Library and the Royal Society of Medicine Library, for example.

At the more local level there are the libraries of such institutions as the Ironbridge Gorge Museum (Shropshire), St Deiniol's Library (Hawarden), Leadhills Miners' Library (Biggar), the Linen Hall Library (Belfast) and the libraries of cathedrals, such as Hereford, Canterbury and York (which has a databank on Yorkshire people before 1600), and St Columb's, Londonderry, as well as the local archaeological and history societies described earlier.[27]

ARCHIVES[28]

Archives range 'over the records of medieval and modern government, both central and local, the archives of the Church and universities, the papers of great dynastic landed families, and collections made from various sources by scholars or antiquarians' and the categories and number of UK institutions holding archival records are quite considerable. Even with some exclusions, the current edition of *British archives* lists over 1,100 institutions[29] 'where archives in the widest sense of the word, are held and made relatively accessible'[30] and, in addition to record repositories, includes collections in some museums, libraries, other institutions and in private hands. The term 'archive' has also been applied to subject collections of material, which may or may not contain manuscript and record material, such as the National Jazz Archive, Loughton, Essex, or the Black Cultural Archives, Brixton, London, and to those of film, sound recordings and pictures.

The National Register of Archives (of which there is also a Scottish office), collects information about manuscript sources outside the public records, and has copies of the published guides and the unpublished lists of archival collections for those repositories which have produced and submitted them. A number of other institutions will help locate particular records.[31]

Although archival collections may be unsatisfactorily housed, posing problems of preservation, access and use, a number of archive buildings, national, county and local, have been erected in recent years: the Public Record Office (1977, extended in 1997); Hampshire Record Office (1993); Hammersmith and Fulham Archives (1992), and Jersey Archive (2000).[32]

NATIONAL RECORD OFFICES

The Public Record Office (PRO), established in 1838, acquires all government archives selected for permanent preservation. In addition to government and legal records, the PRO contains much deposited and donated material, has numerous semi-official and private collections of public figures and the archives of some national non-governmental organizations. Non-manuscript material includes photographs, maps and plans, some film, and a staff library strong on English topography. Some official records are not in the PRO but with other bodies or in approved local repositories. Together with the Office for National Statistics, the PRO also operates the Family Record Centre.

Set up in 1946, the House of Lords Record Office is responsible for the records of both houses of Parliament and various deposited papers. With the exception of its journals dating from 1547, the House of Commons records are post-1834, as earlier ones were lost in a fire of that year. National legislation that has had a local effect and local legislation (for canals, railways, roads and bridges, for example), attract the interest of local historians, and there is a large record office collection consisting of plans of such enterprises dating from 1794.

The National Archives of Scotland (NAS), formerly the Scottish Record Office, is the repository for the government and legal records of Scotland but also receives other records on deposit. The NAS's main collections include legal and administrative records before union with England in 1707, the records of various government agencies and departments, records of the Scottish central and local courts, records of local authorities and churches, and the records of families, institutions, businesses and industrial firms. Non-manuscript material includes a large collection of maps and plans, and photographs in certain record groups, and there is a library covering Scottish history and topography.

Established in 1923, the Public Record Office of Northern Ireland (PRONI) takes responsibility for official records – government departments, courts of law, statutory bodies, imperial records (created by the Westminster government) – and accepts records on deposit. It also acts like the manuscript department of a national library, has much pre-1922 archival material and additionally has several large photographic collections. In the absence of local record offices, local archives are centralized at PRONI. There is an Isle of Man Public Record Office, charged with holding Manx government records, as well as archive services in Jersey and Guernsey holding official records.

The National Archives of Ireland, established in 1988 through the amalgamation of two earlier institutions, holds the records of government departments from 1922, the archives of the Chief Secretary's Office (1790–1922), parish records, estate archives, family papers, business records, census records and trade union archives. Two special collections are the archive of the Ordnance Survey of Ireland and records of convict transportation to Australia.[33]

The Irish Genealogical Project is endeavouring to make genealogical information in Ireland more readily available. Computer indexing centres have been established both north and south and various levels of progress reported.

REGISTER OFFICES

Registration of births, deaths and marriages in England and Wales began in 1837 and there are indexes to the registers at the Family Record Centre (FRC). The decennial census returns are transferred to the PRO but microform copies are held at the FRC, along with death duty registers (1796–1858) and copies of wills before 1858 from the Prerogative Court of Canterbury and non-parochial registers. The Principal Registry of the Family Division has custody of all wills admitted to probate in England and Wales since 1858 and the public is able to purchase copies.

Established in 1855, on the introduction of compulsory registration of births, deaths and marriages in Scotland, the General Register Office for Scotland provides a unique UK research facility, as it also accommodates in one place the registers, old parochial records (before 1855) and census records.

The General Register Office (Northern Ireland) was set up in 1922 to register births, marriages and deaths in the province. Registration records from the mid-19th century, for what is now Northern Ireland, are also available for consultation. In the Republic of Ireland the General Register Office has indexes to births, deaths and marriages in all Ireland (1864–1921) and (exclusive of the six north-eastern counties) those registered from 1922 onwards.

There are also registry offices for the Isle of Man, Guernsey and Jersey, as well as local registry offices throughout the UK.

Questions of land ownership can be answered by reference to records of the Land Registry and the district land registries for England and Wales. For further sources of personal information (including financial information), and that relating to real and other property, commercial and professional bodies and organizations, available from official and public records, the *Directory of registers and records* provides useful guidance.[34]

Other national archive collections of a specialized nature include those of the National Army Museum, the Royal Air Force Museum, and the Oriental and India Office Collections at the British Library.

COUNTY AND LOCAL RECORD OFFICES

Prior to the most recent local government reorganization, each English and Welsh county (with the exception of Avon) had an archive service – county record office (CRO) – with branches in some cases. There were in addition in England other local authority record offices maintained by cities, boroughs and district councils. In Scotland, archive services were provided by regional councils, island authorities and district councils, but it is generally recognized that archive services were not as well developed as in England and Wales.

In Wales and Scotland, the new system of unitary councils (April 1996) broke up most of the county units in which archive services were based. 'In Scotland, indeed, large areas had no archive provision. The challenges facing archive services in these countries have been different than those in England, and in many ways more acute.'[35]

Local government reorganization in England in the 1990s, however, turned out to be less disruptive for archive provision than expected. There was fear it would result in fragmentation and the multiplication of small underresourced services but this was avoided. Wales has suffered in this way, but on balance there has also been some improvement.[36] The role of the Keeper of Records of Scotland (now Head of the National Archives) 'in advising all new unitary authorities on their record keeping ... provided the opportunity to issue specific guidance' and 'there are now more archives and more archivists ... than before reorganization'.[37] In Wales, a similar arrangement requires all authorities to draw up schemes for the management of archives and records for approval by the national assembly.

In England and Wales, the county record offices continue to be responsible for official and local authority records (both past and present) and also contain church and chapel records, the private records of businesses, local societies and political parties, for example, and may also include manuscripts. All English CROs (but not the Isle of Man Public Record Office) are also diocesan record offices and, where permitted, may also house manorial, tithe and specified classes of public records.

Like public libraries, archive services are enjoined to generate income and secure lottery funding, and the latter is seen as the way to support developments in archive services. As in libraries, there is 'an emphasis on standards and performance', but also an appreciation of the need for improved legal protection for archives.[38]

England

Local government reorganization in 1998 created 46 new unitary authorities and abolished the counties of Avon, Cleveland and Humberside. Of the shire counties, only Berkshire ceased to exist and urban areas in 18 counties became unitary authorities, affecting archive services and budgets in some of the counties from which they were created. Hereford and Worcester's association was abrogated and the Isle of Wight became a single island authority. Various solutions to these changes were effected or are in the process of negotiation.

In many instances existing county record offices remained unchanged or operate through joint arrangements. For example, Cleveland (now Teesside) and Berkshire CROs are funded by the constituent local authorities. In the former county of Avon, the area is mostly covered by the Bristol Record Office.

In some cases the new unitary authorities may choose to run their own archive service: Portsmouth and Southampton in Hampshire, for example, or Plymouth (which includes the West Devon area) and the Medway towns, which run independent services based on former Devon and Kent branch offices.

Archive services continue to be provided by those local authorities untouched by reorganization: the London boroughs and metropolitan district councils, such as Birmingham, Bolton and Sandwell, whose archive services are often provided in association with local studies collections. In London, the boroughs are legally permitted to collect records relating to their area, but not all do so. Major groups of records for the former counties of London and Middlesex and outer London boroughs are held by the London Metropolitan Archives and the CROs of Essex, Kent, Hertfordshire and Surrey, respectively. The London Metropolitan Archives is administered by the Corporation of London, which acts under its own archive legislation in respect of its records held at the Guildhall Library.[39]

Wales

Boundary and name changes make it less than easy to describe archive services in the 22 new unitary authorities in relation to what preceded them. Powys remained unchanged while the county of Dyfed was split into the Pembrokeshire, Carmarthenshire and Ceredigion county record offices. Clwyd was divided into two – there are thus record offices for Denbighshire and Flintshire – and lost areas to the newly independent Conwy and Wrexham who have established their own services. Gwynedd also lost part of its area to Conwy, and Anglesey (which re-established an independent archive service), but continues to maintain a record office at Caernarfon together with Merioneth Archives at Dolgellau. Gwent, Glamorgan and West Glamorgan were dissolved into a number of new authorities but the 'county' record offices continue following joint management agreements.

Scotland

Archives in Scotland are in a state of flux following the local government reorganizations of 1996, resulting in 32 unitary authorities. In some regions, such as Strathclyde and Central, centralized archive services were split up, along with their archive holdings, but island authorities continue to operate a service on Shetland and Orkney, as do the city authorities of Aberdeen, Dundee, Edinburgh and Glasgow. Completely new archive services, however, were established in South Lanarkshire, West Lothian and Clackmannanshire, with 'a significant strengthening of small services elsewhere'.[40]

Northern Ireland

In Northern Ireland, local records continue to be centralized at the Public Record Office of Northern Ireland.

OTHER ARCHIVES

There are many other types of repository: university, hospital, military, religious, industrial, business and sporting. Many will have material relating to individual localities or social groups and therefore knowledge of and access to such collections is important.[41] Some will be institutions, companies and private individuals who do not collect archives but may be prepared, like the BBC, for example, at the BBC Written Archives in Reading, to make their own records available for research. The *Directory of corporate archives* lists some of the members of the Business Archives Council which maintain archive facilities, for example the Bank of England, the John Lewis partnership, W.H. Smith Ltd, Young & Co's Brewery.[42] Private collections of estate and family records, for example the Duke of Norfolk's Library and Archives, Arundel Castle, and the Devonshire Collection, Chatsworth, are listed by the Historical Manuscripts Commission, and may be available for consultation, possibly for a fee.

Archives of types of material

Film, video and other non-book materials share many of the problems of much local studies material: the absence of a legal deposit requirement, the problems of bibliographical control and the difficulties, such as acquisition, associated with unpublished materials. Graham Cornish's booklet provides a guide to national archival collections of non-book materials,[43] but there are also a number of regional resources which local studies enquirers may wish to investigate.

National moving image archives

Established in 1935, the National Film and Television Archive, London, collects a wide variety of film (including amateur film) as well as recorded TV programmes. Amongst other things, the collection provides a record of contemporary life and people, ethnography, transport and exploration. The Scottish Film Archive in Glasgow, established in 1976, places its collecting emphasis on Scottish material. The collection is almost entirely non-fiction and includes local cinema newsreels, advertising, educational, amateur, documentary and local TV news material. As indicated below, moving image material may also be held by other national institutions, as in Wales, for example.

National sound archives

The National Sound Archive at the British Library is international in scope but is also the national repository of sound recordings of all kinds, including music, literature, drama, speeches, historic events, language and dialect, and wildlife. Material comes in from a wide range of sources, including public libraries, private collectors and the BBC. The collection and preservation of material illustrating Scottish literature, local history and traditions is carried out by the University of Edinburgh, School of Scottish Studies. It houses recordings of the numerous Scottish oral history projects. In Wales, there is the Sound and Moving Image Collection at the National Library. This includes published recordings of Welsh interest, radio programmes from Radio Cymru and Radio Wales, oral recordings, recordings of S4C, HTV Wales and BBC Wales, and also films. There is also a substantial collection of oral history, spoken literature, language and music at the Museum of Welsh Life, St Fagans and, in Northern Ireland, a similar collection at the Ulster Folk and Transport Museum.

The Folklore Archive, University College, Dublin, has many sound recordings, photographs, films, video, etc of folk culture material (including song and dance), covering all the Irish counties.

Regional film and sound archives

Complementing national film, television and sound resources are a number of regional archives, whose aim is to obtain and preserve items about their own region and forward material of national importance to a national archive. For sound there is, for example, the North West Sound Archive (Clitheroe). For film (and sometimes also television or sound) there are, for example, the North West (Manchester), East Anglian (Norwich), Northern (Gateshead), Wessex (Winchester) and Yorkshire (Ripon) film archives.

At the local level, sound recordings, particularly oral history recordings, are held by many libraries, museums, record offices and community groups. The *Directory of recorded sound resources in the United Kingdom* lists over 480 collections of all kinds and is compiled from the national register of collections of recorded sound database at the National Sound Archive, British Library.[44] The British Universities Film and Video Council, which fosters the production, study and use of film, etc for higher education and research, has published a researcher's guide to British film and television collections, including regional and local ones.[45]

Picture archives

Libraries, museums and conventional archive repositories may all have substantial pictorial collections. However, there are a number of large general, historical, news or subject photographic collections. These include the Hulton Getty Collection, the Museum of London Picture Library, News Team International (Birmingham), Victoria and Albert Museum Picture Library and the Francis Frith Collection of photographs of many British towns and villages, which may also be of interest in local studies research. There are a number of published guides to help the local studies picture researcher, including directories of British photographic and slide collections.[46]

MUSEUMS[47]

A museum is 'an institution which collects, documents, exhibits and interprets material evidence and associated information for public benefit', and there are about 2,500 museums and galleries open to the public in the UK.[48] Of these, many are funded by the state and local authorities but there is a large number of independent museums, represented by the Association of Independent Museums (AIM), founded in 1977. The largest group of independent museums consists of local history museums (215 in an AIM survey), 'collecting primarily for themselves material which reflects their own need to identify with the place in which they live and the evidence of its history'.[49] Museums are usually contained within a building but some, consisting of rescued historical buildings or buildings in their original location, are open-air sites, for example Weald and Downland Open Air Museum, West Sussex, and the Chiltern Open Air Museum, Buckinghamshire.

County and local museums (sometimes called 'heritage centres') are administered by local authorities, national museums by government departments (for example the Ministry of Defence) or bodies, or by boards of trustees. There are also museums administered by military regiments, universities, colleges and schools, hospitals, societies, professional associations, industrial, commercial and private organizations, operating in a number of cases as charitable trusts.

Museums, other than national institutions, are supported by technical services and advice on conservation, display, documentation and publicity provided by the area museum councils; there are also autonomous regional museum federations which promote the development of their members through meetings and training, for example, and provide feedback to other bodies.

While there are examples of modern purpose-built museums in the UK, for example the Burrell Collection, Glasgow, the National Museum of Scotland, Edinburgh, the Shakespeare Globe and Education Centre, London and the Jorvik

Viking Centre, York, the museum is typically housed in converted premises, often of historical and architectural interest. In addition to their galleries, museums may house a range of additional facilities, such as cafeteria/restaurant, auditorium, shop or museum library, and provide a variety of services: temporary exhibitions, item identification, publications and educational services, for example.

Some museums may call themselves a heritage or visitor centre (or similar description) and may be centres devoted to an exhibition on a special subject or place and may be based in a historic building. Examples include Thurso Heritage Centre, Weavers Triangle Visitor Centre (Burnley), Stafford Castle and Visitor Centre and Upton Heritage Centre.

NATIONAL MUSEUMS

The UK national museums and branches include both general institutions and those covering specialist areas such as science, arms and armour, and art. Their libraries are usually major subject collections in their field: for example, the Department of Printed Books at the Imperial War Museum.

The British Museum houses the national collections of art and archaeology from prehistoric to modern times and among its departments are those concerned with prehistoric and Romano-British, mediaeval and later antiquities, coins and medals, prints and drawings.[50] In Cardiff, the National Museum and Gallery contains geology, botany, zoology, archaeology, industry and art exhibits relating to the history and cultural life of Wales. The National Museums of Scotland, Edinburgh has collections that include those on the decorative arts, archaeology, geology, natural history and working life. The Ulster Folk and Transport Museum, Holywood houses major collections illustrating the way of life and traditions of the people of Northern Ireland. The museum also has a sound archive and operates the BBC Northern Ireland Radio Archive. Ulster Museum, Belfast houses the province's major collections of fine and applied art, as well as extensive collections that include archaeology, history, botany and geology. The Ulster–American Folk Park, Omagh features traditional rural buildings from Ulster and America and includes original 19th-century shopfronts. In 1998, these three Ulster institutions were merged to form the National Museums and Galleries of Northern Ireland. Ireland's National Museum in Dublin covers archaeology (with artefacts from every Irish county), history, the decorative arts, folk life, geology and zoology; there is a large picture archive.

National museums may have branches, such as the Royal Armouries at HM Tower of London, a branch of the Royal Armouries Museum, Leeds, or be responsible for institutions with a special subject focus – the Bethnal Green Museum of Childhood comes under the umbrella of the Victoria and Albert Museum. Among other specialist museums in this national group is the National

Maritime Museum, Greenwich, illustrating Britain's maritime history through its collection of nautical artefacts, which include models of ships and boats, astronomical and navigational instruments, uniforms, weaponry, paintings and prints. Its library covers such subjects as shipbuilding, shipping companies, piracy and biography and includes rare books and Lloyd's Register from 1764 onwards. Other important specialist sources include the National Museum of Photography, Film and Television, Bradford where, for example, equipment and printed ephemera are collected, and the Museum of the Moving Image, South Bank, London, which traces the development of cinema and television.

COUNTY MUSEUMS

Not every county has a county museum but those that do usually provide a picture of the county in all its aspects, particular concern being given to local industry, agriculture and crafts. Examples in England include the Museum of Kent Life; Buckinghamshire County Museum, Aylesbury, which illustrates the county's geology, natural history, archaeology and history and has a small collection of local paintings; and Warwickshire Museum, Warwick, that illustrates the wildlife, geology, archaeology and history of the county.

In Wales, there is for Pembrokeshire, for example, the Tenby Museum and Art Gallery, with changing exhibitions of local artists and archive and library, while Carmarthenshire County Museum, Abergwili, in the former palace of the Bishop of St David's, shows the history, archaeology, costume, folk life and natural history of the region; it includes local prints and drawings. In Scotland the Shetland Museum, Lerwick describes Shetland life through the ages through collections of archaeology, folk life, history, maritime and natural history, as well as a photographic collection and archive. The Armagh County Museum, Northern Ireland, is considered one of the best in Ireland, and also has a well regarded reference library. The Monaghan County Museum and Art Gallery in the Republic of Ireland, established in 1974, was the first local authority museum in the state and has a large local history section.

OTHER LOCAL MUSEUMS

There are plenty of examples of town museums, both local authority and independently run, which reflect the history of the place in which they are located, although some may have a wider geographical remit. In Wales, Abergavenny Museum, Monmouthshire portrays the history of the town from its origins in Roman times to the present day. Across the border, Birmingham Museum and Art Gallery's Local History Gallery is concerned with the origins and growth of that city and its suburbs from the end of the Middle Ages to the present day. There is heavy use of printed and other materials – prints, paintings and photographs – to support the artefacts. Guildford Museum, Surrey is the archaeological and historical museum for the county, especially West Surrey and Guildford, and has a large collection of photographs and drawings of the Guildford area. Harborough Museum, Leicestershire holds the collections of the Market Harborough Historical Society, in addition to local history material relating to the 50 villages within a ten mile radius.[51] The Museum of London provides a visual, chronologically arranged biography of the London area, starting 250,000 years ago, and there is a print room and library. In Scotland there is the Gairloch Heritage Museum showing past life in a west highland parish, and in Northern Ireland the Balleymoney Museum and Heritage Centre for exhibits on Balleymoney and north Antrim. The Republic of Ireland has, for example, Cork Public Museum, covering national and local history, and Dungarvan Museum, County Waterford which illustrates the history of the town.

SPECIALIST MUSEUMS

There are numerous specialist museums representing a whole range of different subjects, such as agriculture and rural life, brewing, costume, industrial history, maritime history, Irish linen, transport and the armed services. The last-named group is particularly large (about 140 service museums), some only open by appointment. As well as museum items, many service museums also contain archives and other documents, photographs and souvenirs. The Army Museums Ogilby Trust provides information about the collection of regimental and military museums, while a classified list of specialist museums is to be found in the *Local historian's encyclopedia*.[52]

ART GALLERIES

Local authority art galleries are often found housed in association with museums, as well as operating as separate institutions.[53] From a local studies point of view, the significance of art galleries lies in the works they house by local artists, works portraying the locality, and the portraits of people of local (sometimes wider) fame. Such local art may take many forms: paintings, drawings, watercolours, sculpture, photographs and video. While art galleries of national importance, such as national galleries in London, Cardiff, Edinburgh and Dublin, may have works of interest to local studies research and enquiry, the local art gallery, where such exists, is the likely starting place.

NATIONAL GALLERIES

In the search for pictures of individuals, appropriate enquiries could be made of the National Portrait Gallery, London, with its portraits of famous British men and women in a variety of media; the Scottish National Portrait Gallery, Edinburgh, which houses portraits of famous Scottish men and women, and the Department of Pictures and Maps, National Library of Wales, Aberystwyth, whose collection includes portraits of Welsh people from all walks of life and has been designated the Welsh Portrait Archive.

LOCAL GALLERIES

In the absence of a local art gallery, it is worthwhile remembering that examples of pictorial art may be found in some local studies collections.[54] However, where a gallery is provided, the following examples give some indication of what might be available locally. In the Aberdeen Art Gallery, both Scottish and local artists are well represented; the Victoria Art Gallery, Bath includes works of local topography; Derby City Museum and Art Gallery has an extensive topographical collection and the works of Joseph Wright; Salford Museum and Art Gallery's collection covers social and local history but its collection of L.S. Lowry's paintings and drawings has been moved to the purpose-built Lowry Centre; Glyn Vivian Art Gallery, Swansea, is a fine arts museum that includes local pottery, porcelain and glass; Orchard Gallery, Londonderry has local history paintings as well as photographs and recordings; York City Art Gallery exhibits works by York artists and also has watercolours, drawings and prints of York topography.

HISTORIC HOUSES

A historic house, whether stately home, cottage or ruin (such as a castle), and its associated buildings and gardens, may be of interest to the local historian for a number of reasons: its residents, the architects, designers and craftsmen associated with it, its furniture, its works of art (including portraits) or other collections, such as library, museum or archive. While such buildings may be publicly owned or in the care of the National Trust, others are in private hands and their presentation to visitors is very varied.

Examples include Claydon House, Buckinghamshire, with its Florence Nightingale Museum; more famous ones such as Longleat House, Wiltshire, an Elizabethan building with Capability Brown landscaped parkland and collection of rare books, and Castle Howard, North Yorkshire, designed by Vanburgh, with its collection of pictures, statuary, furniture and costume. Further examples include those associated with other families, such as Lanhydrock House (Robartes family), Cornwall or Erddig Hall (Yorke family) Wrexham, and those associated with individuals, such as Milton's Cottage (Chalfont St Giles), the Elgar Birthplace Museum (Lower Broadheath), the Brontë Parsonage (Haworth), Hogarth's House (Chiswick), Barrie's Birthplace (Kirriemuir) or Hill House (Helensburgh), by the architect Charles Rennie Mackintosh. Historic buildings, but with no special association, may be used for museum, heritage or other purposes, as with Aberconwy House, Conwy, which includes an exhibition on the history of the town, as well as furniture relating to the house's history.[55]

SOCIETIES AND INSTITUTIONS

In addition to the resource providers for local studies described in this chapter there are many institutions and organizations, funded independently or by national and local government, that offer guidance, information, publications and services, such as training in the fields of concern to local studies: family and local history, the environment, etc. These range from professional organizations for librarians, archivists and museum curators to local and family history organizations, publishing societies and national organizations.[56] Useful lists of such bodies are to be found in *British archives* and elsewhere.[57]

CONCLUSION

This chapter has provided a framework for an understanding of the various types of institution that provide resources for local studies in the UK (and to a lesser extent in the Republic of Ireland) and the different levels – national, regional and local – at which they function. It is a picture that in broad outline remains fairly constant, but one where significant change can occur following government and local authority decisions.

For various reasons the chapter has dealt almost solely with resource providers of interest to local and family historians but there is a good case for such an account to be extended to cover areas such as geography, natural history and environmental questions, for example.

NOTES

1 For guidance on source materials of the recent past, see Lord, E. (1999), *Investigating the twentieth century*, Stroud: Tempus.
2 See, for example, *World guide to libraries* (1998), 5th edition, Munich: Saur; *Museums of the world* (1995), 5th edition, Munich: Saur. The latter includes a person and subject index.
3 For a gateway to family history resources held in public libraries see Familia (*www.earl.org.uk/familia*). For the archives gateway, see Archon (*www.hmc.gov.uk*). For the museums gateway, see the 24-Hour Museum (*www.24hourmuseum.org.uk*).

4   Collins, P. (1998), *Pathways to Ulster's past: sources and resources for local studies*, Belfast: Queen's University, Institute of Irish Studies; Cox, M. (ed.) (1999), *Exploring Scottish history, with a directory of resource centres for Scottish local and national history in Scotland*, 2nd edition, Hamilton: Scottish Library Association; Campbell-Kease, J. (1989), *A companion to local history research*, London: Alphabooks; Nolan, W. (1982), *Tracing the past: sources for local history in the Republic of Ireland*, Dublin: Geography Publications.

5   For a comprehensive coverage of libraries, museums, archives, etc, which includes a 'local history and studies' heading in the index, see *Aslib directory of information sources in the United Kingdom* (1996), 9th edition, London: Aslib; for similar coverage but excluding museums and covering the Irish Republic and with a detailed subject index, see *Libraries directory 1996–98* (1998), edited by I. Walker, Cambridge: Clarke. For Ireland, with specific references to local studies libraries in its subject index, see *Directory of libraries and information services in Ireland* (1996), 5th edition, Dublin: Library Association of Ireland and Library Association (Northern Ireland Branch).

6   The importance of branch collections is endorsed by Library Association Local Studies Group (2002), *Local studies libraries: Library Association guidelines for local studies provision in public libraries*, 2nd edition, London: Library Association, para B6.2.1.

7   Crabb, S. and Gordon, R. (2000), 'Dronfield's local history zone', *Local studies librarian* 19 (1), 10–12.

8   *Local history news* (2000), (54), 7 (*www.saddleworth-historical-society.org.uk*).

9   *Local history magazine* suggests that regional heritage plans (see Chapter 1) should involve local history societies and that their work, including collecting, should be encouraged and supported: 'A local history role for MLAC?' (2000), *Local history magazine* (78) March/April, 9.

10 'Horley's past is in safe hands: Horley Local History Centre' (1998), *Public library journal* 13 (5), 73–7.

11 Crosby, A. (2000), 'By his postcode ye shall know him', *Local history news* (57), 2.

12 Pinhorn, M. (comp.) (1995), *Historical, archaeological and kindred societies in Great Britain..., a geographical list*, Colbourne, Isle of Wight: Pinhorns; Pinhorn, M. (comp.) (1997), *Local history/studies libraries in Great Britain: a list*, Colbourne, Isle of Wight: Pinhorns. For county, regional and general organizations, see also 'Local history directory' (1999), *Local history magazine* (74), 39–44. In Northern Ireland, the Federation of Ulster Local Studies (FULS) has more than 90 affiliated local history societies and publishes *Local history link*.

13 The society appoints a member of its committee as a liaison officer, and a committee member attends user panel meetings. Its computer group is creating a database of the index to settlement and removal papers. Accommodation is not provided for the society but a proposed new building would enable this. Information from Susan Flood, Collection Manager, Hertfordshire Archives and Local Studies.

14 For a list of family history societies in the UK and elsewhere, as well as much other useful information, see *Genealogical services directory with British local history* (2000), edited by R. Blatchford and G. Heslop, 4th edition, York: GR Specialist Information Services.

15 There is a list of family history centres in the *Genealogical services directory*, 343–4.

16 Friggens, G. (1998), 'Local studies centres', *Local studies librarian* 17 (2), 8–11, a summary of Friggens, G. (1996), *Local studies centres in theory and practice*, Aberystwyth: Department of Information and Library Studies, University of Wales, Aberystwyth (thesis).

17 Rimmer, D. (1998), 'The organisation of local studies: a permissive approach', *Local studies librarian* 17 (2), 11–13.

18 Graham, M. (1992), 'Local studies: a new approach', *Public library journal* 7 (3), 65–8; Buxton, H. (1996), 'There's more to it than money! [management of the Surrey History Centre project]', *Library Association record* 98 (8), 410–11; Robinson, D. (1998), 'Surrey's new history centre', *Local history magazine* (70) November/December, 23–6.

19 For the full story, see Day, A. (1988), *The British Library: a guide to its structure, publications, collections and services*, London: Library Association. More recent developments, omitting the historical background, are chronicled in Day, A. (1994), *The new British Library*, London: Library Association.

20 For information about the national and other libraries, see *Scottish library and information resources* (1999), 11th edition, Hamilton: Scottish Library Association.

21 For information about the national and other libraries, see *Directory of libraries and information services in Ireland* (1996), 5th edition, Dublin, Library Association of Ireland and the Library Association (Northern Ireland Branch).

22 For an account of another college collection, see Armsby, A.F. and Morgan, L. (1990), 'Newcastle College local studies collection', *Local studies librarian* 9 (1), 9–13.

23 *Academic libraries in the United Kingdom and the Republic of Ireland* (1994), edited by A. Harrold, London: Library Association; includes subject and special collections indexes.

24 Paul, D. and Dewe, M (1987), 'Local studies collections in academic libraries', in *Local studies collections: a manual*, vol 1, edited by M. Dewe, Aldershot: Gower, 52–69.

25 Camp, A.J. (1992), 'Society of Genealogists', *Local historian* 22 (2), 68–73.

26 Doughan, D. (1993), 'Local heroines: the Fawcett Library and women's history', *Local historian* 23 (2), 92–7.

27 For further guidance, see *Aslib directory of literary and historical collections in the UK* (1993), edited by K.W. Reynard, London: Aslib; *A directory of rare book and special collections in the United Kingdom and the Republic of Ireland* (1997), edited by B.C. Bloomfield, 2nd edition, London: Library Association.

28 For a fuller, yet concise, account of this section, see Olney, R.J. (1995), *Manuscript sources for British history: their nature, location and use*, London: University of London Institute of Historical Research. Publicly funded archive institutions are listed in *Record repositories in Great Britain* (1999), 11th edition, London: Public Record Office.

29 *British archives: a guide to archive resources in the United Kingdom* (1989), compiled by J. Foster and J. Sheppard, 2nd edition, London: Macmillan, vii; *British archives* (1995), compiled by J. Foster and J. Sheppard, 3rd edition, Basingstoke, Macmillan, vii.

30 *British archives* (1989), viii.

31 A useful list of addresses is given in *British archives* (1995), xlviii–liv.

32 Case studies and a list of buildings are given in Kitching, C. (1993), *Archive buildings in the United Kingdom 1977–1992*, London: HMSO.

33 For fuller information about the Republic of Ireland, see *Directory of Irish archives* (1993), edited by S. Helferty and R. Refausse, 2nd edition, Dublin: Irish Academic Press.

34 Abraham, B. (1993), *Directory of registers and records*, 5th edition, London: Longman.

35 Dunhill, R. (1998), 'Living with change: English county archives', *Local history magazine* (70) November/December, 11.

36 'Welsh record offices and local government re-organization' (1997), *Local history magazine* (59) January/February, 12.

37 *Archives at the millennium: the twenty-eighth report of the Royal Commission on Historical Manuscripts, 1991–1999* (1999), London: Stationery Office, 44.

38 O'Sullivan, M. (2000), 'Government policy on archives', *Local history news* (54), 4–5.

39 For details, which include relevant CROs and special repositories, e.g. hospitals, see *London local archives: a directory of local authority and other record offices and libraries in the London area* (1999), edited by C. Cotton, London: Greater Archives Network.

40 *Archives at the millennium*, 44.

41 For example: Allinson, J. and Hooper, K. (1999), 'A record of Romani heritage [Archives at University of Liverpool]', *Library Association record* 101 (11), 647–9; 'Poll tax archive [At the University of Paisley]', (2000), *Library Association record* 102 (2), 74.

42 Richmond, L. and Turton, A. (1997), *Directory of corporate archives: a guide to British businesses which maintain archives*, 4th edition, London: Business Archives Council.

43 Cornish, G.P. (1986), *Archival collections of non-book materials: a listing and brief description of major national collections*, London: British Library.

44 Weerasinghe, L. (1989), *Directory of recorded sound resources in the United Kingdom*, London: British Library.

45 Ballantyne, J. ed. (1993), *Researcher's guide to British film and television collections*, 4th edition, London: British Universities Film and Video Council.

46 For example: *BAPLA directory of picture libraries 2000/2001* (2000), London: British Association of Picture Libraries and Agencies; McKeown, R. (1990), *National directory of slide collections*, London: British Library; Wall, P. (1977), *Directory of British photographic collections*, London: Heinemann.

47 For a listing of museums, see *Museums yearbook* (1999), London: Museums Association.

48 *Britain 2000: the official yearbook of the United Kingdom* (1999), London: Stationery Office, 260.

49 Cossons, N. (1992), 'Independent museums', in *Manual of curatorship: a guide to museum practice*, Oxford: Butterworth–Heinemann, 114.

50 For a description of the museum's holdings in this area, see Griffiths, A. and Williams, R. (1987), *The Department of Prints and Drawings in the British Museum: user's guide*, London: British Museum.

51 Pursglove, R. (2000), 'Harborough Museum', *Local history magazine* (80) July/August, 17–18.

52 Richardson, J. (1986), *Local historian's encyclopedia*, 2nd edition, New Barnet, Herts: Historical Publications. Further information is to be found in *Museum and special collections in the United Kingdom* (1993), edited by P. Dale, London: Aslib; *Museums of the World* (1995), 5th edition, Munich: Saur.

53 *Museums and galleries 1999/2000* (1999), London: Johansens; lists over 1,800 UK institutions.

54 Nurse, B. (1991), 'Prints, drawings and watercolours', in *Local studies collections: a manual*, vol 2, edited by M. Dewe, Aldershot: Gower, 329–51.

55 *Historic houses, castles and gardens* (1999), London: Johansens; lists over 2,000 places in Britain, Ireland and parts of Europe.

56 Jamieson, I. (1991), 'Institutions and societies in local studies', in *Local studies collections: a manual*, vol 2, edited by M. Dewe, Aldershot: Gower, 80–101.

57 *British archives* (1995), xlviii–liv; Pinhorn (1995), *Historical, archaeological and kindred societies*, 1–8.

3 Management

Elizabeth A. Melrose

INTRODUCTION

Local studies collections have evolved, and continue to evolve, over the years. The last decade, however, has seen radical changes in UK library structures, as well as many outside pressures on library authorities that have had an impact on the internal management of public libraries and thus also on local studies provision. As Margaret Kinnell says, 'Perhaps the most telling impact of the political environment on managers ... has been simply the amount of change to which they have had to respond in recent years.'[1] Many of these changes influencing library provision, such as the redrawing of local authority boundaries, regionalism, the emergence of standards and Best Value, and the growing number of local studies users (including 'electronic' users), have been referred to in Chapter 1.

Although never as rapid as now, change has always been a constant factor, and local studies librarians must realize that they are affected as much as any other colleagues in the library service. In so far as these changes have impelled senior staff to take a more planned and strategic approach to library management, it is necessary for local studies librarians to manage their resources in the best possible way. Skills in planning and strategic management are needed not only to coordinate and develop individual departments but also to ensure that these meet the planned expectations of the library service as a whole.

In 1987, Michael Dewe made 'a plea for the utilisation of a management approach to the administration of the local studies collection, particularly through the formulation of objectives and policies, and to the resources it needs to attract'.[2] If local studies librarians wish to continue to oversee a priority service – one that is not overtaken by more effective or more flexible providers – this approach is now an imperative.

In managing the local studies department, the senior local studies librarian must be aware of matters of strategic importance to the authority. These will have an impact on the library service, since library strategy is dependent on and related to the concerns of the authority and subject to the same pressing, external initiatives from national government and statutory organizations, initiatives such as lifelong learning, social inclusion and access for all. The section head should be familiar with the planning and policy timetables set out by the library service and should take part in the overall planning process. Where, as in East Dunbartonshire Libraries, the reference and information librarian in charge of local studies is a member of the senior management team, he can keep informed about those strategic issues uppermost within the authority. He can immediately comprehend any likely impact on the local studies department. At the least, departmental concerns should be seen to contribute to the debate preceding the compilation of the annual library service plans. Where the local studies librarian does not have this advantage, managers must inform those working in the department so that local studies staff understand and accept the background in which their department is working, and do not concentrate on their own particular area of responsibility.

LOCAL STUDIES DEPARTMENTAL AUDIT

The local studies librarian should accept the discipline of a business plan, and taking stock is an essential first step. Time should be spent on a total departmental audit, as this process requires objective consideration. Progress can indeed be made otherwise, but if the local studies librarian does not fully comprehend the position from which the department starts, much effort may be dissipated by moving in conflicting and false directions.

A structured assessment of the entire local studies service in the context of its parent body as a whole will give the local studies manager an idea whether:

- the present collection is being managed satisfactorily as an active and current service, responsive to the demands of the public, both from a distance and from within the local community,
- access to the collection and the expertise of the staff is made available to as many different sections of the public as possible, and whether efforts are made to encourage those not using the service at present,
- the existing funding and other resources, including staff, are being used to the best effect,
- the departmental development plan includes building up the collection for the future while conserving the heritage of the past,
- priorities have been set and are relevant to an informed prediction of future trends in research and in the provision of relevant local studies material.

CONSULTATION WITH USERS

Throughout the whole process of planning and the follow-up implementation, there must be a dialogue with those who come into the department, use the local studies resources or have any contact with local studies staff within the local studies area or at any official outside events. What do the readers think of the quality of the service? Any audit of the department should include consultation with the users about their perception of local studies as provided and as they might suggest it could be provided to the community.

A specific customer consultation survey conducted by Derby and Derbyshire libraries in 1999 gives a picture not only of the people using those local studies libraries but also of the materials that they are using and the suggestions they noted for future development of the service.[3]

Documentation, such as the compliments and complaints files and other feedback resulting from questionnaires, are indications of the success, or otherwise, of the departmental attitude to the customers, and the stock and the facilities supplied. These, along with any other performance indicators, give a first indication on which to base decisions and, as any changes are made within the department, a validation of any success as far as the public is concerned.

CURRENT AND FUTURE SERVICES

Local history should promote all the topics concerned with the locality and thus any activity or event or person that might be part of the local community. However, local studies staff need to be responsive, with an understanding of the changing nature of historical research and of the people undertaking it – the different subjects that concern the public. This will help towards an examination of the department's service delivery and the manager's consideration of what programmes the present collection supports in terms of customer research, community outreach, promotion or publishing. Librarians must ask therefore:

- What are the priorities of the collection and are these still relevant to the users and any potential customers?
- Are there any noticeable gaps in the service provision? With changes to local authority boundaries and employment patterns, there could be geographical areas and settlements unrepresented in the collection or time periods that have been neglected. Could readers be disappointed should they begin to research the history of ethnic communities only to find that the local studies department has ignored or been unable to find this aspect of the local story? Are all forms of source material collected or are some excluded by default or on the grounds of expense?

- What subject areas does the collection include that could be promoted but have been ignored – perhaps because of an unmanageable format? Very large-scale ephemeral theatre posters, for example, may have been hidden away and neglected for lack of time to promote them.

USERS AND ACCESS

As in any other library department, local studies librarians need to assess the community that the department serves in order to know their users. Some national surveys, such as the Chartered Institute of Public Finance and Accountancy (CIPFA) public library user surveys, or more local library questionnaires, can be too general and may not take the many types of local studies enquiries into account. 'Even libraries live in a competitive environment ... The decline or growth of institutions depends on how they can make their activities appear relevant to their contemporary world. Being seen as relevant is important, because from that funding flows.'[4]

The City of York libraries recently sent out a questionnaire on the use of the local studies photographic collections, not only to current users, but also to other members of the public, through the local family history society. The results will allow the library authority to make considered judgments on the popularity of the illustrations. As more local studies work is being introduced into the schools curriculum, both at primary and secondary level, the numbers of school students may increase, with all the demands that school classes can bring. The study of family history is no longer the preserve of the young or the retired but appeals to all age groups. Even those with little formal academic training may have information about their own historical topics that could be useful to others. Media programmes on local history, while encouraging the public to research the history of their localities, have enlarged the prospective local studies audience. The clientele of each local studies library will include a differing demographic mix. Local studies librarians must also cooperate with heritage units and other organizations to discover those who could be using the local studies department but are prevented from doing so by disadvantage, or distance, or a separate living language and culture – or to discover those who have never heard about the available source material.

'Collections aren't about what you have but about what you provide access to'[5] and so the local studies manager must here deal with another issue, not just access to source material, investigating the concerns of the partially sighted and those unused to computer technology, but also access to the library building and to the local studies department itself. Is there disabled access to the department? Is there a wide enough space for a wheelchair and a seated companion at desks of a convenient height in the local studies area; a hearing loop system; information on a moderated website suitable for those disadvantaged by physical disability or learning difficulties? In the audit all these factors should be examined.

ASSESSMENT OF BUDGETS AND AVAILABLE RESOURCES

While compiling the audit, the local studies librarian should look carefully at all the resources at the disposal of the department. The financial audit is important and should include a careful appraisal of the financial budget allocated to local studies, since this underpins all aspects of the service: the acquisition of material, staffing and any development of the department as a whole. Eventually decisions will have to be taken over each heading, such as staffing, possible refurbishment of the department, outreach activities, material in print or electronic format, with its subtle associated costs for hardware, line charges and rising licensing fees. So it is important that each charge is documented to assist choices made more difficult by the speed of technological changes.

In some libraries, such as Wimbledon, the local studies funding was part of the information services fund, but from April 2000 is linked to the Heritage Centre as a single cost centre. In North Yorkshire, local studies material is purchased from each of six delegated group reference funds. In Swansea Library Service, the local studies librarian is responsible for the purchase of local and Welsh lending material as well as for the local studies collections held within the reference library. This budget system allows branch libraries to have the resources necessary to support school projects and other research. In Belfast Public Library, operating for the first full year from April 2000, a percentage of the general reference budget is being allocated to the Irish Collection. If the manager does not have the experience to investigate and analyse the specifics of the local studies funding, he must take advice from others.

The local studies manager will estimate the value of every operation that contributes to the running of the department. The area occupied by the local studies department within the library building, along with the furniture, the equipment and the facilities, should be costed. This will include facilities required for storage and conservation and for the exploitation of the new electronic media: 'public library authorities will have to manage their budgets in the future with regard for the needs of the NLN (New Library Network).'[6]

Are there any programmes in place to underwrite the cost of the department and how effective are these income-generating projects? Some such are the local studies publications series and the production of associated items, reproductions of illustrations, and CD-ROMs of local studies virtual tours such as the one produced by Sheffield Libraries, 'The Sheffield Time Machine: a virtual tour of historic Sheffield'. Are the staff progressing appropriate funding bids that could win the library service grants, such as those offered by Wolfson, the New

Opportunities Fund or the British Library, to set up projects that would benefit the department and the collection?

STAFFING

A survey of the present staffing should be taken and consideration given to the accumulated experience that each staff member possesses, especially in the field of local studies. The staffing establishment is a major expense, but it makes a difference not only to the assistance that can be given to users but also to the amount of background work that can be organized within the collection. The local studies manager should emphasize the importance of the staff, their expertise, their ability to organize and interpret material in the collection and to communicate this knowledge to the users. However, with new developments in library practice – devolved responsibilities and flexible working hours on the one hand and the requirement for cooperative working arrangements between local studies providers at all levels on the other – good teamwork is essential. This runs parallel with a need for new skills demanded by the extension of the new technology, underlined by the obligation on all library staff to complete the European Computer Driving Licence syllabus.

The audit will survey the staff provision in the particular service. Across the country this is extremely variable, much dependent on the historic circumstances of individual local authorities. In Gloucester County Library Service, the main county local studies service, the Gloucester Collection, is open for 46½ hours a week. It is administered by a senior librarian (local studies) at third-tier level with a full-time team librarian (local studies) and 200 hours per annum extra time from library assistants. There are also six local studies centres with local area collections and these have time-budgeted team librarian hours allocated to them. In Northern Ireland, in Ballymena, where the local studies department is open for 52 hours a week, there are two full-time members of staff in the department, a local studies development officer and an enquiry-cum-research assistant. North Yorkshire County Library Service, on the other hand, has no designated local studies librarians. Work for local studies is part of the reference and information service. Six information librarians have the responsibility for the service within their districts and they discuss local studies provision at the regular Information Services meeting chaired by the third-tier information services adviser and attended by the assistant county archivist. Special projects, such as the indexing of large illustrations collections at Harrogate, can be delegated to members of the group reference team. Countywide local studies events such as the Libraries National Year of Reading month featuring local newspapers and periodicals are coordinated by the information services adviser. At Chesterfield Library, where there is a librarian (local studies) and an assistant librarian (local studies) the clerical staff are allocated to local studies for a couple of years before they move on to other responsibilities.

While cataloguing the present provision and any reasons for this, such as an administrative formula that may have been devised to increase or decrease staff hours, the manager must be aware of any duties that are undertaken outside and in addition to work hours. Staff in local studies departments are in demand as speakers to outside groups and societies and frequently attend weekend and evening functions to promote the collections. On the other hand the hours given by any members of Friends of the libraries, archives and museums groups, assistants on short-term contracts and trained volunteers must be collated and defended.

FUTURE DEVELOPMENTS

With an ever-increasing range of history sources and ways of providing this material, all requiring training not only for the staff but also for the users, the manager must measure the new trends in information technology. These can be invaluable in giving access to sources that take up storage space in the original, are unique or in need of conservation, or are local but held at distant repositories. However, the need for IT skills does encroach on the traditional staffing structure. Enquiries come by e-mail in a less formal manner; website technology and the desire to display jewels of the collection on the Internet for all does require time and effort. The technology is developing and changing so quickly that it can only continue to alter service delivery. Staffing levels and skills must echo this but not reduce the value of tested routines. Listing and prioritizing work patterns should be a main intention of the audit.

Government strategy is encouraging regionalism and cooperative partnerships and this has a bearing on the way the service is delivered. Such cooperation is already in place. In Suffolk, each of the three local studies collections in the county is housed in one of the three branches of the record office in Bury St Edmunds, Ipswich and Lowestoft. The day-to-day running of the collections is supervised by the county local studies librarian with archive assistants carrying out the routine work. Walsall Metropolitan District Council runs a local studies centre with a full-time local studies librarian and a part-time archives/local studies assistant. The consortia proposed by the New Opportunities Fund (NOF) has produced other more extensive heritage partnerships in the second round of the *'nof-digitise'* funding bids and these have included libraries with the Public Record Office, independent museums and local history societies, among others. It is useful to list any existing collaborative ventures or potential endeavours in the local studies field in the audit.

There is a need to treat changes positively and optimistically: staff should be persuaded that such transitions can be seen as an opportunity. It need not mean that striving for a better funded service should be abandoned or that there should not be a search for new ways in which to meet readers' needs. However, the alternative is to be reactive and fall behind other organizations who can deliver a service in different, more participative, ways while the library, allowing itself to be bound by internal apathy and external constraints, receives less support.

SWOT ANALYSIS

A SWOT analysis is a common device that lists the key features of the service, to establish areas of Strength and Weakness as well as Opportunities and Threats. For example, with a local studies department strength might be the local situation of the library with its immediate contacts within the community. Weaknesses could involve lack of funding and staff, which are likely to affect the quality of the service offered to the readers both at branch libraries and at the main local studies collections. Designated opening hours could be few. Opportunities would be evident where the library becomes a focal point for the local historical society. The growing number of Internet sites providing historical information to distance learners could also provide opportunities to a small local library with little printed local studies stock but with public Internet access. Real threats to the established existence of the local studies department in its traditional form will come from other organized establishments such as the BBC Sound Archive, Barnardo's Photographic File or commercial firms, with a keen eye for profit, digitizing popular material such as trade directories, for example. A SWOT analysis must focus on looking for key issues, and not concentrate on peripheral or unrelated matters.

BEST VALUE

The Local Government Act 1999 obliges local authorities to produce best value performance plans, and library services will not be exempt from the programme of best value reviews which focus on service delivery and will be subject to independent inspection. Even if the local studies department has not already been involved in the forward planning for best value, the manager must be prepared for the application of the four best value principles when the review takes place. These principles cover the '4Cs':

- challenge why, how and by whom the service is provided;
- compare performance with other providers;
- consult users, partners, local taxpayers and others;
- compete to secure efficient and effective services.

Pembrokeshire Libraries began their best value project in 2000 and the reference and local studies librarian was part of a team planning for best value in local studies. Many library authorities have opted to review the whole of their service but others may favour a rolling programme, reviewing separate departments such as the local studies department, over a period of time. The local studies staff must be prepared to be positively involved.

In the assessment of current practice, some imagination and perception must be exercised. It is not enough to contemplate procedures that served a useful purpose in the past, enduring though these may appear to be. All procedures must be carefully examined. The future is uncertain, apart from the truism that more change is likely. Staff should be encouraged not only to appraise current practice, but to be intuitive and take risks within a total management plan.

PLANNING

'Few [local authorities] have taken the opportunity to stand back from the daily pressures and think strategically about what it is they hope to achieve now and in the long term, or to quantify and then find the resources necessary for that purpose.'[7] Both national government and local authorities can change course, announcing new priorities or instigating new programmes. There is a need for the department to provide input into local library plans and local information plans. The current obligation for interdepartmental cooperation in the museums, archives and libraries sector is not yet always fully integrated. A background of political and financial change does not allow much time for effective planning, but the importance of this process cannot be overemphasized. If, in a period of accelerated competitive and technological change, the local studies department ignores the need for a systematic approach, there can be no surprise if more aggressive organizations attempt to usurp some of its key features.

Another aspect that emphasizes the need for planning is that one model cannot be used for all local studies departments. On the one hand there has been some fragmentation resulting in smaller authorities in England and Wales, and at the same time there has been a building up of regional ties and alliances with the universities and colleges. It is not unusual for local studies departments to be allied loosely or more cooperatively with county record offices, while in other cases there is a strong connection with the museums service.

Nevertheless, having considered the audit of the local studies department, including the present provision of staff, an assessment of future trends and the SWOT analysis, the local studies manager should be in a position to devise a local studies plan. This plan should underpin all the departmental operations, not just in the field of collection management but in the administration of the department as a whole. All members of staff should understand the purpose of planning. It is not only a management necessity but requires cooperative effort, observation and research to set out the local studies objectives and to map out ways of achieving these. Planning provides the framework that enables all other activity to take place.

STAFF INVOLVEMENT WITH THE PLANNING PROCESS

Some staff may not be enthusiastic about assisting in the process, believing either that formal planning only documents what they are already doing or that the time taken in preparing the departmental plan is better spent in front-line activities with the readers. Enthusiasm for the practice of what could be seen as a commercial, business discipline may be limited, but the local studies manager needs his colleagues to share the forward planning process, not least because it is they who can more easily assess the service from the user's perspective. Every member of staff can make a contribution. As well as maintaining contacts with branch librarians, local studies staff must forge connections with the senior managers in all other library departments and across their partner organizations. Good alliances will support local studies and introduce aspects of the service into other appropriate service plans.

Despite their acknowledged workloads, professional staff must be motivated to exercise relevant business skills. In this way each member of the local studies team can be inspired to make a contribution to the planning process. Like their business colleagues, they too are responsible for the use of scarce departmental resources and the setting of priorities.

The local studies manager must try to anticipate what kind of local studies service should be provided in the future, within the circumstances of the community and the organization as a whole. He must formulate aims which will achieve this outcome. These objectives and goals, derived from the local studies departmental audit and the external scan of the community and its needs, are the detail of the management plan. A professional management approach to the aims of the department must now be considered. Uncertain working conditions and budget changes may leave little time for effective planning, but local studies librarians need to provide documentary evidence in support of their belief that theirs is a key service, highly regarded by the community.

THE MISSION STATEMENT

The local studies department could summarize its purpose in a short form of words, a mission statement. This statement should be compatible with the stated mission statement of the service as a whole and even with departmental aspirations, should the library subscribe to a joint local studies centre or be in the same unit as archives, museums or a heritage department. This ensures that the librarians do not get diverted into unplanned activities or the acquisition of unwanted material. Along with the mission statement of the entire service, the local studies statement of purpose should be reviewed at frequent intervals.

AIMS AND OBJECTIVES

Local authorities are now obliged to publish a Best Value Performance Plan for each financial year and library services will not be exempt from this scrutiny. This plan will include an examination of the strategic aims and main objectives of the council with a performance comparison and a listing of future priorities. Analysis of service delivery will be backed up by steady consultation with the service users. Within a programme of Best Value Reviews, the local authority is likely to have decided on a time for the evaluation of the library services.

A key service aim for libraries concerns local studies, in that the library service is expected to be a major repository for the recorded history and life of the area it serves.[8] The annual library plan, required by the Department of Culture, Media and Sport, will be a requisite document for inspection within the Best Value programme. It will also be a foundation for the government's local cultural strategy in the near future. The local studies manager must take part in this overall planning cycle.

Local studies libraries: Library Association guidelines for local studies provision in public libraries (Library Association Local Studies Group (2002) demonstrate that services should work towards formulated aims and objectives according to agreed standards in order to promote lifelong learning and social inclusion.[9] This strategic planning develops the service for the future. The structure of such planning should combine past and present experience but also take account of new developments, new attitudes, new knowledge and the need for new types of resources.

Local studies departments may not have a formal written mission statement, relying rather on a statement of aims and objectives. If the local studies department has such a document, based on the local studies audit, the aspirations of users and partners and on an analysis of the available resources, this does need to be re-examined and updated very regularly. The document should set out guidelines for the management of the local studies collections and for the delivery of the service. It should clarify the direction in which the service will move and function in the future. If no such statement exists, the process of compiling a rational set of aims and objectives can only be prudent. There have to be clear objectives for a consistent approach to planning and decision making. These are the goals of the department, the plan for a proactive departmental response to present conditions and aims for the future. Staff need to be included, for the objectives will guide the operations of the department and support their daily routine.

A priority timescale could be given to various goals. Some, perhaps related to promotional display work, will be immediately achievable. Some, perhaps where the section intends to establish and maintain a publishing programme, will take longer, perhaps on account of budget restrictions or the need for staff training. Some, affected by outside pressures, such as a wish to establish and maintain links with all area and national agencies working in the field of local studies, could be long-term. These timescales, though helpful for the authority's planning cycle, must be adaptable and continuous.

LOCAL STUDIES POLICIES

Faye Phillips has written: 'The local history collection manager requires policies and procedures, a staff, a budget, and a plan in order to properly administer the organisation.'[10] She goes on to quote a writer on archival management who believes that the application of management principles are not only straightforward but 'largely a matter of common sense'.

From the objectives and goals of the local studies department comes naturally the need for policy and procedures, to assist the administration of the department. Although most library managers subscribe to the idea of a local studies policy linked to the documents produced for the whole service, many services are at different stages of strategic development. Suffolk Libraries and Heritage Department has a document, which includes local studies, but there is no particular policy document specific to the section. Islington has a collections policy document but nothing else. Some authorities contain aspects of local studies work, such as stock management, in more general policy documents. The Telford and Wrekin policy document for local studies provision (1998) gives paragraphs on 'What are local studies?', 'Why local studies?', 'Where?' – grading the collections in the nine libraries within the Telford and Wrekin district – 'Content and collections policy', 'Care and conservation', 'Staff', and 'Promotion'. This is not a long document, but one that covers the necessary information about provision. More advanced is that of Plymouth City Libraries who are completing a local studies policy arranged under the headings, aims, corporate/library service objectives and policies, target user groups, user consultation, scope (geographical and by format), standards/performance indicators, budget, selection criteria, selection methods, management and inter-library loan policy. In Nottingham Libraries, Information and Museums Service a principal librarian convened a working party that included the head of local studies, a senior library assistant and two other staff members. Their report (1998), *Local studies beyond the millennium in county and city*, provides the aims and objectives of the local studies service and addresses delivery, the structure of the service, resources, staffing and training. The report also contains recommendations on, for example, the development of four family history centres across the county, minimum stock levels and the establishment of a promotions and marketing group.

Within any set of policy documents many issues can be addressed. From an assessment of the community and its needs will emerge a definition of the users of the local studies section, emphasizing those differing groups that come into the local studies department, and defining the non-users who do not, either through choice, through disadvantage or through lack of knowledge of the material available. Here the policy could outline ways in which the department aimed to encourage their present users while conducting outreach projects to promote its work to non-users. The local history collection and local studies enquiry work in a small community is likely to differ in extent from a large metropolitan public library and the policies will take this perspective into account.

Other policies could include decisions on the access that the public should be given to the source material. Within a newly refurbished central library, Lincoln Local Studies has a policy of open public access for most of their stock, including a large collection of pamphlets and ephemera. However, other authorities believe that allowing readers to consult the shelves without staff intervention could lead to overuse, damage and loss of material that could be difficult to replace. Should there be a room or designated area for local studies with opening hours at times when staff can be available, both to assist and to supervise? Should the researchers be allowed a specified number of local studies items at one time? Will the service be prepared to provide duplicate copies of fragile or unique items? Record offices take more precautions, issuing readers' tickets and providing pencils for visitors, for example.

Other policies could indicate options on access and space requirements for the collection and the area for attending to the background work. Resolution of such questions in a convincing policy has far-reaching implications for the kind of accommodation provided for both the readers and the stock. If this is unsuitable or insecure it should be improved to a standard which supports the policy. Deciding on the service to be provided and the way in which it should be delivered also affects staffing levels and is dependent on the finance available. All these factors must be taken into account.

The types of programmes to be supported by the staff and by the collection could be part of a policy statement along with a definition of the resource-sharing element in any regional cooperative projects such as NEWSPLAN, for example. Part of the policy could be a plan for future progress, identifying what needs to be done within a specific timeframe. In the event, all the policies should contain procedures that can be used as guidelines for different parts of the service – on acquisitions, enquiry handling, staffing, promotion, and so on – which can be applied to the training of staff.

THE ACTION PLAN

The action plan could deal with the implementation of the objectives in more depth and also concern itself more fully with future development. These should be prioritized and thought given as to how results can be obtained. A practical and achievable timetable will encourage the staff and give them targets to reach. The timetable must be realistic and must be reviewed regularly to take account of unforeseen eventualities. There can be different end-dates for separate objectives:

- some deadlines could be immediate – staff training could be put in place to eliminate bad practice and to increase knowledge of the source material;
- a short-term objective could be the delivery of an outreach programme of talks to local societies within a specified time, or the completion of an index to give further access to part of the collection;
- medium-term objectives might include the writing of a grant proposal for funding a collaborative bid to digitize regional photographic collections;
- long-term goals could be the planning of a new local studies area in a new library, or a programme to improve local studies provision by designing a local studies website.

Although the results should be attainable, the plans should be flexible and subject to continual review.

Primary issues that must be decided in particular areas of local studies management could be dealt with and set out in policy papers to be agreed by the library service. One of these could be the duties of local studies staff. From the departmental audit, decisions could be made about what duties were critical, what work had accumulated or been added since the previous staffing review and what routines would therefore have to be abandoned. This is especially relevant with the increase in local studies involvement in digitization, the creation of local studies websites and the preparation required for large funding bids. This is work that was not expected some years ago and, as staff numbers have not increased, managers must adjust staff duties, or consider the role of volunteers or Friends of the library groups, with the accompanying obligations and time constraints. Some historic responsibilities may have to be rationalized and discarded and this should be agreed with the staff.

Decisions could be taken on staff training and awareness with pre-appointment training being assessed at the interview stage. Would local studies staff training be more effective given in-house, by external trainers or by distance learning through the internet and CD-ROMs? Training and lifelong learning in the field of local studies should be a constant throughout any staff development plan, both for all library staff and for other user groups where the opportunity occurs. The spread of information and communication technology (ICT) tutorials has made distance learning a much easier option, so long as the authority gives background support and takes a liberal view on study leave. How much is it considered that attendance at professional functions should be classed as training? Networking with colleagues to talk over issues at conferences and workshops may fall victim to any funding difficulties, so it is important to have a clear view of the advantages that can be gained from these informal discussions and contacts.

MONITORING AND EVALUATION

The effect of the management plan will be lost unless there is a mechanism for monitoring the way the local studies department reaches those targets it has set itself. Standards should be set and managers should be aware of other national standards and international standards where they are applicable to the service. Whereas the draft library standards produced by the Department for Culture, Media and Sport, *Comprehensive and efficient – Standards for modern public libraries; a consultation paper* (June 2000), held little that was relevant to local studies librarians in particular, *Local studies libraries: Library Association guidelines for local studies provision in public libraries* will assist authorities in drawing up standards relating specifically to the service. There is a need, for example, to have benchmarks for access, user satisfaction, conservation issues and security of stock and technology.

The 1964 Public Libraries Act stated that local authorities had to provide 'a comprehensive and efficient library service' and to ensure that there are books and other materials 'sufficient in number, range and quality to meet the general requirements and any special requirements'. Comprehensiveness, efficiency and quality are hard to identify statistically, though most managers realize the necessity for comparisons at a time when all library departments are attempting to do more with less. The Greater London Archives Network (GLAN) has endorsed the Historical Manuscripts Commission's recommendation that they 'might work with the Audit Commission and others to develop standards for records management':[11] in their case in the London area. Evaluation, through recognized standards and the sharing of models of good practice, will ensure that staff do not lose sight of the aims of the department. It will provide principles for a consistent level of service. Monitoring will allow any failing performance to be addressed quickly and the promotion of good standards will support every aspect of the library service as a whole.

Most library authorities have a basic evaluation system in place. Some have worked towards customer charters, charter marks or Investors in People, or will be considering whether standards produced by the Guidance Council or the Community Legal Service are appropriate. Present evaluation of local studies' services consists mainly of enquiry surveys, statistics of enquiries and letter enquiry counts, use of the microfilm/microfiche readers and the word-processors and hits on the Internet. Devon has a users' register and counts 'items filed' along with statistics of enquiries and website use. More in-depth evaluation is taken by Plymouth Local and Naval Studies Library which maintains regular contact with a local studies forum of individuals and organizations and Blackburn with Darwen, who are setting up focus groups comprising members of Blackburn's local history and family history societies plus a couple of members of staff. Telford and Wrekin echo the wish of other local studies librarians, especially those about to be involved in best value reports: 'We are still trying to work out how to assess usage … any advice or example of successful practice would be appreciated.'[12] There is a growing need for good practice studies dealing with the management of local studies collections. The president of the national Local Studies Section of the Australian Library and Information Association wrote: 'As a national group we also are planning to do a survey of the country … and this is entitled "Who is managing what?" – because we don't know enough of what is going on in the field.' Writing on the subject was complicated, she felt, 'mainly because of the difficulty of getting up to date material' and 'because there is simply not enough committed to paper'.[13]

CONCLUSION

A combination of personal experience and discussion with local studies professionals in other heritage organizations should encourage any local studies manager to pursue a particular concept of what the local studies department could and should be in the future. This is the central vision. The management plan should encompass this, but should expand by stating where the service is at present, where it aims to go and how it will arrive there. The service audit is an essential part of this, along with an analysis of the work of the department and staff in relation to the objectives of the library service as a whole. There needs to be a thorough, systematic investigation into how the department operates, what it does and the resources with which this work is accomplished. From this the senior manager can conduct a SWOT analysis, examining the strengths and weaknesses of the department and contrasting the opportunities and threats that it might face. At this point there may be alternative opinions on what courses to follow. A best value review must apply the additional '4Cs' principles (challenge, compare, consult and compete). In any case priorities can be set and departmental aims and objectives agreed by all the staff before these strategies are developed into detailed programmes for action. A realistic timetable should be devised and the entire plan should be reviewed regularly to ensure that unexpected events, from inside or outside the organization, have not overtaken or derailed the set targets. A final stage is to establish an evaluation and monitoring system against which the department can measure its achievements. These steps are similar to those used in most business environments and, adapted to local studies delivery, are as valid.

The vital ingredient in planning for the future of local studies, in a time of competitiveness and the need for cooperation without subjection, is not the discussion of the need for planning but a commitment to planning itself.

ACKNOWLEDGMENTS

I would like to thank all those colleagues who assisted me while I was engaged with this chapter, especially those who responded to a questionnaire I circulated via the EARL-contacts discussion list, March 2000, and those who took time to discuss other enquiries. I have used specific information sent by the following: Joan Bray, Head of Local Studies, Nottinghamshire Libraries, Information and Museum Service; Joyce Brown, Local and Naval Studies Librarian, Plymouth City Libraries; Lynn Buick, Information Development Officer, Northern Ireland and North Eastern Education and Library Board; Ed Button, Local Studies Librarian, Suffolk Record Office; Ruth Gordon, Local Studies Librarian, Derbyshire Libraries and Heritage Department; Stephanie Green, Librarian, Brighton and Hove Libraries and Museums; Linda Greenwood, Irish and Local Studies Librarian, Belfast and Library Board; Marilyn Higson, Senior Librarian, Telford and Wrekin Libraries and Heritage Department; Nick Hollis, Information Services Co-ordinator, Bracknell Forest Libraries; John Hughes, Group Librarian, West Gloucester County Library, Arts and Museums Service; Marilyn Jones, Local Studies Librarian, City and County of Swansea; Gina Lane, Finsbury Library, London; Ian Maxted, County Local Studies Librarian, Devon Library and Information Services; Pam Rew, Information Services Librarian, Wimbledon Reference Library; Diana Rushton, Local Studies Manager, Blackburn with Darwen Library and Information Service; Philippa Stevens, County Local Studies Librarian, Hampshire County Library; Cath Yates, Local Studies Librarian, Walsall MBC.

NOTES

1   Kinnell, M. (1996), 'Managing in a corporate culture', in Kinnell, M. and Sturges, P. (eds), *Continuity and innovation in the public library*, London: Library Association, 179.

2   Dewe, M. (1991), 'Management: objectives, policies and finance', in Dewe, M. (ed.), *Local studies collections: Vol 1*, Aldershot: Gower, 97.

3   Matkin, C. and Gordon, R A. (2000), 'Consulting the customer: a survey of local studies library users in Derby and Derbyshire', *Local studies librarian* 19 (1), 2–5.

4   Greenhaigh, L. and Worpole, K. (1995), *Libraries in a world of cultural change*, London: UCL Press, 116–17.

5   Greenstein, Dan (1999), 'Coping with the stuff: collection management in a networked environment', EARL Council meeting presentation (*http://www.earl.org.uk/events/presentations/ 990524/dan/sld002.htm*).

6   Library and Information Commission (1999), 'New links for the lottery: proposals for the New Opportunities Fund. LIC response' (*http://www.lic.gov.uk/publications/responses/linksresp.html*).

7   Royal Commission on Historical Manuscripts (1999), *Archives at the millennium: the twenty-eighth report of the Royal Commission on Historical Manuscripts, 1991–1999*, London: Stationery Office, 43.

8   Her Majesty's Stationery Office (1991), *Setting objectives for the public library services*, Library and Information Council, quoted in Watson, A. (2000), *Best returns. Best value guidance for library authorities in England*, London: Library Association, 10.

9   Library Association Local Studies Group (2002), *Local studies libraries: Library Association guidelines for local studies provision in public libraries*, information from 2nd edition, London: Library Association, para A1.3.

10   Phillips, F. (1995), *Local history collections in libraries*, Englewood, Colorado: Libraries Unlimited, 119.

11   Royal Commission on Historical Manuscripts (1999), 40.

12   Information from Marilyn Higson, Senior Librarian, Telford and Wrekin Libraries and Heritage Department.

13   E-mail from Jan Partridge, Department of Information Studies, Curtin University of Technology, Perth, Western Australia.

FURTHER READING

Evans, M. (1991), *All change? Public library management strategies for the 1990s*, London: Taylor Graham.

Feather, J. (1996), *Preservation and the management of library collections*, London: Library Association.

Hasson, A.C. (1996), 'Reaching out', in Kinnell, M. and Sturges, P. (eds), *Continuity and innovation in the public library*, London: Library Association, 148–166.

Haythornthwaite, J. (1995), 'Skills for today and tomorrow', in *New roles, new skills, new people*, Hatfield: University of Hertfordshire Press, 41–8.

Kinnell, M. (1996), 'Managing in a corporate culture: the role of the chief librarian', in Kinnell, M. and Sturges, P. (eds), *Continuity and innovation in the public library*, London: Library Association, 167–188.

MacLachlan, L. (1995), 'How to manage more on less: the management challenge of the new world', in *New roles, new skills, new people*, Hatfield: University of Hertfordshire Press, 56–71.

Morgan, S. (1997), 'Future academic library skills: what will they be?', in Layzell-Ward, P. and Weingand, D.E. (eds), *Human development: competencies for the twenty-first century*, Munich: K.G. Saur, 19–29.

Ward, P. and Washington, J. (eds) (1990), *Managing local studies collections*, Sydney: Australian Library and Information Association, Local Studies and Public Libraries sections, New South Wales.

Winterbotham, D. and Crosby, A. (1998), *The local studies library. A handbook for local historians*, Salisbury: British Association for Local History.

Wyatt, M. (1990), 'Managing local studies resources: arrangement, description, access and preservation', in Ward, P. and Washington, J. (eds), *Managing local studies collections*, Sydney: Australian Library and Information Association, Local Studies and Public Libraries sections, New South Wales, 36–43.

4 Materials

Jill Barber

The local studies collection is constantly being renewed. It is a contemporary resource, not purely a retrospective one, in which current and historical materials are of equal value. This chapter provides an overview of the range of materials that are to be found in most local studies collections. The scope of its materials reflects an evolving interdisciplinary focus encompassing geography, economics, social science, planning, commerce, politics and culture. In form, as well as content, local studies materials are extremely diverse. Printed books and pamphlets are still at the heart of the collection, but maps and plans, prints and photographs, visual and sound recordings, and increasingly electronic forms, are all part of the rich resource which exists to meet the needs of users, and enable staff to answer every kind of enquiry about the local area.

Historically, as public libraries were set up some 60 years before the first county record office, a considerable amount of archive material was acquired by libraries. It is now recognized that the storage of documents requires special environmental conditions, and much of this material has been transferred to record offices. Similarly, where artefacts have been collected by libraries, these are now seen to belong in museums. Even where archives and local studies are combined, as in many London boroughs and metropolitan districts, responsibility for the collections is usually divided between specialist professional staff. Today, it is an unwritten rule that printed works are classified as local studies materials, whereas manuscript sources are the province of archivists.

The value of materials in the local studies collection is that many are rare or unique, a fact that is not always appreciated by users or librarians. Every local studies library is a specialist resource, and part of the strength of the collection lies in its long history.[1] Libraries have been building up collections of material published locally, or relating to the local area, from the mid-19th century: the first book presented to the Cambridgeshire Collection in 1855 is still on the shelves and ready for use.[2] Because public libraries are 'on the spot' they have been able to acquire small, often privately printed, publications and benefit from collections amassed by local antiquaries.[3]

BOOKS AND PAMPHLETS

The diversity of the local studies collection will be evident in its range of printed books, covering topics as varied as transport, health, housing, tourism, politics, industry, entertainment, law and order, architecture and literature. Local histories may make up a surprisingly small proportion, although standard works such as the Victoria County History (see p. 71) will be central to the collection. Essential reference tools will include guides to research, guides to sources, bibliographies and indexes, biographical and topographical dictionaries, as well as guide books, government publications, electoral registers and directories.

REGIONAL HISTORIES

Some of the earliest books in the collection will be county histories. First appearing in 1576,[4] by 1800 only seven counties in England were without one, with Scotland and Wales tending to be later.[5] The first town history was John Stow's *Survey of London* (1598), followed closely by Great Yarmouth, Exeter, Canterbury, Stamford and Newcastle. Further growth in urban history was slow, and many major towns, including York and Norwich, had to wait until the 18th or 19th century. As interest increased, the unit of study became smaller. The first parish history was published in 1695,[6] but it was not until the 19th century that most communities had one. Written by country gentlemen or clergymen, these early histories focused on landed families and church monuments rather than social history, and tend to lack references and indexes (see Chapter 1).[7] However, the authors often had access to documents in private hands, or buildings that have disappeared. Many local studies collections contain grangerized copies. These are extra-illustrated versions of published histories, often rebound in several volumes, interleaving the original text with illustrations, maps, newspaper cuttings and other items gleaned from a number of sources. These copies are unique, and of great value.[8] Under the influence of W.G. Hoskins, there has been a revolution in local history writing since 1950. The history of an area is now defined by social rather than administrative boundaries, and the emphasis is on development and change, comparative studies and the lives of ordinary people.[9] Many local studies are thematic, focusing on women, the poor or public health. The local studies collection will seek to bring together in one place all the studies that have a bearing on the local area.

VICTORIA COUNTY HISTORY

As noted in Chapter 1, the Victoria County History (VCH) was founded in 1899, with the optimistic aim of writing an outline history of the whole of England (Scotland and Wales were excluded) place by place. In 1989 a celebration was held to mark the publication of 200 volumes, but the task is still far from complete. The aim is to produce a general volume for each county, followed by the history of each parish. About a dozen counties have been completed and others are in progress, but so far there are no volumes for Northumberland, Westmorland or the West Riding. The earlier volumes focused on manorial history, ancient monuments, ecclesiastical buildings and archaeological remains, but since 1947 the approach has been modernized to include economic and social history, population studies, the landscape, education and nonconformity. This widening scope has doubled the volume of the project – it is now anticipated that Wiltshire will need 20 volumes. The VCH is noted for its consistent methods and high scholarly standards. A similarly authoritative work is the series produced by the *Survey of London*, which was set up in 1897 to carry out a similar task for London.[10] These will both be the first point of reference for local historians.

REFERENCE WORKS

Where local studies collections are housed with reference libraries, they will be able to share resources, including standard reference tools.[11] These should include guides to local and family history research, such as *Ancestral trails*,[12] and guides to sources, such as the *Gibson Guides*. This is an excellent series of individual booklets covering a wide range of sources from licensed victuallers' to probate records, indicating their location and use. Published by the Federation of Family History Societies (FFHS), many libraries will have standing orders for these, and the research aids produced by the Society of Genealogists, such as *My ancestor was a Methodist*.

Bibliographies and indexes may be regional in scope, such as the extensive *Bibliography of North West England*, a retrospective bibliography in 14 volumes, and the *Bibliography of printed works on London history to 1939* which lists books and articles found in libraries in the area. The *Bibliography of Scotland* lists recently published items, and *Irish periodicals first published before 1901* is a complete list of library holdings in Northern Ireland. Subject bibliographies, such as the *Bibliography of railway history*, may be of particular value for certain areas.[13] An index of illustrations in *The Builder*, 1842–3, for people (including architects, builders, stonecarvers, manufacturers, engravers, etc.), places and subjects will be useful for family and other historians, listing local buildings such as schools and churches, as well as individual houses.[14] Gazetteers and encyclopaedias such as the excellent *London encyclopedia* (1983), are available for some areas.

The *Dictionary of National Biography*, which is being updated at the time of writing to be more representative of minority groups, is one of several biographical dictionaries. Local gentry families can be found in the various editions of *Kelly's Handbook, Burke's Landed Gentry, Walford's County Families* and *Who's Who*.[15] *Alumni Oxonienses* and *Alumni Cantabrigienses* give biographical details of those who went to Oxford or Cambridge. For Church of England clergymen there is *Crockford's Clerical Directory*, first published in 1858, and Foster's *Index Ecclesiasticus* covering the earlier 19th century. *Halls' Ministers and Circuits* does the same for Methodist ministers. In Wales, many nonconformist ministers can be found in *Eminent Welshmen*. Professions have their own listings, such as the *Law Lists* and *Navy Lists*.[16] Obituaries, often found in local newspapers, are another source of biographical information. *Musgrave's Obituary* covers the 18th century, and there are indexes to marriages and obituaries in the *Gentleman's Magazine*.

GOVERNMENT PUBLICATIONS

Parliamentary reports of select committees and royal commissions were published in the 19th century on a variety of topics, including the employment of women and children. These contain invaluable first-hand evidence of witnesses. They are often concerned with local communities, such as the straw plait schools of Buckinghamshire, and child labour in the Nottingham lace factories. Original copies are rare, but many are now available on microfilm.[17] HMSO also publishes census reports every ten years, the county statistics providing valuable evidence for population change in local communities throughout the United Kingdom from 1801, as well as information on occupations and housing. Since 1981 small area statistics are available which provide a more detailed social and economic breakdown.[18] Local Acts of Parliament, giving special powers to organizations or people, often relate to canals, railways, new roads or, more recently in Doncaster, a waste treatment plant (1988). Sometimes these Acts are accompanied by evidence from a Commission of Enquiry, undertaken to gauge community feeling before the Act was passed.[19]

LITERATURE

Literature by local authors now has an accepted place in the local studies collection.[20] In many areas the local studies library has become a specialist repository for this genre.[21] Novels set in the locality, including children's historical fiction, may provide useful background information and atmosphere. Literature will include autobiographies and reminiscences, diaries (often written by 18th- and 19th-century travellers before the advent of guide books), letters and journalistic reporting, such as John Hollingshead's *Ragged London* (1861).

PAMPHLETS

A wide range of promotional literature is produced today by local businesses, including annual reports, trade catalogues and other commercial material. Local government publications cover a wide range of topics, and are often small booklets or pamphlets. In the 19th century these included reports of the medical officer of health, useful for investigating, for example, cholera and women's health. Today they will cover finance and statistics, social surveys, school prospectuses, development plans and policy documents.[22] Some libraries also act as a repository for council minutes and agenda papers. The volume of these can be phenomenal and it may be difficult to ensure that all are reaching the local studies collection. Ultimately, because many have short runs and include ephemeral material, the local studies collection may have the only surviving copy.[23] A guide has been produced to holdings of local government minutes in Northern Ireland.[24] In the 20th century most local authorities issued guide books (first produced in the 18th century for tourists) and, as these have been updated at regular intervals, often annually, each edition is of value for the information it contains on local services, personalities and events.[25] Sometimes special pamphlet collections are held, often donated by local people or institutions. At times their local subject content may be tenuous, but normally it reflects the interests of local individuals and sometimes the spirit of the community as a whole.[26] Also included in the pamphlet collection will be archaeological reports relating to local sites.

SALE CATALOGUES

Sale catalogues of the 19th and early 20th century are particularly useful, as they may contain detailed plans of estates, brief histories, names of owners and tenants, and photographs. Tunbridge Wells has a large collection (1870–1940) donated by a local auctioneer. Modern estate agents' literature also contains photographs of houses, including interiors, but their ephemeral nature means that few are kept.

DISSERTATIONS AND THESES

Unpublished dissertations, usually in typescript, contain original and important research and a copy is often donated to the local studies library, where much of the research may have been done, as well as the copy kept by the university. Today, many Open University students undertake local projects, which can make a significant contribution to knowledge about the area,[27] and in rare cases GCSE and A-level projects may warrant inclusion.

DIRECTORIES

Directories, listing names, addresses and occupations, began in London in 1677 in response to a demand for trade information. Dublin had its first directory in 1751, and Edinburgh and Glasgow were included in Bailey's *Northern Directory* of 1781.[28] Rural areas appear in county directories by 1832, which give useful brief descriptions of the village or township. From about 1850 directories were produced annually, when Kelly's began producing street directories for major towns and cities. They disappeared in the 1950s, when telephone directories took over the market. Many county and town directories are being reissued on microfiche by commercial publishers, but local studies libraries may contain unique copies for their locality.[29]

ELECTORAL REGISTERS

Electoral registers, or lists of voters, have been published annually since the Reform Act of 1832. Poll books may exist from before 1870, when the secret ballot was introduced, which record voters' names and how they voted, and some of these have been reprinted. Electoral registers are frequently used by companies wanting to check how long people have lived at a given address, or by people looking for relatives. Being arranged by ward and then by street, they are not always straightforward to use. It is important to remember that they are not a full record of the male population until 1918, and for women not until 1928. Information may be a year out of date as the registers are usually drawn up in the autumn previous to the year when they are in force.[30]

NEWSPAPERS

Provincial newspapers began in the 18th century, the first being the *Norwich post* in 1701. By the mid-19th century most towns of any size had a weekly newspaper and some of the larger towns had several. Today, there may be many more. Hendon local studies library, for example, maintains 12 local newspapers. Many of these are free newspapers, which mushroomed during the 1980s and often appear in multiple variant editions in which most of the contents is duplicated.[31] Newspapers provide the most extensive source of local information, but their sheer bulk makes them difficult to store and handle. The microfilming programme initiated by NEWSPLAN and the British Library Newspaper Library does not mean, however, that libraries should necessarily dispense with hard copies once a microfilm version is available.[32] However, many local studies collections still hold files of provincial newspapers before 1830 which contain unique editions.[33] Regional and local newspapers may prove richer sources than national newspapers; for example, the most vivid early accounts of the *Titanic* disaster can be found in Liverpool newspapers.[34] But the information is difficult of access, as few libraries are fortunate enough to have inherited indexes to local newspapers. Most are now involved in some sort of indexing programme, although it may be current rather than retrospective. Newspaper cuttings, arranged by subject, are maintained in some collections, and others may have scrapbooks, often on topics such as transport or the theatre, donated by private collectors.[35]

PERIODICALS

As well as church and school magazines, a range of journals are produced by local and regional societies. These range from those of family history societies to scholarly publications like *The Welsh history review* and *Northern history*, containing articles that may present the latest research on a local subject or area, but they need to be indexed to make the information accessible to users. Other publications, often referred to as serials because of their frequency,[36] will be the volumes produced by local history or record societies, such as the Thoroton Society in Nottinghamshire, the Catholic Record Society, the Jewish Historical Society or the Huguenot Society. Some periodicals in the collection will relate to research interests, they include *Local historian*, *Local history magazine*, *Local population studies*, *Family history news and digest*, *Family and community history*, *The journal of regional and local studies*, *Oral history*, *Rural history* and *Urban history*. Others will reflect particular local interests, such as leather at Walsall and car manufacture at Coventry, or particular communities; Brent and Wolverhampton, for example, both take ethnic minority magazines.[37] Articles of particular local interest, in journals which are not kept in stock, are usually copied and treated as pamphlets. As well as being of interest to users, periodicals can serve as selection tools for the librarian as they often highlight small-scale publications which are easy to miss.[38]

MAPS AND PLANS

Maps and plans are often considered to be some of the most important materials in the local studies collection.[39] As primary sources for the study of a local area they provide an unsurpassed record of change over time. Maps may account for as much as 24 per cent of the material requested by local studies users, and sheer numbers may be considerable: there are 3,300 maps and plans at Worthing.[40] The range, outlined below, is extensive: land use, geology, administration, as well as those showing individual roads and houses. Others may attempt to reconstruct the past, or provide a vision for the future, but these may be traps for the unwary, as many plans for road schemes or rebuilding of town centres were never put into practice.[41]

COUNTY, TOWN AND PARISH

The earliest printed maps of England and Wales were produced by Christopher Saxton (1574–9) and the first survey of Scotland was by Timothy Pont (1590–1610). The first maps to show roads were John Norden's maps of Middlesex (1593) and Hertfordshire (1598). John Speed produced an atlas of county maps for England and Wales in 1611, with more general maps of Scotland and Ireland, many of which have been reproduced, but these are too lacking in detail to be of much use to local historians. John Ogilby's *Britannia* (1675) contained strip maps showing main roads with the towns, villages, inns, churches, bridges and even gallows along their route. The 18th and 19th centuries saw an explosion in map making, with county and parish maps varying in detail. Town plans also began in the 16th century, including the first map of London (1553–8). Other towns have been mapped from the 16th century, noticeably at periods of economic prosperity.

ORDNANCE SURVEY

Founded in 1791 to map the south coast under threat of a French invasion, the Ordnance Survey produced its one inch to the mile series from 1801 to 1873, beginning with Kent, and ending with the Isle of Man. Scotland was covered in 1845–78. Facsimiles of this first edition have been produced by the publisher David and Charles. The success of the one inch series quickly led to a demand for larger-scale surveys. In 1872, the New Series or second edition began, based on 25 inch surveys for cultivated land and six inch surveys for other areas, for the whole of Britain. These large-scale Ordnance Survey national grid sheets were only produced in editions of about 20 copies, so they are now very rare. Their heavy usage means that many local studies libraries are now making them available on microfiche aperture cards, instead of producing the originals. The production of town plans at a scale of 60 inches to the mile began in 1840. The first series does not include sufficient detail, but the second series produced in the 1860s and 1870s shows not just the streets, but every building, including details of factories, schools and institutions, and the complete track layout of railways and tramways. Three further editions were produced in the 1890s, 1910s and 1930s, providing invaluable sources for the study of changes in a local area.[42]

Reprints of many large-scale maps, usually taken from the 25 inch editions, have been produced by Alan Godfrey. The eventual aim is to cover all major towns and urban areas in Britain and Ireland. Current large-scale maps are heavily used by architects, surveyors and civil engineers for a range of planning and building needs (including site surveys), by local residents (applying for planning permission) and by students. The scale was changed from imperial to metric in 1945, and the sheet size reduced, so they are not directly comparable with earlier editions.[43] One of the challenges for local studies collections is that these maps are now updated digitally, and are subject to constant revision, so there are no longer the fixed points of reference supplied by published editions. There is the danger that traditional printed plans may be discontinued as commercial users gain access to digital information. For future use, it is important that local studies collections maintain a historical record of revised sheets acquired at periodic intervals.[44]

GOAD MAPS AND PLANS

Frequently requested by GCSE geography students are Goad shopping maps. These developed out of the fire insurance plans first published in Britain by Charles E. Goad in 1886. These large-scale plans of selected town-centre areas were produced at a scale of 40 feet to the inch. To assist insurance companies to assess clients' risks, they show the building materials used and the nature of the business in each building, often with the name of the company or individual concerned. They were updated periodically, enabling changes in use and ownership of property to be identified. By the time they were discontinued in 1970, they covered 53 towns and cities. In 1967, as use by insurance companies declined, Goad began producing maps of shopping centres. These now exist for over 1,000 areas, including smaller towns like Aberystwyth. Produced at a scale of 88 feet to the inch, they show the names and businesses of individual shops, enabling changes in use to be followed. They can provide a modern substitute for directories.[45]

MAPS FOR SPECIAL PURPOSES

A growing social concern, especially with public health, produced a new type of map in the 19th century. These were social surveys, of which perhaps the finest example is Charles Booth's Poverty Map of London (1889). Every street is colour-coded according to social class, from 'aristocratic, very wealthy' to 'vicious, semi-criminal class': an early attempt to link criminality with poverty. Improvement schemes, which proliferated in 19th-century towns, gave rise to a number of significant printed maps, often linked to schedules listing individual property owners. These were often linked to slum housing, but might be related to canals, railways or road schemes. Transport maps may be outline maps, indicating routes, or show railways or other lines of communication superimposed on a general topographical map. The proliferation of 20th-century bus maps is often a mixed blessing for local studies collections, given the sheer quantity produced. In coastal areas, marine charts can be important for the development of ports and harbours, and also for details of the coastline. Systematic published charting of Britain's coastline was begun by the Admiralty in 1795. Local authorities continue to produce maps for a range of special purposes. These may indicate the location of schools, car parks or even air raid shelters. Two world wars have produced some fascinating civil defence maps, plotting the nature and location of every bomb that fell.

EPHEMERA

'Ephemera' has been used since the 1960s to describe items which are of a transitory nature, such as tickets, posters, theatre playbills and programmes, menus, invitations, certificates, timetables, political propaganda and holiday brochures.[46] Because it was not designed to last, the survival of this material is haphazard, its physical form often fragile, and the sheer volume for the present day can be overwhelming. It can provide unique evidence for prices, local businesses, fashion trends and developments in printing or design.[47] Early trade cards are now highly prized for the light they throw on occupations, streets and people.[48] Ephemera can portray the views of 'alternative' groups and their activities, which may be ignored or misrepresented in more conventional sources.

ILLUSTRATIONS

Pictorial sources include photographs, prints and engravings, original drawings and watercolours by local artists.[49] Oil paintings are usually passed on to museums or galleries. Slide collections may be a useful resource for talks, and include copies of items relating to the local area held elsewhere.[50] Visual evidence found in ephemera, such as posters and bill-heads, may provide unique evidence for changes to buildings, particularly theatres, inns, shops and factories. Many local studies libraries will also have special collections, often extremely valuable, obtained by purchase or donation from private individuals.[51]

PHOTOGRAPHS

Many libraries have extensive collections of photographs – 20,000 at Strathkelvin near Glasgow[52] – although it is rare to find local views before 1865. In Cambridgeshire one collection alone contains 100,000 photographs, the work of

Lillian Ream, who had a studio in Wisbech, 1921–61.[53] Aerial photography surveys, often carried out by commercial companies or planning departments, may be deposited in the local studies collection, and are popular with schools studying the development of their local area. Old postcards are sometimes kept as a separate collection. Thousands of these were produced between 1894 and 1919, when their popularity began to decline with increased postage and the coming of the telephone. They continued to be produced, but not in the same volume. The National Library of Wales has over 13,000 postcard views of Wales. Views of villages and hamlets were produced as well as street scenes of towns and cities, and many have survived because of the craze for collecting postcards in vogue in the Edwardian era.[54] They provide a unique record of communities, often just before a period of great change. Black and white photographs have been preferred to colour, as being more stable, but this may now need to be reconsidered. Many libraries are now digitizing their photographic collections to make them more widely available.

PRINTS AND ENGRAVINGS

During the 18th century a new interest in travel and the 'picturesque' led to a demand for engravings of local views.[55] Many topographical engravings were published in separate volumes, or as illustrations to county histories. Samuel and Nathaniel Buck produced over 80 town views for England and Wales, as well as more than 400 of castles and ancient monuments (1720–53). News events would be drawn by artists on the spot and then etched onto copper plates, or wood blocks, for reproduction. Print shops sprang up, and illustrations were eagerly collected by those who could afford them. In a pre-literate age, prints often told a story without words, using conventions by which people would recognize key political or local figures. Although sometimes difficult to interpret today, they give a fascinating insight into contemporary values and attitudes. The satirical cartoons of the late 18th and early 19th centuries are particularly intriguing, and local studies collections may include unique copies of these, often preserved in special collections.

ORIGINAL DRAWINGS AND WATERCOLOURS

Many libraries have drawings and paintings portraying the local area, or produced by local artists.[56] Watercolour artists tend to show a concern for the careful and realistic recording of places and buildings, which makes their works such a useful source. Oil paintings are not usually considered to be such accurate representations, which is why they are not usually part of the local studies collection.[57]

SOUND RECORDINGS

Audiotapes may include talking books for the blind and commercially produced recordings of local choirs or bands.[58] Many libraries are actively engaged in oral reminiscence work,[59] and a wealth of advice is available for those embarking on oral history.[60] Tameside was one of the first to see its potential for filling gaps in the collection, such as a lack of information about ethnic minorities, launching a competition in 1995 for an oral history interview giving insight into the experiences of an immigrant from another country.[61] Transcripts and indexes are needed if the best use is to be made of oral history recordings.

FILM AND VIDEO

Visual recordings may be particularly important for industries, sport, performing arts or local events. Film is still the most permanent means, although video can be viewed more easily, and is now being used to make rare film more accessible. Many local studies libraries have a useful, if small, collection of films dating back to the early 20th century, such as 'Historic Kensington's housing problems' and 'Bexley's municipal baths and clock tower unveiling ceremony' (1912).[62] The use of video for oral history is still under debate but may have a useful place for recording dying crafts and customs.[63] In 1988 the British Video History Trust was set up to encourage the collection of first-hand testimony and scenes of everyday life. The Scottish Film Archive has compiled videos on various topics, such as holidays and work, and is looking to deposit local interest material in libraries. Home videos have not yet gained acceptance as appropriate materials for the local studies collection, but this may have to be reassessed in the near future as video opens up a 'whole new area of local studies provision'.[64]

MICROFORMS, CD-ROM AND THE INTERNET

Technological advance, and new demands from users, have led to a new category of material that is now seen as the core of the local studies library. This is primarily material used by family historians.[65] Microform publishing is low-cost and has led to an explosion in the number of indexes and original sources becoming available for inclusion in the local studies collection.[66]

CENSUS RETURNS

The first census of England and Wales was taken in 1801, since when it has been taken every ten years, with the exception of 1941, the returns becoming available to the public after 100 years.[67] Until the 1970s, the census enumerators' books could only be consulted at the Public Record Office, but microfilming transformed their use, making them available at local level. Most local studies libraries now hold the 1841–91 census returns for their area.[68] The 1901 census will be released on the Internet, but microfilm copies will still be available for libraries. From 1851, the returns give exact ages, relationships, marital status, occupations and place of birth. In Wales a 'W' in the first column indicates where a family responded in Welsh.[69] In 1891 information was recorded about the number of rooms occupied by a family if less than five. For towns this can provide useful evidence of overcrowding and social mobility. Arranged by street, the information given is invaluable for local as well as family historians, providing evidence for population change, migration, employment and housing. In Ireland, although a census was taken every ten years from 1801, many of the records were destroyed in 1922. The returns for 1861–91 were totally destroyed, but portions of the returns for 1821–51 have survived for certain counties. Street indexes are available for major towns, and name indexes have been produced by local societies for many areas. In the 1990s the Mormons produced a transcript of the 1881 census for the whole of England and Wales on microfiche, by county, with indexes for names and birthplaces. This means that it is now theoretically possible to trace any individual who was alive in April 1881, anywhere in the country.

CIVIL REGISTRATION INDEXES

Another central source now available on microfiche in many local studies collections is the indexes to Births, Marriages and Deaths for England and Wales, from 1837 to the present day. To obtain access to detailed information, copies of the original certificates still have to be ordered from the Family Records Centre,[70] where the original indexes may be consulted. However, the often lengthy process of searching for the right reference can now often be undertaken locally. The indexes are arranged under quarters for each year. Many users are undertaking one-name searches, extracting all the references to a particular surname. This can identify which local area a family has come from.

FAMILY SEARCH AND THE IGI

The International Genealogical Index (IGI) produced by the Mormons for every county in England and Wales, and now worldwide, was one of the first microfiche sources acquired by many local studies collections. Arranged alphabetically by county, it provides an index to baptisms and marriages in parish registers, and some non-conformist registers, although it is not complete, and it is important to know which local parishes are covered. Several editions have been produced and it is constantly being updated. In the 1990s it was largely replaced by the more extensive Family Search. Many local studies collections now hold Family Search on CD-ROM, which includes ancestral files and websites as well as the IGI. This can now be searched on the Internet (although not yet in as full a version) and demand for this is high.

CD-ROMs

An increasing range of material is available on CD-ROM, some produced locally and some nationally, such as the British Library's *Medieval Realms*, which was produced to provide resource material for the National Curriculum at Key Stage 3. The local studies library may even have produced its own CD-ROMs. Many contain visual sources, while others, like the *Westminster Historical Database*, provide access to printed sources such as poll books and rate books. A recent innovation has been the use of CD-ROM for the text of dissertations produced by students on the Open University's course, Studying Family and Community History, most of which are on local topics.[71]

ELECTRONIC RECORDS

Computer technology was initially seen as a means to access local studies materials at off-site locations, through projects such as the *Durham Record*, an interactive database of photographs, maps and archaeological records, and *Hackney 2000*, which links illustrations and maps.[72] In some areas, members of the public are encouraged to lend material for digitization, which means that the electronic record may become the only copy in the collection. *Collage*, an image database containing 20,000 works from the Guildhall Library and Guildhall Art Gallery, London, is now available via the web.[73] As well as the rapidly increasing range of family history sources which can be accessed on the Internet,[74] this medium is being used for other sources which would formerly have appeared in limited printed editions, for example Ofsted reports for local schools. Local information may only appear on a website, which is continually being revised. Periodicals are also looking to electronic publishing as a more cost-effective alternative; the *West country heritage*, for example, no longer appears in traditional form.[75]

CONCLUSION

One of the greatest challenges facing the local studies collection today is that, while the nature and content of the core materials of the collection remain the same, in many cases the format in which they are made available is changing rapidly, and seems set to continue to do so in the foreseeable future. It is now rare for libraries to keep original copies of local newspapers, and the advent of digitization is revolutionizing access to maps and illustrations. At the same time microforms, and more recently the Internet, have created an explosion in the range of sources available locally.[76] Although it could be argued that many of these non-traditional sources are not strictly related to the local area, their inclusion has brought many new users to the library. Many of these, through an initial interest in family history, have discovered for the first time the wealth of other materials in the local studies collection.

NOTES

1   A study of 864 items in the Westcountry Studies Library found that only 20 per cent were held by the British Library. Recognition of the value of material in local collections has led to proposals that responsibility for local and regional material might transfer from the national libraries to 'well managed local collections'. See Maxted, I. (1998), 'Local studies libraries as rare book collections', *Local studies librarian* 17 (1), 2–7.

2   Petty, M. (1996), 'Networking local studies', *Local studies librarian* 15 (1), 2–5. See also Jamieson, I. (1994), 'Editorial', *Local studies librarian* 13 (2), 1.

3   Some important collections in local studies libraries have been highlighted by project EARL. See Phillips, A. (1998), 'Preserving the nation's collection of rare local materials: towards a coalition', *Local studies librarian* 17 (1), 8–17.

4   William Lambarde's *Perambulation of Kent*. More than 25 county histories had been produced by 1750 and a further 22 by 1800.

5   The first history of Cardiganshire was produced in 1810.

6   The history of Ambrosden, Oxfordshire, by White Kennett.

7   There is a good overview in Winterbotham, D. and Crosby, A. (1998), *The local studies library: a handbook for local historians*, Salisbury: BALH, 14–26.

8   Dorchester Library has a magnificent 13-volume set of Hutchin, J. (1796–1815), *History and antiquities of the county of Dorset*, originally issued in four vols. The term originates with James Granger (1723–76), who published his *Biographical history of England* (1769) with blank pages for inserting extra illustrations.

9   For example: Spufford, M. (1974), *Contrasting communities*, Cambridge: Cambridge University Press; Prior, M. (1983), *Fisher Row: fishermen, bargemen and canal boatmen in Oxford, 1500–1900*, Oxford: Clarendon Press.

10   The first volume was published in 1900, and over 40 have now been completed, the most recent being Knightsbridge (2000).

11   *Local studies libraries: Library Association guidelines for local studies provision in public libraries* (2002). London: Library Association, Introduction.

12   Herber, M.D. (1997), *Ancestral trails: the complete guide to British genealogy and family history*, Stroud: Sutton Publishing/Society of Genealogists.

13   Other examples are given in Winterbotham, D. and Crosby, A. (1998), *The local studies library*, 7–8.

14   Richardson, R. (1990), 'The *Builder*'s illustrations', *Local studies librarian* 9 (1), 13–15.

15   A cumulative index of families which have appeared in the many different publications by Burke's Peerage can be found in *Burke's family index* (1976), London: Burke's Peerage.

16   These and other works can be traced through Raymond, S. (1992), *Occupational sources for genealogists: a bibliography*, Birmingham: Federation of Family History Societies.

17   See Winterbotham, D. and Crosby, A. (1998), *The local studies library*, 61–8.
18   Ibid., 58–9.
19   Ibid., 69–72.
20   At a local history workshop in 1986, it was asked why libraries do not collect literature: *Local studies librarian* (1986), 5 (2); Melrose, E.A. (1991), 'Books and pamphlets', in *Local studies collections: a manual*, vol 2, edited by M. Dewe, Aldershot: Gower, 258–9; *Local studies libraries: Library Association guidelines . . .* (2002), para B5.1.1.
21   The British Library holds only 47 per cent of Surrey titles held by local studies collections published since the 1970s, 38 per cent of Leicestershire titles from the 1990s, and 45 per cent of North Yorkshire titles from the 1980s and 1990s. This is partly because local collections often hold all the editions and reprints of works of local authors. See Phillips, A. (1998), 'Preserving the nation's collection of rare local materials: towards a coalition', *Local studies librarian* 17 (1), 10.
22   See Winterbotham, D. and Crosby, A. (1998), *The local studies library*, 73–80.
23   See also Melrose, E.A. (1991), 'Books and Pamphlets', 254–5.
24   *Local government minutes: Northern Ireland library holdings with locations* (1990), Omagh: Library Local Studies Panel.
25   See Melrose, E.A. (1991), 'Books and Pamphlets', 248–9.
26   A notable example is the Buxton Collection of 200 Civil War pamphlets at Bath. Redruth has the Hamilton Jenkin collection on mining, and there are naval history collections at Portsmouth and Plymouth. See Maxted, I. (1998), 'Local studies libraries as rare book collections', *Local studies librarian* 17 (1), 4.
27   See below under CD-ROMs.
28   A good account is given in Winterbotham, D. and Crosby, A. (1998), *The local studies library*, 42–53. See also Shaw, G. and Alexander, A. (1994), 'Directories as sources in local history', *Local history magazine* (46) September, 12–17.
29   For example, the only known copies of the 1841 and 1851 Exeter directories are in the Westcountry Studies Library. See Maxted, I. (1998), 'Local studies libraries', 4. For further information see Melrose, E.A. (1991), 'Books and Pamphlets', 249–51; Atkins, P.J. (1990), *The directories of London, 1677–1977*, Mansell.
30   See Winterbotham, D. and Crosby, A. (1998), *The local studies library*, 53–4.
31   Smith, G. (1995), 'Free newspapers: a national policy for their collection and preservation', *Local studies librarian* 14 (1), 13–14.
32   This is not always recommended; see *Local studies libraries: Library Association guidelines . . .* (2002), para B5.1.2.
33   The British Library Newspaper Library at Colindale holds *Trewman's Exeter flying-post* from 1807, but the Westcountry Studies Library has unique copies from 1763 to 1807; Maxted, I. (1998), 'Local studies libraries', 3.
34   A good guide to their use is Murphy, M. (1991), *Newspapers and local history*, Chichester: Phillimore for BALH.
35   See Winterbotham, D. and Crosby, A. (1998), *The local studies library*, 34–41.
36   See the definition given in ibid., 27–33.
37   Westmancoat, J. (1991), 'Newspapers and periodicals', in *Local studies collections: a manual*, vol 2, edited by M. Dewe, Aldershot: Gower, 304–5.
38   *Local studies libraries: Library Association guidelines . . .* (2002), para B5.1.2.
39   See Winterbotham, D. and Crosby, A. (1998), *The local studies library*, 81–90.
40   Hayes, M. (1996), 'Local maps in West Sussex: the reorganisation of the county library collection', *Local studies librarian* 15 (1), 11–13.
41   For example, Westminster holds three different plans for the building of Victoria Street, none of which represents the final version, and as many plans for Trafalgar Square and Regent's Park.
42   Many users want to locate a particular building. There is a need for street indexes to identify the appropriate sheet number. For London, the LCC's *Index to Street Names*, in several editions, gives the reference numbers for both the pre-1945 and post-1945 series of large-scale maps.

43   For a more detailed look at Ordnance Survey maps, see Abbott, R. (1991), 'Maps and plans', in *Local studies collections: a manual*, vol 2, edited by M. Dewe, Aldershot: Gower, 270–76.

44   *Local studies libraries: Library Association guidelines* ... (2002), para B5.1.4.

45   Copies of the fire insurance and shopping centre plans, and details of their coverage, can be obtained from Charles E. Goad Ltd, Salisbury Square, Old Hatfield, Hertfordshire.

46   See Winterbotham, D. and Crosby, A. (1998), *The local studies library*, 102–5.

47   Ephemera can also be successfully used as a trigger in reminiscence work. See Armstrong, N. (1991), 'Reminiscence work with local studies material', in *Local studies collections: a manual*, vol 2, edited by M. Dewe, Aldershot: Gower, 194–224. Barnet has a collection of locally produced Second World War propaganda posters which is ideal for this.

48   Contemporary ephemera being collected in Westminster includes cards left in public telephone boxes by local prostitutes, which may vanish if local government 'clean-up' campaigns prove successful.

49   See Winterbotham, D. and Crosby, A. (1998), *The local studies library*, 91–101.

50   *Local studies libraries: Library Association guidelines* ... (2002), para B5.1.5.

51   Westminster's Gardner collection, bought from Sotheby's in 1923–4, contains hundreds of prints, drawings and watercolours.

52   Martin, D. (1994), 'Local studies at the new Kirkintilloch library', *Local studies librarian* 13 (2), 3.

53   A series about local photographers appeared in the *Local historian*. The first featured James Barber, a Hendon photographer, whose work is preserved in Barnet local studies library; *Local historian* (1988), 18 (2), 80–81.

54   By 1909 over 800 million postcards were posted each year in Britain.

55   See Nurse, B. (1991), 'Prints, drawings and watercolours', in *Local studies collections: a manual*, vol 2, edited by M. Dewe, Aldershot: Gower, 329–51.

56   *Local studies libraries: Library Association guidelines* ... (2002), para B5.1.5.

57   Nurse, B. (1991), 'Prints, drawings', 329.

58   *Local studies libraries: Library Association guidelines* ... (2002), para B5.1.6.

59   'Upstairs, Downstairs' was started by Westminster in 1998 to collect the reminiscences of female servants in the 1920s and 1930s. For details of a Tameside project, see Lock, A. (1994), 'Living memories of Hyde: using volunteers in an oral history project', *Local studies librarian* 13 (2), 11–15.

60   Llwyd, R. and Evans, G. (1987), 'Oral history recordings', in *Local studies collections: a manual*, vol 1, edited by M. Dewe, Aldershot: Gower, 309–44. A particularly useful handbook is Caunce, S. (1994), *Oral history and the local historian*, London: Longman.

61   'Notes and news', (1995), *Local studies librarian* 14 (1), 19.

62   Sargent, J. (1992–3), 'A London Regional Film Archive', *Library Association Local Studies Group, London and Home Counties Branch Newsletter*. A survey of local studies collections in London found films were held at Southwark, Bexley, Kensington and Chelsea, Lewisham, Tower Hamlets and Westminster.

63   Baggs, C. (1987), 'Visual materials', in *Local studies collections: a manual*, vol 1, edited by M. Dewe, Aldershot: Gower, 351, 355–6.

64   Bligh, S. (1991), 'Video history: planning for the future', *Local studies librarian* 10 (2), 7–9.

65   *Local studies libraries: Library Association guidelines* ... (2002), para B8.2.2.

66   Raymond, S.A. (1999), *British genealogical microfiche*, Birmingham: FFHS; lists material produced by commercial and private publishers, arranged by county.

67   See Winterbotham, D. and Crosby, A. (1998), *The local studies library*, 55–60.

68   Names were not officially recorded until 1841, but some survive in local enumerators' books. Some for 1801–31 have survived locally, usually in local record offices, and many are now available on microfiche.

69   In 1891, an additional question asked was whether Welsh or English was spoken. Unfortunately, the answers are open to misinterpretation as no distinction was made between those who were bilingual and those who could only speak Welsh.

70   At 1 Myddleton Street, London EC1R 1UW (*www.pro.gov.uk/about/frc*).

71   482 of these have been released; Petty, M. (1996), 'Open University dissertations on CD-Rom', *Local studies librarian* 15 (2), 19–20.

72   Watson, I. (1996), 'The Durham Record', *Local studies librarian* 15 (2), 2–6.

73   At *http://collage.nhil.com*. See also Qstrow, S.D. (1998), *Digitizing historical picture collections for the Internet*, Washington: Council on Library and Information Resources; Amsterdam: European Commission on Preservation and Access; Carpenter, L., Shaw, S. and Prescott, A. (1998), *Towards the digital library. The initiatives for access programme*, London: The British Library.

74   Several guides are now available, e.g. Lamb, T.S. (2000), *Teach yourself today: e-Genealogy, finding your family roots online*, Indianapolis: Sams, Macmillan.

75   (1996), *Local studies librarian* 15 (2), 21.

76   A survey of sources used at Bolton found that 54 per cent were printed materials, and 40 per cent microforms. See Campbell, K. and Mills, B. (1995), 'Bolton archives and local studies: a customer survey', *Local studies librarian* 14 (1), 10–12.

5 Collection management

Diana Dixon

Harrod's librarian's glossary defines collection management as 'The organisation and maintenance of library stock, starting from collection development policies, keeping the needs of users a priority objective, and considering alternative means of document and information supply to supplement local holdings'.[1] This means that the concept of collection management includes all the processes, from selection to conservation of library materials, to meet the needs of users within budgetary and other resource constraints. This chapter, therefore, considers these various elements that constitute collection management of local studies collections: establishing and implementing a collection development policy; collection review and evaluation; preservation and conservation.

COLLECTION DEVELOPMENT

Collection development can be defined as 'the process of planning a stock acquisition programme not only simply to cater for immediate needs, but to build a coherent and reliable collection over a number of years, to meet the objectives of the service'.[2] Clearly, local studies collections must also consider the needs, not only of users today, but also of those in the future.

The American Library Association has published guidelines for drawing up collection development policies that state: 'a written development policy is a tool that assists acquisition personnel in working consistently toward required goals, thus ensuring stronger collections.'[3] Faye Phillips emphasizes the importance of having a written collection development policy and draws an analogy with a road atlas that shows where the collection is, where it wants to go and how best to get there.[4]

Whilst it is generally agreed that all local studies collections should have a written collection development policy, not all local studies libraries in the UK have one. Where policies exist they may be regarded as a selection or acquisition policy with, perhaps, separate policies for preservation and disaster management. Often, however, there is no separate policy for the local studies department, but it has input into the parent authority's policy, as in Birmingham Libraries. Collections of local studies material in learned societies or universities clearly need a policy in line with the mission statement of the parent body. There is an implicit understanding that the library should be committed to providing appropriate storage facilities and suitably qualified staff to house, administer and promote the local collection. 'Funding must be sufficient to provide an adequate range of books and other local studies resources. To this end it is desirable that local studies libraries have their own separate budget, of sufficient purchasing power.'[5]

SELECTION

The advantages of having a written selection policy for local studies are that the collection will

- reflect the aims and objectives of the local studies department,
- meet the needs of users,
- be built up in a consistent manner.

The policy will

- consider, for example, problems of relevance and selectivity and offer guidance,
- take into account resourcing: staffing, accommodation and budget,
- facilitate partnerships with local organizations.

In particular, the collecting policy 'should define (a) the topographical scope of the collection and (b) the forms of material to be collected, always retaining the option of redefinition at a future date to meet changed circumstances as these may occur. Once the definitions have been agreed upon, comprehensiveness should be their aim,[6] but selective or representational collecting may be more appropriate for some formats and subjects (e.g. ephemera, local authors and celebrities) as defined by the collection development policy.

TOPOGRAPHY

Although defining the area served may seem straightforward in terms of current administrative boundaries, it may be less clear-cut for local historical societies, or academic collections, and there are a number of points to consider as, for example, administrative boundaries may change. For instance, in the UK, local government has been reorganized twice in the past 25 years, with the result that many library authorities now cover very different areas. The county of Rutland disappeared in

1974 and was reinstated in 1997; in Wales, Cardiganshire was subsumed into Dyfed in 1974, and in 1996 it reappeared as Ceredigion; similar reorganization occurred in Scotland. The question for local studies librarians is complex: does the collection embrace all former administrative areas as well as the present? If an area has a clear cultural coherence as a region but crosses administrative boundaries, such as Merseyside or the Peak District, should the library also take this into account? Similarly, linguistic and cultural groupings may ignore national frontiers, as for example on the Hungarian and Romanian borders.

Users, too, may find administrative boundaries artificial and irrelevant to their own needs. For instance, although the River Dove separates Derbyshire from Staffordshire, many farms straddle the boundary and some readers whose postal address is Staffordshire prefer to use the Derbyshire Library Service for convenience. Thus Derbyshire took a conscious decision to collect material relating to Staffordshire Moorland to assist users. How far material is collected relating to bordering counties may well depend to some extent on the level of provision in the neighbouring authorities. Rich local collections in Sheffield and Manchester enable Derbyshire to be less assiduous in collecting material of cross-border interest in the north west of the county. Birmingham Central Library takes the view that a 15 to 20 mile radius of the Central Library will ensure that most relevant material is collected.

MATERIALS

Stock for the studies collection must satisfy the information needs of its users, potential as well as actual, and this should be the prime consideration in any selection process.[7] The difficulty for local studies librarians is that they need a crystal ball to ensure that their collection will be able to satisfy the information requirements of future generations as well as the present. Such a policy should be frequently revised to take account both of changing information needs and of new information sources, whether hard copy or electronic. The following policy criteria need to be kept in mind when selecting material.

- All stock should satisfy the informational needs of the community served, reflecting all sectors of society, and should ensure that the collection is not biased in favour of any economic or cultural group.
- The library service should be able to provide on demand, and largely from its own resources, information on all topics of public interest and concern relating to the locality served by the library; such information may be drawn either from hard copy, from electronic sources or from networks.
- Materials should cover a wide range of levels and be suitable for all age groups in the community.

- The selection policy should ensure that the needs of those with visual disabilities are met.[8]

REPRESENTING THE COMMUNITY

Local studies libraries should cater for all sectors of the community they serve. Increasingly, there is recognition that women and ethnic minorities should be served by local studies collections. Indeed, a recent conference of Black library workers[9] noted the contribution ethnic communities make to British history and this implies that local studies libraries could be more active in representing their needs. Often libraries are organized so that community services and local studies are separate departments and the need for skills in Asian and other minority languages means that responsibility for collection building falls outside local studies. The answer seems to be closer liaison between departments. Sharp[10] recognized that local studies librarians seemed aware of the problem and in many cases had taken active steps to work closely with cultural minority librarians. Birmingham has a definite policy of liaison and, for example, produced leaflets in various languages to publicize the service, and there have been various initiatives to stimulate awareness of the multicultural heritage and nature of many cities and regions.

WORKING IN PARTNERSHIP

Local studies libraries do not operate in isolation. To be effective they need to work in close partnership with other organizations providing similar material.

Therefore: 'The policy should take into account the aspirations of other local repositories seeking similar material especially museums and record offices, and full discussion should take place with the professional staff in charge of such repositories. In this way joint agreement can be reached, eliminating both competition and unnecessary duplication, and facilitating convenience of user access.'[11] Although a number of British local studies libraries have joined together with record offices to form heritage centres, as in Suffolk, many remain physically and administratively separate. Close liaison between archives and local studies libraries will be mutually beneficial in the context of collection management. Similarly, local universities may have strong local collections, as with the East Midlands Collection in Nottingham University. Many museums and local historical societies, for example the Norris Museum in St Ives, family history societies or private subscription libraries, often contain valuable local resources. Cooperation prevents duplication of expensive material like census returns and cooperative microfilming projects can make previously less accessible material more widely available. It can also, as in the case of Croydon,[12] lead to the creation of an integrated database combining holdings of the libraries, museum and archives.

Sometimes, as in Horley, mentioned earlier, the local history stock has been combined with that of the local history society to form an exceptional local studies resource.[13] The success of the NEWSPLAN project[14] (see Chapter 1) demonstrates the effectiveness of local cooperation in microfilming local newspapers and filling gaps in collections. Many local authorities contribute 1 per cent of their materials budget for filming and enhancing their holdings of provincial newspapers.

SERVICE POINT PROVISION

As a matter of policy, some local studies material should be provided at all service points in an authority.[15] Careful distinctions, however, need to be made for minimum levels of stock provision for libraries serving different sizes of population. Authorities will differ in the terminology used for these service points, but there should be provision in a central collection, larger district collections, urban and rural libraries as well as small branch libraries and mobile libraries. Derbyshire and Nottinghamshire have both produced detailed lists of local studies requirements for all service points. Not only do such lists ensure that all local books, periodicals and newspapers, directories, guidebooks, electoral registers, timetables, maps, illustrative material, ephemera and council minutes of local interest are collected but they also reinforce the need for local librarians to notify the central local studies library of any recently published local material. Smaller community libraries also have the responsibility to monitor demographic and economic changes in their locality and to alert the main service point of changing informational needs as a result of these developments. The local studies *Guidelines* recommend that 'they should include extensive collections of extracted cuttings and documents, perhaps in the "parish pack"[16] format in binders ... or alternatively as individual indexed and laminated documents'.[17] Good collection development plans state these requirements and place the onus for effective collection development on all libraries in the authority, rather than expecting all responsibility to be taken centrally.

LOCAL AUTHORS AND CELEBRITIES

The question of collecting material relating to local authors and celebrities is a contentious one and each case needs to be considered on its merits. Distinctions may become hazy when an author who was born in a particular area leaves early in life and has no current contact, literary or personal, with the region. Most local studies collections will try to collect literary work from those born or living in a locality whose work contains some local interest but many will fight shy, for example, of collecting all the academic books published by the staff of the local university, regardless of where they were born. Even this approach can cause problems: no one would doubt the necessity for Liverpool Libraries to collect popular fiction set in Liverpool by authors such as Lyn Andrews, Joan Jonker and Helen Forrester, but the difficulty arises with authors such as Birmingham-born Barbara Cartland, whose prodigious fictional output is not set in Birmingham. The pragmatic solution adopted by Birmingham Libraries is to collect a sample of her books rather than the complete set and to collect biographical works about her. The problem is compounded by the fact that a whole range of books may result from the popularity of particular authors, such as Beatrix Potter. Additional problems arise when the local author has a major scholarly reputation, as for example in the case of Shakespeare or D.H. Lawrence, as lavish collectors' editions are produced and these may fall outside the library's acquisition budget. In Nottingham, the policy is to buy selectively, so that, for instance, Byron facsimiles would not be bought on grounds of cost, although the Cambridge D.H. Lawrence edition would. Similarly, reviews, criticisms, biographical material and cuttings are actively collected. Staff need to be vigilant in watching for significant anniversaries to ensure that the material generated at that time is not overlooked.[18]

The problem is exacerbated when deciding what to collect on or about local celebrities: Members of Parliament, prominent businessmen or entertainers, sportsmen and notorieties. A pragmatic approach is to collect all autobiographical and biographical material but to limit overall coverage when individuals leave the locality. It is prudent to keep a watchful eye on the local media to spot emerging celebrities early enough, to ensure that relevant material is not missed.

FAME AND THE LOCALITY

Another collection development problem faced by local studies librarians is when a locality becomes the setting for a soap opera or film. Whilst it may be appropriate for North Yorkshire to collect extensively material relating to *Heartbeat* or for Auckland City Libraries on *Shortland St.*, how far is it relevant to collect material because the radio series *The Archers* is recorded in Birmingham? Decisions have to be made on an individual basis, dependent on public expectation, interest and demand. Screenplays, novels and picture books of the locality deserve their place, but how far is it legitimate, for example, to collect the recipe books that such series spawn? Nottingham collects any item relating to Robin Hood, including graphic novels and toys.

LOCAL PRINTERS AND PUBLISHERS

The output of local printers and publishers may be of local interest and in such cases a policy should be determined on what is to be represented in the collection, but in many cases the work is of no local interest and to collect it would stretch storage and budgets beyond justification. This is especially true when printers such as Richard Clay of Bungay serve an international market.

BACKGROUND MATERIAL

Television programmes and evening classes on family history or tracing the history of buildings generally stimulate increased interest in the local studies collection. Researchers expect to find not only the relevant documentary resources but also general material on using family history and archival sources, and manuals on local history and genealogy methodology. For this reason, although the local studies collection is primarily responsible for collecting material relevant to the heritage of a particular area, it has some responsibility to assist its clients in exploiting its resources. Libraries need to support those studying for certificate courses in family and local history and for school projects. Many local studies libraries actively collect books and periodicals on genealogical sources and this is a practice to be encouraged. Certainly, Birmingham and Derbyshire have up-to-date guides to family and local history and relevant magazines on the shelves.

ACQUISITION

One of the problems with local studies publications is that a very high proportion is not published through the conventional book trade and thus is not available via library suppliers. Neither is it always listed in national bibliographies or trade sources such as *The bookseller* or CD-ROM book trade sources: *TES Bookfind* and *Global Books in Print*; nor is it available from the Internet suppliers such as *Amazon.co.uk*. Some periodicals contain useful annual bibliographies such as the *Agricultural history review*, *Economic history review*, *Business archives* and the *Urban History Review*. Although such sources should be scanned on a regular basis, most acquisitions to the collection will not be listed in them. Chris Makepeace provided a useful overview of the principal British lists of local studies publications in *The reference sources handbook*,[19] and similar listings appear for North America and for Australia.[20] Nonetheless, the observation that 'there is no set list of sources that can be recommended for systematic searching' remains valid today.[21] A recent research project confirmed the findings of Andrew Phillips, that a substantial proportion of local publishing is not represented in the *British national bibliography* and escapes legal deposit.[22]

The specialist and local nature of much local studies material means that much is produced by local printers, small publishers specializing in work of local interest, or author/publishers. The material will often be a worthwhile contribution to knowledge, but it will prove hard to trace through the book trade. Chris Makepeace drew attention to this problem: 'there are many publications which do not reach the pages of the usual bibliographic tools and which are traced after a great deal of hard detective work on the part of the staff of the department'.[23]

Ephemera presents its own problems. The difficulty is in establishing realistic guidelines about what to collect. Should posters, train and theatre tickets form part of the local collection or not? Failure to collect systematically according to an agreed policy can lead to serious gaps in collections; for example, a recent survey revealed that of the 44 football clubs in the English premier and first divisions only 19 programmes were collected on a regular basis by local libraries.

In the 1990s a research project, 'A collection policy for printed Welsh ephemera',[24] looked at what printed ephemera was currently being collected by Welsh institutions, especially local studies libraries and the National Library of Wales. A pilot study in July 1992 centred on public libraries in Aberystwyth and Mold. One of the aims of the project was to make recommendations to libraries and other institutions in Wales for the formulation of a national collection policy for Welsh ephemera. The authors stressed that a 'collection policy is essential if the printed ephemera is to be acquired and managed in an effective manner'.[25]

For older material, librarians need to consult second-hand and antiquarian booksellers' catalogues and auction and sales catalogues in order to fill gaps in the collection. Most local studies librarians have regular contacts with second-hand booksellers and many notify the library about appropriate material. Cultivating reputable and reliable second-hand booksellers will reap rewards. Increasingly, the Internet is proving an invaluable means of tracing out-of-print titles and time should be allowed for regular searching. However, it should be remembered that financial constraints may prevent libraries from acquiring extremely high priced topographical works and literary facsimiles.

There is no substitute for the expertise and knowledge of the local studies staff and it is recommended that new staff should be trained to look for relevant material when they visit book shops. Larger authorities such as Birmingham City Libraries are able to timetable bookshop visits on a regular basis for staff to look out for new publications that might otherwise be missed. Jumble sales, charity shops, junkshops and second-hand bookshops may also yield the occasional worthwhile gem.

It is particularly hard to acquire limited circulation publications which are not sold through conventional book trade outlets. Most local studies librarians admit they rely heavily on unconventional sources to acquire material. Local newspapers, radio and television stations often feature new local publications and most bookstores have shelves dedicated to books of local interest. For this reason local studies librarians have to take a proactive role in acquiring material by keeping a vigilant eye on the local newspaper for announcements of new publications, as well as reviews in periodicals, especially from local history societies, general local history magazines, such as the *Local historian* and community newsletters, like the *Blyth bugle* in Southwold. These normally make a policy of featuring any new publication of local interest. Accordingly, it is normal practice in many libraries to scan the local newspapers on a regular basis, as is done in Derbyshire. Likewise, staff should listen to book programmes on local radio and television, as they often transmit short features on new publications by local authors. There is no doubt that the Internet is an increasingly useful source of information for publications, with many societies mounting websites listing new titles. It is worth keeping a regular eye on all of these to ensure that material is not missed.

It is essential to collect material published by the local authority, and also from district and parish councils, but tracing and acquiring this material is difficult because it emanates from a variety of departments and is produced in small print runs.[26] Establishing personal contact with key individuals in departments is the only way to ensure material comes to the librarian's attention. It is vital to maintain an up-to-date list of contacts and to send regular reminders that material is needed. The hardest part is often maintaining the momentum when personnel change and the initial enthusiasm wears off. However, the benefits of such a practice cannot be underestimated.

Local societies, schools, churches and organizations all publish material that should properly find its way onto the shelves of the local studies collection, but because much of it escapes standard bibliographic sources it is difficult to trace what has been produced. Librarians bemoan the problems of ensuring a regular supply of free publications that cannot be ordered in a conventional way. For this reason, local free newspapers and community newsletters are often missed, as it may be impossible to ensure a regular delivery. These are often brought in by members of the library staff. Suffolk local studies collections in Ipswich and Lowestoft certainly acquire their community newsletters in this way.

Election manifestos and the newsletters produced by political parties are hard to acquire formally and again staff should be alerted to their importance and encouraged to collect them for the library. Regular library users can also be persuaded to donate such material.

It is necessary to build up a list of contacts to supply the library with material from local branches of national organizations which produce regional newsletters, like the Victorian Society, and clubs and societies, churches, schools, universities and colleges, and leisure and recreational facilities. Estate agents often publish newsletters as well as property details and their literature is especially important for its illustrations, for example, of the sought-after Tarrant Houses built in Weybridge in the 1930s, about which there is now great interest among architectural historians. Local businesses publish house journals, such as the Everard's Brewery's *Tiger talk*, often containing obituaries and photographs, and their promotional advertising material will also be potentially important.

The local studies library needs to be proactive in its acquisition practice in order to implement its collection development policy successfully. Interviews in the local press and radio and publicity appeals can be used to encourage the public to deposit material of interest. This is particularly important for photographs of buildings and people and the benefits can be great, as in Newcastle, where the library received 8,000 slides and 2,000 photographs on the changing face of Newcastle. Often people will be willing to supply precious material for copying. The Birmingham History Van (mentioned in earlier chapters) visits community centres and old people's residential homes and encourages people to bring along their photographs for copying for the collection. The increasing popularity of digitization means that people are happy to lend material to form part of the digital record.

Microforms are useful supplements to local studies collections and relevant parts of important sources such as the census and the International Genealogical Index are necessary and popular additions to stock. However, sufficient microform readers, and reader printers, must also be purchased and administrative issues such as maintenance of equipment and film, booking procedures and possible charging all need careful consideration before providing material in this format. Whilst libraries may collect name indexes to the census for a wider area, most cannot afford to collect the entire countrywide census, or the GRO registers of births, marriages and deaths, however desirable their readers may think it would be to have them available locally.

CREATION OF MATERIAL

The interest in reminiscence as a historical source is important to the local collection. With a unique pool of the collective memory of local inhabitants, local studies librarians are ideally placed to be involved in creating this potentially valuable resource. Possibilities include stimulating interest and initiating a project, acting as coordinator and supplying equipment. Local studies libraries have played an important part in a number of projects involving oral history or video recordings. For example, based on oral history interviews, the Rockhampton biographical register[27] was formed, and a similar project used reminiscences in Franklin Lakes, New Jersey.[28] Recently, Oadby library was given a CD-ROM about people living in the village 100 years ago, compiled by Oadby Local History

Group.[29] Likewise, local studies libraries have often been involved in detailed photographic surveys, building by building. One of the most famous of these is the continuing Chester Photographic Survey,[30] which began in 1963, in which the library service became involved at an early stage.

DONATIONS

People using the local studies library for research should be persuaded to donate a copy of their work to the library. Research students generally carry out in-depth investigations, containing useful detail, and the library may offer to copy a thesis for the collection. Where the research results in a book or article, authors should be encouraged to donate a copy.

Each unsolicited donation needs to be considered on its own merits. It frequently duplicates material already held by the collection, and may be in poor condition, needing expensive restoration; or owners may impose terms and conditions which make it unacceptable. Many librarians confess to being circumspect in their attitude to donations. Because of the high costs of cataloguing, restoring and housing donations, many libraries now try to discourage unsolicited donations, simply because the costs outweigh the usefulness of the items donated. However, this generally does not apply to local studies materials, especially photographs, and most libraries welcome donations of photographs of the area and often are willing to copy them for clients. Lack of suitable accommodation may play an important part in deciding whether an item is acceptable or not. Fire regulations may mean that, despite its intrinsic value, a donation of a potentially combustible film cannot be accepted. Similarly, floor-loading restrictions may prevent a library from accepting a bulky multi-volume donation. On the other hand, generous donations past and present have contributed to the richness of local studies collections. Sometimes a donor may consult the library before giving an item and a library may benefit from regular and generous donations from individuals. In Derbyshire this has meant that the library has been able to acquire expensive facsimiles that it could not have afforded otherwise.

ELECTRONIC INFORMATION

The rapidly changing market of electronic information sources means that librarians need to keep abreast of new products and developments by regularly scanning media sources, the library and information press, e.g. *Information world*, local history and local government information sources, as well as publicity from the leading producers of electronic products, and the Internet.

Decisions about replacing hard copy with electronic alternatives will be influenced by a variety of considerations, including budget, costs of licence fees, and hardware installation and maintenance, cost of replacement of printer cartridges and paper, as well as whether the public will have free and widely available access to such material.

Electronic products need to be carefully evaluated in terms of their information content, and whether they satisfy an information need that can be more efficiently met than by using hard copy.[31] More and more popular reference sources, especially for genealogists, are now available electronically, and some only appear in multi-media versions on CD-ROM. The reverse also applies and, for the foreseeable future, electronic copy information sources will coexist side by side, and local studies services will need to cater for both. Access to the Internet, too, will be expected by users of the collection and will need to be budgeted for.

COLLECTION EVALUATION AND REVIEW

No local studies collection is static. New products, both in conventional and in multi-media formats, are appearing and these need to be carefully evaluated to ensure that the collection is closely tailored to meet the information needs of those it serves. The collection should be systematically reviewed to identify collection weaknesses and a policy of active collecting or soliciting of material to improve the situation should be implemented. Electronic products need vigilant monitoring before hard copy is discarded, to ensure that they are being regularly updated and that the information they offer is complete and accurate.

The collection must be regularly monitored to take account, not only of new products, but also of changing information needs in the community served by the library. Regular access to community profiling documentation is essential to see that all needs are adequately catered for. Changing emphases in local studies need to be accommodated. For instance, television programmes may stimulate a demand for material on a previously neglected topic and the collection needs to be evaluated to see if it can cater for a rise in demand.

Care should be taken to select materials that will satisfy the information needs of young people. The increasing importance of local studies research projects in schools means that the selection of appropriate learning material should be done in close association with local teachers to ensure that children can satisfactorily complete school assignments.

CURRENCY

Every library authority will be expected to adhere to standards for currency and should publicize these.[32] The local studies department is different from the rest of the library, in that out-of-date materials, for example directories and timetables, need to be retained for their future research potential. Thus the collection of Liverpool directories dating back to 1754 is the envy of many other cities. Similarly, old telephone directories and railway timetables are invaluable to historians and should be retained. Older versions of printed maps, especially large scale, must be retained and print-outs of digital mapping need to be made at regular intervals to ensure that an accurate portrayal of the changing environment is kept.

WEEDING

Although normally libraries are encouraged to discard items where the presentation is dated and there are better alternatives, in local studies these usually have a uniqueness that justifies their retention. It is hard to predict what will be of interest to future generations and sometimes even a rather pedestrian or inaccurate text may be supported by unique illustrative material, or contain factual information that is not available elsewhere. Obviously, such works must be collected and kept.

Libraries generally are expected to discard items physically damaged, defaced, dirty or worn out and this practice is equally valid for the local studies collection. However, in some cases the work may be out of print and hard or impossible to replace. Careful scrutiny will be needed to decide whether its uniqueness and intrinsic value justifies its retention (probably on restricted access) until a replacement can be found. However, outdated CD-ROMs should be removed from public access and users advised if electronic sources, and some sources on the Internet, are inaccurate or not current. As with printed sources, previous versions of a CD-ROM may contain potentially valuable material which should be retained. This is especially true of digitized maps. Material stored in closed access should be monitored, and if it has not been used for, say, ten years, consideration should be given to discarding, microfilming or digitizing it, or alternatively investigating cheaper storage facilities. Out-of-town warehousing may be an attractive option for inner city libraries where storage is expensive.

PRESERVATION AND CONSERVATION

PRESERVATION

The unique and irreplaceable nature of some of the material in local studies collections, for example local newspapers, maps, pamphlets and illustrations, means that a preservation policy is vital if these sources are to survive. In a key text, John Feather offers a definition, 'Preservation is an aspect of the management of the library. Its objective is to ensure that the information survives in an accessible and usable form'.[33]

Libraries were slow to recognize the importance of preserving their collections, but a series of disasters to collections brought the problem to prominence. The Florence floods of 1966 and disastrous fires, including those at Los Angeles (1986) and Norwich Central Library (1994), all demonstrated the vulnerability of library collections and the need to plan a preservation policy. Minor incidents do not capture the headlines but may be just as devastating to local history collections. Flood damage and fire can all but destroy unique material. Libraries need to be aware of the threats and take steps to have a policy for immediate restorative action. Disaster management or disaster plans take into account likely environmental threats to the collection, including floods, hurricanes and earthquakes, as well as man-made threats including fire, bombs, building inadequacies and chemical spillages, and develop a strategy for immediate responses to catastrophe.

In the UK, interest in preservation was stimulated by publication of the Ratcliffe[34] report in 1984 which exhorted librarians to regard preservation as a vital part of their basic responsibility, and advocated training and education. The British Library's National Preservation Office (1984) encourages and coordinates cooperative preservation activities. The International Federation of Library Associations (IFLA) developed a core programme on Preservation and Conservation in 1984 and actively promotes preservation issues by organizing regional seminars with education and training high on the agenda. In 1995 guidelines on *Library disaster planning*[35] recognized that collections are at risk from a variety of threats, including the nature of the material itself, natural and man-made disasters, the environment in which the material is kept and the way in which it is handled. More recently, the IFLA *Principles for the care and handling of library material*[36] reiterate the necessity for being prepared, by having up-to-date written plans, emergency supplies and equipment, and training in disaster response techniques. Disaster plans are now recognized as an important aspect of preservation management.

Clements[37] advocated regular review of a library's preservation policy and thought it should include

- a set of standards for the storage, cleaning and handling of material,
- a programme of education for staff and users,
- a contingency plan for disaster recovery,
- a maintenance programme to clean and repair damaged items,
- priorities for conservation of all kinds,
- use of surrogates to replace originals.

It was the precarious state of 19th-century paper that first set alarm bells ringing in North America in the 1960s. Items at risk need to be assessed and if necessary protected from unnecessary exposure and wear and tear. Newsprint is a particularly self-destructing medium and the recent award of a £5 million Heritage

Lottery grant in the United Kingdom to microfilm local newspapers at risk is one way of preserving this vital historical source for posterity and ensures a continuing commitment to preserve vulnerable newspaper collections. Libraries can also digitize at-risk materials such as photographs, maps and documents.

There is no doubt that the Internet is an ideal medium for exploiting material and a number of authorities are publicizing their collections in this way. In Pittsburgh a hypertext project based on photographs has added a valuable insight into the urban landscape[38] and, in the UK, Knowsley has mounted an ambitious educational project based on photographs and maps to create an interactive website.[39]

On a more mundane level, basics such as the boxing of material in acid-proof boxes is an important aspect of preservation and libraries often include provision for these in their budget. The library should have a binding policy and should ensure that material is regularly inspected to identify material needing to be bound. Similarly, local studies librarians must take reasonable precautions to prevent theft, either by security tagging, if appropriate, or by registering readers of rare and valuable material.[40]

CONSERVATION

Conservation is an important part of preservation activity. Described as 'Specific practices taken to slow deterioration and prolong the active life of an object by directly intervening in its physical and chemical make up',[41] 'It normally implies the repair of a damaged item to ensure the continued existence of individual items. The decision on intervention is essentially managerial or professional'.[42] Nowhere is conservation more important in a public library than in the local studies collection. The unique nature of material means that every effort must be made to restore damaged material. At the same time, ways need to be found to allow the public access to fragile material without further endangering the original. Surrogacy, e.g. the use of photocopies, is a viable option which enables users to have access to material which would otherwise be too fragile for use.

Although local studies librarians will generally argue for the retention of any printed item unless a replacement can easily be found, considerable activity has seen the transfer of films onto video because of their potentially combustible nature. Nottinghamshire was early in this respect and the trend has been followed in most authorities. There is a growing body of literature on care and preservation of library materials.

CONCLUSION

The world boasts a great number of excellent local studies collections, many of which have developed as a result of judicious collection management policies combined with fortuitous and generous donations. Nonetheless, although excellent collections have been built up without the benefit of a systematic collection policy, it can be argued that they could have been even more appropriate to the needs of their users if such policies had been in force. Changing circumstances, however, require local studies librarians to ensure that collections are developed in accordance with vision to ensure that the needs of all their users, real and potential, are met. Sound collection management now will reap its rewards for future generations.

NOTES

1   Prytherch, Ray (1999), *Harrod's librarian's glossary and reference book*, 9th edn, Aldershot: Gower, 163.
2   Ibid.
3   'AAL guidelines for formulation of collection development policies' (1979), in Bonk, W.J. and Magrill, R.M., *Building library collections*, 7th edn, Metuchen, NJ: Scarecrow, 63–8. These ALA guidelines were approved in 1976. Gabriel, M.R. (1995), *Collection development and collection evaluation*, Lanham, MD and London: Scarecrow contains various ALA guidelines for formulating and reviewing library collections.
4   Phillips, Faye (1995), *Local history collections in libraries*, Englewood, Colorado: Libraries Unlimited, 10.
5   Library Association Local Studies Group (2002), *Local studies libraries: Library Association guidelines for local studies provision in public libraries*, 2nd edition, London: Library Association, para B5.1.
6   Ibid.
7   See (2002) *Local studies libraries: Library Association guidelines ...* (2002), see section A2 for a detailed exposition of the various categories of users of local studies.
8   *Guidelines for information services provision in public libraries* (1999), London: Library Association Publishing, 17. They contain much that is relevant for local studies collections. Reference should also be made to Spiller, D. (2000), *Providing materials for library users*, London: Library Association Publishing; *Public library stock management* (1998), BNB Research Fund Report 90, National Acquisitions Group; and Evans, G. Edward (2000), *Developing library and information center collections*, 4th edn, Englewood, Colorado: Libraries Unlimited.
9   The Black Library Workers Conference in November 1999 noted that the contribution of ethnic minorities to British history was often unrecognized or underestimated.
10   Sharp, D.C. (1989), 'Public library provision of a local studies service in a multi-ethnic Society', Leeds: Leeds Polytechnic, Dept. of Library and Information Studies, MA Occasional Publications 5.
11   *Local studies libraries: Library Association guidelines ...* (2002), para B5.1.
12   Harris, O. (1996), 'United we stand – Croydon's multi-disciplinary, historical database', *IT news* 3, 17–21.
13   Wark, P. (1997), 'More power to the CIA', *Public library journal* 12 (6), 125–8.
14   NEWSPLAN is a cooperative project to audit the physical state of Britain's local newspapers and to make recommendations for microfilming the titles most at risk. Ten volumes have been published by the British Library and much has been accomplished since publication of the first volume in 1984.

15   *Local studies libraries: Library Association guidelines* ... (2002), para B6.2.1.

16   Bromwich, D. (1987), 'Parish packs: the Somerset approach', *Local studies librarian* 6(2), 15–16.

17   *Local studies libraries: Library Association guidelines* ... (2002), para B6.2.1.

18   Hayes, M. (1997), 'Sleeping with the enemy', *Local studies librarian* 16(1), Summer, 2–5, discusses the Special Events Group that has been formed in West Sussex to mark important anniversaries such as the bicentenary of the birth of Percy Bysshe Shelley or the 50th anniversary of the death of H.G. Wells.

19   Makepeace, C. (1996), 'Local studies', in Lea, P. and Day, A., *The reference sources handbook*, 4th edn, London: Library Association Publishing, 144–210; Winterbotham, Diana and Crosby, Alan (1999), *The local studies library*, Salisbury: BALH gives a helpful discussion of sources.

20   Useful are Katz, W.A. (1997), *Introduction to reference work*, 7th edn, New York: McGraw-Hill; Bond, M.E. and Carron, M.M. (comps) (1996), *Canadian reference sources*, Vancouver: University of British Columbia Press; Mills, J.J. (1990), *Information resources and services in Australia*, Wagga Wagga: Charles Sturt University.

21   *Standard of provision for local studies: report and policy statement* (1981), Preston: Lancashire Libraries, 5.

22   Phillips, A. (1998), 'Preserving the nation's collection of rare local materials: towards a coalition', *Local studies librarian*, 17 (1), 8–17. A research project at Loughborough University in 1999 investigated publication in Leicester and the adequacy of bibliographic control. The findings were discussed at a seminar at the British Library, 13 January 2000.

23   Makepeace, C. (1987), 'Acquisition', in Dewe, M. (ed.), *A manual of local studies librarianship*, Aldershot: Gower, 189.

24   Dewe, M. (1992), 'A collecting policy for printed ephemera: some contrasting United Kingdom approaches', *Local studies librarian*, 11 (1), 6–11; Drew, P. and Dewe, M. (1992), 'The Welsh ephemera project', *Local studies librarian*, 11 (2), 16–17. A useful comparison with Australian practice is found in Dewe, M. and Drew, P. (1993), 'The collection of printed ephemera in Australia at national, state and local levels', *international information and library review*, 25 (2), 123–40. Dewe, M. and Drew, P.R. (1994), *A collection policy for printed Welsh ephemera: a report and guidelines*, Aberystwyth: Department of Information and Library Studies, University of Wales, Aberystwyth.

25   Drew and Dewe (1992), 17.

26   Sturges, R.P. and Dixon, D. (1983), *Investigation of local publications*, Loughborough, Department of Library Studies, discussed the problems faced in tracing local authority publications in two areas: Leicester and Shropshire. The project also examined the nature of local publishing and made efforts to acquire as much of the current literary output as possible.

27   Tom, N. (1994), 'Collecting a community's oral history', *Link up*, March, 13–14.

28   Cooke, G.W. (1994), 'Building local history collections through guided autobiography', *American libraries*, 25 (9), 825–8, describes how guided autobiography tours with older people have expanded the collection in Franklin Lakes, New Jersey.

29   'History on a hard disk' (2000), *Oadby and Wigston mail*, 6 April, 34.

30   Fisher, G. (1993), 'Thirty years of the Chester Photographic Survey', *Local studies librarian*, 12 (1), 11–13.

31   Guidelines for evaluating electronic information sources are currently in preparation by the Library Association Information Services Group and should be published by the Group in 2002.

32   *Draft standards for public libraries* (2000) have firm criteria for discarding such material but many of them may not be applicable in local studies collections.

33   Feather, John (1996), *Preservation and the management of library collections*, 2nd edn, London: Library Association Publishing, 2.

34   Ratcliffe, F.W. (ed.) (1984), *Preservation policies and conservation in British libraries*, London: British Library (Library and Information Report 25).

35   Skepastianu, M. (1995), *Library disaster planning prepared for the IFLA Section on conservation and preservation: prevention, preparedness, response recovery*, The Hague: IFLA.

36   Adcock, E.P. (1998), *Principles for the care and handling of library material*, The Hague: IFLA.

37   Clements, G. (1991), 'Preservation policies', in Kenny, G. (ed.), *A reading guide to the preservation of library collections*, London: Library association Publishing, 15.
38   Chad, B. (1995), 'Bridging the urban landscape', *Ohio libraries*, 8 (3), 13–16.
39   Marchant, P. and Hume, E. (1998), 'Visiting Knowsley's past', *Library Association record*, 100 (9), 468–9.
40   *Local studies libraries: Library Association guidelines* ... (2002), para B6.1.1.
41   Adcock, E.P. (1998), 4.
42   Feather (1996), 2.

6 Information access and retrieval

Eileen Hume and Alice Lock

INTRODUCTION

Owing to changes in the study of local history and in the range of users of the local collection, local studies staff have faced a number of challenges, of which the latest is the transformation of information retrieval methods offered by new technology. Because local studies libraries are in a period of transition from paper-based to machine-based retrieval systems, this chapter can only indicate a few likely trends and issues. The importance of information retrieval is reinforced by the local studies *Guidelines* that make the provision of a comprehensive range of finding aids one of the aims and objectives of the service.

CATALOGUING

Differing demands on local studies libraries mean there is a tendency still to use card catalogues even when the parent lending systems are computerized. Two recent reports, however, have stressed the importance of electronic cataloguing for local studies and other research libraries: *Virtually new* and *Full disclosure*.[1] While *Virtually new* is primarily concerned with digitization projects, it emphasizes that creating, automating and networking catalogues and finding aids has to be recognized as the priority for many local studies collections, special collections and archives.[2] *Full disclosure* is a welcome first step towards a national strategy for the retrospective conversion of library catalogues and emphasizes that material is essentially hidden and unused if not listed electronically. The economic benefits of maximizing existing investment in the library stock and manual finding aids by conversion are important, but 'loss of our collective memory' must also be halted.[3] It has been argued also that special collections are 'jewels of a library's holdings' and should be given prominence on computer opening pages and websites.[4] A further benefit is that electronic catalogues can be easily duplicated and copies stored off-site as a disaster precaution.

RETROSPECTIVE CONVERSION AND CATALOGUING

Retrospective conversion is an enormous problem and in 1997 it was estimated that about 50 million records awaited conversion, with a likely cost of £80–100 million.[5] Meanwhile, many libraries are using a mixture of systems, which makes searching very difficult. In one university, library users could find themselves consulting up to eight files, five in manual forms and three on-line, while other material may be totally uncatalogued.[6] LASER's needs assessment survey of heritage material in 1998 found 30 per cent of collections were uncatalogued, 11 per cent were catalogued only at collection level, 50 per cent at item level and 8 per cent at item level in part.[7] These collections are being held for the future and, as levels of use of older material will be the same, or greater, than for new material the problem will not disappear.

Although retrospective electronic cataloguing is to be welcomed, it is worth noting that there are some drawbacks. There is often user resistance, which has led a few librarians in the USA to express reservations and stress the need for more extensive assistance for readers.[8] Users in local studies libraries, perhaps unlike those in lending libraries, often know how to use card catalogues and are usually older and more resistant to change. One study has found that even academics in the humanities are reluctant to use new technology for research; for example, they have less patience with the Internet than those in other disciplines.[9] Users, therefore, will need to learn new searching techniques and may need considerable assistance.

Libraries considering retrospective conversion can benefit from the experience of collections which have already gone through the process, such as Trinity College, Dublin, where a collection of three million books included about one million which had been catalogued by MARC (on fiche) since 1968.[10] The first step was to convert the cards for which a record already existed in the British National Bibliography (BNB) or other sources (about 75 per cent) and combine these with the post-1968 records in an on-line system. The second stage was to convert the remaining cards, but an attempt to use existing records produced a low hit rate and a quality of cataloguing below the cards. Trinity College decided to use the data on its cards. This experience may be repeated in local studies libraries where there is often extensive analytical cataloguing drawing out local themes which might be lost in a simple transfer to electronic records.

A smaller scheme took place at the Moravian Music Foundation in the USA. Surprisingly, records for over 68 per cent of holdings were found in existing databases.[11] It was estimated that from 16 to 38 minutes were taken to convert a record from another database, but it required more than 50 minutes to create a new machine-readable record. Local studies libraries will often be holding the only copy of a book or other item, thus creating the need to make new time-consuming records.

In Britain, Westminster, Wolverhampton and Chethams Library in Manchester are planning to computerize their local studies catalogues by digitizing the cards or as part of a digitization project for maps, cuttings and photographs.[12] Many other libraries have developed machine-readable catalogues for new accessions or selected stock. One of these is the Malta State Library, which holds the island's Malta material and produces the national bibliography. Its catalogue entry will therefore become the master entry for libraries in Malta.[13]

In 1994 Gloucestershire libraries decided a union catalogue of local studies materials was needed.[14] The main collection of over 200,000 items was held at Gloucester, but as local studies centres had been set up in six main libraries after 1991, the union catalogue had to be accessed from all these sites and had to accommodate different work patterns and classification schemes. A core record with site-specific elements was created along with a thesaurus and keyword authority file. Staff at Gloucester were closely involved in creating the system which allowed expertise which can be used on other projects to be developed in-house.

These initiatives are valuable first steps, but both *Full disclosure* and *Making the most of our libraries* stress that retrospective cataloguing must eventually apply to the whole of collections, not least to eliminate the irritation of consulting several finding aids. Bryant emphasizes that one researcher's ephemeral document is another's essential source, especially true in local research, and so none can be overlooked. Any document considered worthy of a manual record should be included and, once it becomes visible, use will be increased.[15]

CATALOGUING STANDARDS

Retrospective cataloguing requires the development and use of existing standards, and any scheme will need input from staff conversant with those standards. Both *Full disclosure* and *Making the most of our libraries* recognize this as a problem, as many library schools are no longer producing cataloguers, and the human element in good quality cataloguing is essential.[16] A knowledge of the history of printing is also helpful for local studies cataloguing.

The local studies *Guidelines* stress that there is a responsibility to produce high-quality records because they may become the authoritative record for the national published archive. Anglo American Cataloguing Rules (AACR) standards are an important basis, but extra information, about provenance, special copies and analytical entries, may also be necessary. Local studies cataloguing has always been marked by a need to bring out both subject and place, while AACR puts less emphasis on the place element. Ian Maxted at the Westcountry Studies Library has adapted national standards for that local collection and Devon's book catalogue is now on the Internet.[17] Adapting standards will prove difficult, especially as inconsistencies exist within them: one example relevant to British local and family historians is the difference between the British Library and Library of Congress treatment of material relating to parish churches. The British Library favours the name of the church (St Michael's, Ashton-u-Lyne) while the Library of Congress favours the parish name (Ashton-u-Lyne Parish Church).[18]

Other standards relevant to local studies collections include guidelines for cataloguing rare books produced by the Library Association in 1999 and the English Short Title Catalogue (EngSTC).[19] The EngSTC was developed by the British Library and University of California in 1977 to produce definitive catalogue entries for 18th-century books. In 1987 coverage was extended to all pre-19th-century books published in England, in countries under English colonial rule and items in English published elsewhere. Another important consideration for any system, as the local studies *Guidelines* illustrate, is the need for user-friendly interfaces.

BIBLIOGRAPHIES

As many of the books held in local studies collections are unique, the catalogue entry will become the definitive record and so the standard must be high. This will allow the creation of useful regional bibliographies, a tradition which is thriving in Europe but seems to have declined a little in Britain. British regional bibliographies include the *Bibliography of North-West England*, *Bibliography of printed books on London history to 1939*, the *Devon bibliography*, the *East Anglian bibliography*, the *East Midlands bibliography*, the *Bibliography of Scotland*, and the SCOTLOC database.[20] Other initiatives have not survived; the *Northern bibliography* folded in 1992 and the *East Yorkshire bibliography* only survives in its offshoot, the Humad Project, listing Hull University Library's manuscripts.[21] The *Devon bibliography* and Humad Project are signs of a new trend into electronic format.

On the continent the picture is different. Regional bibliographies in France cover Brittany, Alsace, Burgundy, Languedoc and Normandy.[22] In Hungary an annotated bibliography in Kisfaludy Karoly was being computerized in 1993.[23] Hungarian libraries tend to have county bibliographies dating back 35 years or more.[24] In 1995 the LA Local Studies Group helped sponsor the first volume of Bibliografi-Muresene, for Mures County, Romania.[25] It is intended that the Saami people who live in Norway, Sweden, Finland and Russia, but have a common heritage, will benefit from a bibliography produced by the Berenice Centre, a decentralized network with its headquarters in Rovaniemi, Finland.[26]

This bibliographic tradition can be especially important in developing countries. The *National bibliography of Indian literature*, covering 1900 to 1953, when regional literature was developing, showed that many books were in local collections, at risk from the tropical climate, poor quality paper and heavy use. The bibliography helped create a microfilming project, which will improve cataloguing information and preservation of the titles.[27]

NETWORKED CATALOGUES

The major advantage of an electronic catalogue, and a primary cause of the need for standards, is the opportunity for remote access. It is important, therefore, that local studies catalogues are Z39.50 compliant, and can be accessed from one point, perhaps the UK's Project EARL. The people's network report of 1997 provides encouragement for a library network with facilities for access from all public library service points.[28]

The wider use of the Internet for local studies is discussed below but, as noted by the local studies *Guidelines*, the opportunity for remote access to catalogues of unique collections is a major benefit. Large American and Australian local studies collections have already achieved high-quality websites allowing access to their catalogues of printed, manuscript and oral materials, along with digitized image collections. One example is the Minnesota Historical Society Library whose catalogue is part of the PALS on-line union catalogue and can also be visited through MNLink, a Minnesota libraries network. Over ten years' work has gone into building up the catalogue and website, but many parts of the collection are still not included.[29] The American Heritage Project is a wider initiative to create a national catalogue of finding aids relating to the 19th and early 20th centuries.[30] It adopts a subject approach, bringing together material from various institutions. This is another benefit of remote access, which is illustrated by smaller projects such as the Yorkshire Quaker Heritage Project based at Hull University. This aims to create an electronic list of materials relating to Quakerism wherever they are held, and the British Waterways Project to create a catalogue on the Internet of relevant holdings in 15 different repositories.[31]

Similarly, material in related libraries can be brought together, as in the Cathedral Libraries Project, which aims to catalogue these collections in a compatible, machine-readable format.[32] Remote access thus allows the recovery of relevant material from unlikely locations.

ELECTRONIC MATERIAL IN LOCAL STUDIES LIBRARIES

As more and more electronic source material becomes available in local studies libraries, it brings its own cataloguing problems. The British Library CD

Demonstrator Project showed that it could take up to four times as long to catalogue a CD-ROM as to catalogue a book.[33] Commercially produced material is acquired now and home-made databases are likely to be acquired in the future, as British history students are being encouraged to create them.[34] There will also be the need to access and contribute to outside databases such as the proposed Black and Asian Studies Association database, the History Data Archive and the Archaeology Data Archive.[35] There will be problems in this field with obsolete formats and software; early computer-based research, such as Landsat satellite data from the 1960s, is already lost. Publishers in electronic formats are constantly developing new ways to prevent pirate copies, which will hinder attempts to transfer digital material from obsolete to new mediums.

INTEGRATED CATALOGUES

The development of subject-oriented catalogues bringing together material from different locations is mirrored by work on creating fully integrated local catalogues bringing together material from museums, record offices and libraries. It is generally accepted that researchers want information regardless of its format, whether manuscript, printed or object, but this remains an area where many cataloguing problems are unsolved.

According to L.E. Sherwood of the Canadian Heritage Information Network, the Internet encourages the trend towards integrated collections.[36] Although standards have developed to allow cross-domain searching, there are still disputes, within individual disciplines, over what is acceptable. The development of Croydon's proposed multidisciplinary database illustrates some of these problems. This scheme began with the very attractive idea that visitors would be led from the entertaining interpretative displays in the museum straight into detailed access to the raw materials in the archive, local studies and museum collections. The project was made possible by the setting up of a new central library containing a local studies collection, archives and museum. Finance was available and, as the museum and archive collections had no existing finding aids and the local studies catalogues were eccentric, a system could be built from scratch. The first casualty was the link from museum displays to the catalogue, as the requirements of the two systems proved incompatible. The second problem was the seamless integration of finding aids for the three disciplines. Museums and libraries deal with items as individual objects, with museums concerned with the appearance and composition of objects and libraries with their contents. Archivists concentrate on hierarchical relationships between groups of material. It proved impossible, therefore, to develop integrated cataloguing, but integrated indexing was achieved. Croydon's archivist concluded that the differences between these systems had developed for good reasons and in order to suit the needs of different materials and their users. He said, 'the ultimate goal of integration was not so vitally essential as to justify any compromise of the principles of the individual professions involved'. After five years' work the search element of the database needed development, but it was felt 'a modified version of the dream was realisable'.[37]

Sherwood's solution to this problem was to suggest that libraries and museums may need to adopt the collection-level descriptions which are common in archives.[38] However, a further problem may be that any integrated system would produce too much material, already a feature of electronic catalogues. 'Screen fatigue' means that researchers tend to give up after looking at about nine entries.[39]

The archives world is developing a separate strategy for electronic cataloguing, *Archives-On-line* being the first step, and different standards are developing for archives, libraries and museums.[40] Many archive collections use CALM software, which also has a library version, which may be particularly useful for local studies libraries. The issue of integration is further complicated because relevant materials are held in academic libraries, research bodies, learned societies and government departments. The scale of the problem can be seen in the West Midlands alone, where 700 collections were surveyed to assess their value, scope and accessibility. The audit itself took two years, but the methodology developed may help other projects.[41]

Local studies catalogues should have links with parent lending catalogues to aid general readers, but should not be fully integrated, as neither group of readers would benefit from the inevitable retrieval of irrelevant material. The local studies *Guidelines* stress that cataloguing and management methods are very different for each type of stock. Local studies libraries need more detailed cataloguing and do not require techniques to deal with loans and discards.

CLASSIFICATION

The problems of unfamiliarity and incompatibility with other collections caused by the various, often unique, classification schemes used in local studies libraries seem to have receded as electronic finding aids have developed and as more material tends to be stored on closed access. In lending libraries browsing is thus the most important searching tool for readers, but it is no longer a viable option for many local studies library users.[42]

The local studies *Guidelines* recommend that Dewey, or a version of the Dewey classification system, should be seriously considered for any open access collection or classified subject catalogue simply because it is the most familiar to users and standardized electronic catalogues can use it. The spread of closed access collections, however, puts even more pressure on the quality of finding aids and, in particular, indexing.

INDEXING

As information retrieval in all its aspects is particularly crucial in the field of local studies collections, this section on indexing is intended to complement the previous section on cataloguing.[43] As what distinguishes an index from a catalogue or bibliography is not always understood, definitions are perhaps useful.[44] A catalogue is a record of the documents in a particular collection, whereas a bibliography is a record of the documents in general; but an index is a record of the detailed contents of a particular document. The official definition of an index, according to ISO 99:1996, is that 'an index groups together in a systematic arrangement information scattered throughout a document, database or other collection, and is designed to enable readers to identify and locate relevant information and to retrieve it quickly and efficiently'.

If material is not retrievable because no one has indexed the contents of an item, then, in effect, that information remains invisible. The impact on local studies material could be potentially devastating, since the value of documents will remain unknown and this will perhaps jeopardize their retention for future researchers.[45] Indexes are therefore an essential part of a finding aid system and in the local studies library materials can be divided into three categories:[46] materials needing cataloguing but not indexing (for example, a parish guide), indexed items that do not require cataloguing (such as newspaper cutting files) and catalogued items that need indexing as well (for example, a run of local periodicals).

Indexes can usually be created by using the facilities of an automated system to create a machine-generated index, by tagging key words in the text, or by putting key words into dedicated fields. This in turn leads to the need for a control of vocabulary terms and usually a thesaurus is used.[47] A thesaurus is not a dictionary, and it does not normally contain authoritative terms, but it is there to match the terms brought to the system by the inquirer with the terms used by the indexer. In fact the local studies *Guidelines* emphasize the need for a hierarchical thesaurus to aid consistency in indexing.

There are three main rules in compiling an index.[48] First, use a limited list of indexing terms, but plenty of entry terms. Link these with USE and USE FOR relationships. Wherever there are alternative names for a type of item, a choice needs to be made of the term used for indexing. Provision should be made for an entry under each of the others, saying what the preferred term is; for example, if all types of *industrial* premises are indexed as *factories*, someone who searches for *cotton mills* must be told to look for *factories* instead:

Factories USE FOR *Cotton Mills*
Cotton Mills USE *Factories*

The second rule is to structure terms of the same type into hierarchies. Link these with BROADER TERM/NARROWER TERM relationships. If there are many types of *labour disputes*, under a single item it would be too difficult to look through easily, so a more specific term needs to be used: for example, *labour disputes* as the broader term with the narrower term including *strikes, lockouts, work-to-rule, sit-ins* etc.

The third rule is to remind users of other terms to consider. Link these with RELATED TERM relationships. If the hierarchical relationships are restricted to true specific/generic relationships, another mechanism is needed to draw attention to other terms which an indexer and searcher should consider. Related terms may be of several kinds: objects and the discipline in which they are studied, such as *rush carts* and *folk lore*, processes and their products, such as *weaving* and *cloth* and *tools*, and the process in which they are used, such as *power loom* and *weaving*.

No new material concerning the indexing of local studies collections has been written since 1987, although in 1981 work on indexing local studies collections was undertaken in Australia;[49] key word indexing was a topic discussed by Ian Maxted at a local studies seminar in 1983, but unfortunately unpublished.[50] This is perhaps an area that needs to be examined by local study practitioners. The compilation of an index is a very time-consuming affair, but with ever-increasing pressure on staff time and financial cutbacks from departmental budgets it is often one of the first areas to be neglected. A lack of subject indexing of local studies collections in local authority public libraries in the UK was revealed in a survey undertaken by one of the present authors during the late summer of 1999. More than half the people responsible for local studies collections that replied said they would welcome a hierarchical management system to allow for detailed indexing of their collections.[51]

PRODUCERS OF LOCAL STUDIES INDEXES

Indexes for a local studies collection may be produced by some of the following means:

- library staff;[52]
- volunteers. The Federation of Family History Societies web pages (*http://www.ffhs.org.uk*) illustrate many examples of indexes produced by volunteers;
- independent workers, whose indexes can often represent a lifetime's work. The Guild of One-Name Studies (*http://www.one-name.org*) illustrates the tremendous amount of work completed by independent workers;

- professional indexers, whose work can be used via some of the large abstracting and indexing databases, e.g. *Historical abstracts*;
- search engines on the Internet. The Internet offers a different type of index from the ones that are traditionally available in the local studies library. Indexing in this case is achieved by the use of search engines. A word or phrase is typed in as a 'search term' and the resultant number of matches, with a brief description, displayed on the computer screen. There are many search engines that can be used on the Internet, such as Alta Vista (*http://altavista.com*), Yahoo (*http://yahoo.com*) or Web Crawler (*http://webcrawler.com*).

INDEXES IN THE LOCAL STUDIES LIBRARY

Most of the indexes that are available in local studies libraries would benefit from the application of information technology, to simplify the retrieval of information and eliminate errors when searching. However, indexes are usually available in the form of a card index with often minimal cross-referencing. The local studies *Guidelines* recommend that any indexing system should develop headings, which are applicable to all types of stock held in the collection.

LOCAL NEWSPAPERS

These represent one of the largest sources of information in the local studies library and can be used for some of the following:

- to find a contemporary account of an event,
- to fix the date an event occurred,
- to gain an insight into the social history of a particular period,
- to find articles about places and or events of a local historic interest.

The user's first step is to find a relevant newspaper, and in Britain the general guides are still in paper form, although it seems likely that the regional NEWSPLAN volumes will eventually become searchable databases on the net. The first to appear was LASER's, which lists 2,500 titles.[53]

The US Newspaper Program has developed with many of the same aims as NEWSPLAN, and is intended to locate, catalogue, preserve on microfilm and make available newspapers to researchers. The first step has been to catalogue holdings state by state, the lead usually being taken by a major research institution in each state. It is hoped that a national database will result.[54] As part of this scheme, the Illinois Newspaper Project decided to classify newspapers by geographical area to improve access.[55]

The user's second step is to gain access to the contents of the relevant newspaper, which often requires the use of an index, cuttings file or electronic retrieval of a digitized image. The latter option is a possibility with modern newspapers, many of which are published in electronic form, but so far has not proved viable with older newspapers.

Several English provincial newspapers have begun publishing electronically: the *Northern echo* first appeared on CD-ROM in 1990 and went on-line in 1991.[56] The on-line paper is different from the printed version, containing different stories, links to background material and an 'archive' dating back to its first electronic appearance. It therefore provides its own index for selected recent stories, but presents the local studies librarian with a dilemma, common to all information on the web, of preservation of these news stories.[57] It is claimed that the web has a 'memory' of about two months.[58] A search in 1999 revealed about 40 regional newspaper websites in the UK, many including searchable archives.[59]

NEWSPLAN believes it will be some time before this kind of technology is available for early newspapers, although attempts have been made at the British Library and at Norfolk Local Studies Library.[60] The British Library's Burney Collection of newspapers was digitized because the originals are too fragile to handle, and the microfilms are of poor quality. It proved possible to scan the images to a high enough quality, but was not possible to produce an index using OCR (optical character recognition).[61] Norfolk lost its cuttings collection, which acted as an index to local papers for 1920 to 1994, in the fire of 1994. It was decided to try to replace the index by electronic means, but, so far, the technical problems relating to the density and quality of the image have proved difficult or expensive to solve. Norfolk decided that the heavy costs of being a pioneer in the field were too much to bear.[62] In Australia digitization has also been used as a means of preservation of newspapers.[63]

Even if the technical problems of digitizing papers and indexing by OCR are solved, the technique may have limited usefulness for detailed historical research and may raise false expectations in users. Nineteenth-century terminology is very different from present-day usage. In the field of labour history, for example, the words 'strike' and 'unemployment' are not used, being described, in Lancashire at least, as 'turnouts' and 'short time working'. These are not obvious search terms, especially for anyone new to the subject.

The local studies *Guidelines* suggest that newspaper indexes created by human indexers are likely to be with us for some time, though they will increasingly be in electronic format. Recent examples include the index to the *Canton repository* at Kent State using dBase IV and made available on the Internet, and the *Daily herald* at Provo, Utah using WordPerfect.[64] These projects stress the need for locally compiled lists of subject headings using standards, such as the Library of Congress Subject Headings, as a basis. They also recommend that careful decisions about the scope of the index be made in advance.[65] Many large newspapers have their own libraries which provide subject access to back copies and are also moving into electronic indexes compiled by library staff.[66] Computer professionals should be consulted at the planning stage, as an indexing project for *The guardian* in Nigeria discovered.[67]

Existing manual indexes, in the form of cuttings files which also allow immediate access to the text, can be scanned, as planned in Port Talbot.[68] The Chartered Insurance Institute Library, however, abandoned cuttings in favour of an electronic index to journals and because it was felt important to have the index integrated with the book catalogue. Most readers were remote users, to whom the reference was often as useful as the article.[69]

THE INTERNATIONAL GENEALOGICAL INDEX

This index, compiled by the Church of Jesus Christ of the Latter Day Saints, is available in three formats: microfiche, CD-ROM and via the Family Search web pages. These last two versions simplify the retrieval process; however, the CD-ROM version contains more information. The index works on a geographic basis, for example the old (pre-1974) counties in England. The names are arranged alphabetically and then chronologically. The details include surname, given name(s), parents (if baptism or birth) or spouse (if a marriage), codes for the individual, that is, male, female, husband, wife, and type of event. The date and place of the event is also listed. It has to be remembered that the Index is only an index and does not include any information other than the parties' names. Any additional useful information present in the original document will not be included. The Index is also incomplete, many church registers not having been indexed. The IGI covers the period from early 1500 to 1900 and lists primarily baptisms and marriages. The English section contains entries obtained from parish registers, but it also includes some nonconformist registers and bishops' transcripts. The coverage of the different countries varies considerably.

THE GENERAL REGISTER OFFICE INDEX

The General Register Office Index, sometimes referred to as the GRO or the St Catherine's House Index, covers civil registration of births, marriages and deaths from 1837 to the present and is available on microfiche. The fiche is arranged in numerical order from 1837; within each year it is then arranged in alphabetical order for each quarter of the year. The index indicates the locality of the event by registration district and region. The birth indexes are laid out in the following order: surname, forename(s), supt. reg. district, volume and page. From September 1911 the maiden name of the mother is included. The marriage indexes follow a similar pattern. After March 1912 the surname of the spouse appears alongside each main entry. Death indexes have the same information fields as the birth indexes, but are not always available in local studies libraries because of the cost involved. Libraries may take only a few years of microfiche.

INDEX TO THE CENSUS RETURNS

The census returns, which are usually found in most local studies libraries, are one of the richest sources of information for family history research. The first census took place in 1801. The census is conducted every ten years, but not released for public consultation for 100 years. The census returns are produced on microfiche and microfilm. During the 1970s a project was started to transcribe and index the 1851 census returns, and was mainly tackled by the family history societies.[70] The project is still going on; some counties have been completed and published but the larger counties have yet to be finished. For example, the East of London FHS has been working on the 1861 census, and Huntingdonshire FHS has transcribed the 1841 census returns. Other family history societies have transcribed and indexed other census returns. Collections of most census indexes are held at the Public Record Office or the Society of Genealogists. Some indexes may only contain the surname, the piece and folio number of the census returns, while other indexes contain full details.

In the 1980s the Genealogical Society of Utah, the Society of the Church of Jesus Christ of the Latter-Day Saints and the British Federation of Family History Societies started work on the 1881 census returns. This is available on CD-ROM and lists each person alphabetically by surname. On microfiche, the 1881 index by county is divided into several sections, each section of microfiche being colour coded: for example, yellow – as enumerated, pink – surname index, orange – census place index, green – birthplace index, brown – miscellaneous and notes, brown – lists of vessels/ships, brown – lists of institutions. The reference numbers relate to the Genealogical Society of Utah film numbers and the 'as enumerated' (yellow) section is a transcript of the returns and gives the PRO piece, folio and page number. The surname index lists all people who were in the county on the night of the census. These are in alphabetical order and show forename, age, sex, relationship to the head of household, marital condition, census place, occupation, name of the head of household, where born (county and parish), notes, PRO references and the LDS film reference number.

The Public Record Office is undertaking a major development in 2000, in that it is making available over the Internet the 1901 census. The census taken on 31 March 1901 will be available on the first working day of January 2002. It is part of the vision of the Public Record Office to provide more records electronically. On the Internet the 1901 census will have an index that allows the user to navigate the data more flexibly. It will enable researchers to link directly to the images of the returns. A pilot scheme using the 1891 returns for Norfolk will be available over the Internet from spring of 2001. The basic index will be free to users but a charging system is likely for viewing transcriptions and images of the pages.

There are many census indexes available in the United States, both on microfiche and on microfilm. Most of the federal censuses are indexed and every census from 1790 to 1850 has statewide indexes. Indexers of the 1880, 1910 and 1920 censuses used a 'Soundex' system, a phonetic index putting names together that sounded the same, rather than alphabetically.

NON-BOOK MATERIALS

Books have always been only part of a local studies collection and each type of non-book material has its own strengths as a historical source. Non-book materials have tended to be catalogued and indexed separately, and important developments are taking place in these fields, independently of general cataloguing and indexing considerations, but each has it own problems, including the conflicting demands of high quality and integrated finding aids. Not all types of material can be dealt with here.

Ephemera

Most local studies libraries hold large collections of ephemera, often uncatalogued. A survey of Welsh libraries in 1992 found that, of responding libraries, most classified ephemera, two indexed it and none catalogued it.[71] The local studies *Guidelines* suggest that archival listing techniques may be more suitable for large ephemera collections. Along with practical difficulties, modern ephemera offers a minefield of indexing problems, many shared with alternative literature which Chris Atton has described.[72] Traditional subject-heading lists are often not suitable, as it is preferable to use terms developed by the groups producing the material and not to wait until those terms become respectable. This is part of a problem common to all aspects of local history, as many researchers believe that the contribution of groups, such as black people and women, have been hidden because finding aids do not highlight them. Views of history are not static and, while indexes will usually reflect their time, they should take this indexing problem into account. A large-scale cataloguing project for political ephemera collected since 1968 is taking place at the Linen Hall Library, Belfast. The whole collection is being recatalogued from scratch by electronic means, but finding neutral indexing terms has proved difficult: even the name Northern Ireland is not acceptable to Republicans.[73]

Microforms

Microforms are a heavily used area of stock, yet often with limited finding aids. A survey of microform management in American academic libraries in 1997 found that 77 per cent listed holdings on the library OPAC, but only 54 per cent had more than 90 per cent of microform materials catalogued and classified.[74] Microform sets cause a problem in the USA as many were produced by commercial publishers in the 1960s and 1970s and include a range of publications microfilmed together, but not catalogued separately. Several projects are cataloguing this material properly, including the Slavery Pamphlets Collections at the University of Southern Mississippi and newspapers in the American Periodical Series at Florida University.[75]

Serials

Serial publications produce another set of problems. They require a system which records information about each title, but can also produce data relating to holdings and acquisition and accommodate changes in title, frequency and content. Local studies libraries will often hold runs of antiquarian society transactions and this means that extensive finding aids for their contents are necessary. One project in this area is the Internet Library of 18th and 19th Century Journals, which will eventually allow full text searches.[76] Some modern journals only appear in electronic format. Local studies libraries will also hold copies of one-off articles from journals they do not take, usually catalogued as single items. Sometimes there are articles about a locality appearing in a periodical or serial devoted to that geographic area. This could be included along with newspaper cuttings to form a current awareness bulletin that can be a very valuable information resource.

Film and video

Some local studies libraries hold moving film and video. A state-of-the-art film archive opened in 2000 in Hong Kong. Its catalogue is searchable on the net and allows retrieval of text and still and moving images, using the HORIZON system, also used in New Zealand, Australia and China.[77] The National Library of Wales surveyed academic users in an attempt to improve use of its film and video collection, resulting in a request for the catalogue to be available on the Internet.[78]

THE INTERNET AND OTHER ICT APPLICATIONS

For many years local studies libraries have acted as the guardians of a locality's history and as such the task was often to collect and preserve material rather than exploit the resources.[79] While this still remains true, other factors have caused a

119

dramatic review of the management of resources in the local studies library. The advent, some might even say the explosion, of the Internet as an information medium, and the increased use of information and communication technology in everyday life, have been the catalyst for this change. The use of computers is changing the way information is created, managed and accessed, and digital information forms an ever-larger part of society's cultural and intellectual heritage.[80] The Internet is a new experience in finding information, not only in the field of local studies, since it offers direct access to information and images held in remote locations. This does not necessarily mean remote countries like Australia and the United States of America but also communities perhaps geographically just a few miles apart. Internationally, examples include digitized local history in Australia, accessed through the Australian Libraries Gateway (found at *http://www.nla.gov.au/libraries/*); similarly, the American Local History Network (*http://www.alhn.org/index.htm*), illustrates a good selection with links to sites. In the UK, Glasgow University (*http://www.gla.ac.uk*) through the Humanities Advanced Technology and Information Institute (HATII) page gives many links to digitized collections.

DIGITIZATION

Digitization is the process of capturing and storing information as digital files that can be accessed via a computer terminal. Local studies materials have tremendous potential for digitization and suitable materials include text, documents, images (photographic and video), plans and diagrams, objects and ephemera, sound bites and family trees.

Aims of digitizing

The main aim of digitization is the creation of a digital copy or surrogate of an original item that can be stored, searched, manipulated and retrieved at a location independent of the original source. These items can all be incorporated into seamless presentations of resource material that are of value to all levels of the community, ranging from school children to serious researchers. It is important to bear in mind the local studies *Guidelines* when considering digitization of local studies materials. The guidelines stress the cross-platform approach, in that two levels of digitization are required: high resolution masters for archiving and smaller compressed files for speed of loading on networks and used to deter copyright theft and unauthorized use.

Why digitize?

Digitization projects are usually undertaken to improve access to both open and closed collections and facilitate remote access to the collection from multiple users.[81] It can also offer the facility to sort and order material not usually available to the public, to protect the originals from wear and tear and to save staff time in the retrieval of objects and documents from the storage area.[82]

In *Virtually new*,[83] 100 projects are listed, but, as funding becomes increasingly available to digitize library collections, many more libraries will embark on projects. The advent of the Heritage Lottery Fund (*http://www.portico.bl.uk/ric/*) and other funding sources is providing the impetus for many more digitization projects.

Planning a digitization project

When planning a digitization project for local studies materials various steps should be borne in mind.[84] Firstly an assessment of the need for digitization should be considered. Digitization is not just copying, it is a transformation of materials. Items should be selected for one or both of the following reasons. First is conservation, in that the wear and tear on the originals is reduced. The second is to facilitate easier transmission across time and space, coupled with added value and increased usability. Digitization is not a substitute for preservation, however. It must be remembered that collections are a component of the intellectual capital of an institution. A detailed study of the collection must be undertaken in the first place to ascertain what material is suitable to be digitized and decisions made on how much detail needs to be extracted from the original in the final text. It is very difficult, as noted in the local studies *Guidelines*, to establish criteria to determine whether or not local material possesses 'national interest'. Virtually all material held in local studies collections will be subject to external interest at some time or other, whether by subject specialists seeking local material for comparative or illustrative purposes or by students of genealogy and family history.

Next, a strategic plan should be drawn up that involves users, collection curators, librarians, managers and educationalists. The digitization project should relate to the mission statement of the service and be managed by appropriate project management techniques using standards that are most applicable, that is covering the technical and computing issues as well as the legal issues concerning intellectual property rights and copyright.

Materials selected are usually source-oriented, by content and physical qualities of size, nature and condition. The risk factor must not be overlooked either: material should only be digitized if it is not put at risk. The accompanying data entry, the metadata, should be in accordance with current international standards, i.e. Dublin Core. This will ensure that adequate information can be recorded in a consistent manner, enabling data to be exchanged between projects. Sometimes one digitization project increases the use of other collections held in the local studies library and so this factor should not be dismissed.

Quality assurance checks are essential throughout a project lifespan to ensure that it conforms to the specifications decided at the planning stage of the project. The documents need to be examined for quality control before the process of capturing the image, formatting the file and creating the metadata is begun. Other factors that need careful consideration are the compression of the files, the resultant technical problems of communication protocols and integration with image browsers. It is not within the remit of this book to address these technical issues but there is currently a great deal being written about this topic (*http://www.columbia.edu/cu/libraries/digital/criteria*). One factor which needs consideration, and is often neglected, is the amount of time it takes to remove the item to be digitized from the shelf, digitize and process it, and then return it to the correct place on the shelf. This can use up a lot of staff time.

Finally, some provision for backing up, archiving and preserving the resultant data must be made, and for a mechanism to evaluate the finished project. Hertfordshire University produces good guidelines covering this area (*http://heds.herts.ac.uk/Guidance/JIDI_fs.pdf*).

Once all these steps have been considered, the next question is whether the project can be completed in-house or has to be out-sourced. There are many companies that undertake digitization projects, whether the complete management or the scanning of material only. Two companies with expertise in this area are iBase from Ilkley in Yorkshire and House of Images from Blackburn in Lancashire.[85] There is also the Higher Education Digitisation Service (HEDS) based at Hertfordshire University that will undertake the management of a digitization project.

Images

Images are often one of the first types of local studies materials to be digitized, partly for preservation purposes. This creates a responsibility to provide enough catalogue information to fully represent the original, including details about the medium, creator and circumstances of creation, as well as subject information. Stephen Ostrow, formerly of the Library of Congress, stresses that 'access records for digital surrogates are not ready-to-hand and involve far more than simple digital conversion of records'.[86]

Much work is being attempted on the problems of image indexing, which include the following:

- lack of title pages, which means the indexer has to interpret the image;
- images are often designed to evoke a subjective response;
- there are few indexing standards;
- images may often contain very large amounts of information on a wide range of subjects;

- they may contain an active element, for example illustrating movement.

Some indexers believe that words are inadequate for the task and have tried to develop systems using icons or shapes or colours within images.[87] The problems encountered by the General Motors Media Archive, working in what would appear to be a limited subject area, show the complexity of image indexing. The index was developed to allow detailed access to information about the vehicles, the physical and social background, the active elements of the image (for example, if a truck is moving or heavily laden), the circumstances of image creation (date, place, purpose), its style, its implications (for example, to show that a particular model appeals to women) and the aesthetic element (some images were designated 'wow shots').[88]

Local studies libraries hold a range of images, including topographical drawings, which they may wish to integrate with digitized photographs. At present even basic information is lacking about the holdings of these drawings collections, outside a library's own collection, although a guide was compiled in 1974.[89]

Maps

Maps share some of the problems of newspapers and photographs, in that they are increasingly being produced in electronic format, but some researchers need to consult them as 'objects' as well as sources of information.

The Ordnance Survey and US Geological Survey are both moving towards digital data.[90] Their digital maps present problems because they exist in a range of formats and file structures. Paper maps can be used for a variety of purposes, but digital map data may need different software for each purpose. Digitization of paper originals, as with historical maps, creates further problems, such as the need to compare maps of different sizes and scales, differences caused by pre- and post-Second World War mapping techniques, and the need for very high resolution scanning. However, the Durham Record project shows that these problems can be overcome.[91]

Retrieval systems for these data will have to be developed, as the current standards are for text-based material and they have obsolete elements, including the recording of distance scales, which are flexible in digital versions. Perkins has commented, 'sanity suggests the database not the results' should be catalogued as the content is so enormous. Alternatively, perhaps libraries should concentrate on tailor-making their cataloguing to the needs of their users.[92]

Sound recordings

Local studies libraries may hold a range of sound recordings, including oral history interviews, commercial recordings or even radio broadcasts. Technology is changing rapidly in all these fields and the production of new material in digital format is becoming more common. So far, most retrospective digitization projects seem to focus on accessing materials in formats which can no longer be played, or where sound quality needs improvement, and information retrieval appears a secondary consideration. For example, the National Sound Archive has digitized its collections of wax cylinders and acetate-based tapes.[93]

Slovak Radio is one of the few sound repositories intending to transfer all its holdings into CD format and produce an index.[94] The BBC Radio Archives intends to link its computerized catalogue with its recordings, and the catalogue of the Radio 4 *Analysis* programme, at Bournemouth University, is on the Internet.[95] A more ambitious project to improve access to sound recordings is the National Gallery of the Spoken Word in Michigan, which includes over 50,000 hours of recording on the Internet, and is searchable by keyword, topic, speaker and language.[96]

The National Film and Sound Archive in Australia closed down between 1991 and 1993 to develop an integrated system for all its holdings. MAVIS, the Merged Audio Visual Information System, was the result. It deals with acquisition, accessioning, circulation and cataloguing for sound and visual materials.[97]

Most textbooks for sound archivists and oral historians stress traditional methods of information retrieval, particularly transcripts for oral history interviews, but perhaps using electronic means. Ward stresses that, because tapes hold so much information, many archives develop elaborate retrieval methods which they cannot maintain; the ideal should not outweigh the practical.[98] The strength of oral history is its ability to give insights into older beliefs and attitudes and any indexing system should bring out this less easily retrieved information. As with all historical sources, indexers should have a good understanding of how documents are used.

OTHER NEW TECHNOLOGY DEVELOPMENTS

Developments in new technology are not merely confined to the Internet. In fact the Internet is not the ideal medium for some digital presentations, for example video and sound, as the file sizes are simply too large for more than just a few moments of viewing time. It takes time to download files from the Internet and this factor should be borne in mind when including such files. Many users will be accessing local history Internet sites from their home computers, so the cost of on-line phone time should always be a consideration. This could possibly alter in the near future with the developments that are taking place between the major telecommunication companies and the Internet Service Providers (ISP), for it is probable that in the future access to ISPs will be free. However, there is still the problem of download time, as many users do not have the patience to wait for pages to appear.

The other major 'new' technology medium that is suitable for local studies materials is that of the CD-ROM (compact disc read-only memory). These discs can store vast amounts of information and, provided the personal computer has sufficient random access memory (RAM), can run presentations very efficiently. The advent of hardware that can record onto re-writable compact discs from personal computers is bringing the technology for attempting digital presentations into all local studies libraries. Three examples of projects that are in CD-ROM format are

- the Durham Record, which includes historic photographs, county archaeological sites and monuments records for the County of Durham;[99]
- Hackney on Disk, a project which integrates maps and visual images;[100]
- Gateshead 1900, a compact disc interactive guide to Tyneside in the period 1896–1914.[101]

Just emerging on the technology front is the digital versatile disk (DVD), which is an advanced version of the CD-ROM that can play video with cinema quality sound and pictures, while holding more storage space. This looks like offering even more potential for exploiting local studies collections digitally.

DISSEMINATING COLLECTION INFORMATION ON THE INTERNET

In recent years the pivotal role of disseminating information about local studies collections, as well as general public library information, has fallen to EARL (Electronic Access to Resources in Libraries), the Consortium for Public Library Networking. EARL was established in 1995 to develop the role of public libraries in providing library and information services over the network.[102] Through collaboration, it aims to demonstrate and extend the ability of public libraries to deliver networked information and knowledge-based services (*http:// www.earl.org*).

Local studies feature predominantly in the make-up of the EARL site. This encompasses the Familia database, which lists local history collections that are available within public libraries in the UK. A browse through the Familia pages will reveal the expertise and inventiveness of local studies librarians throughout the country in presenting information in a totally new way. Many sites are outstanding in their information and design concept; for example:

- Devon Library and Information Service
  http://www.devon-cc.gov.uk/library/locstudy/
- Essex County Council Libraries
  http://www.essexcc.gov.uk/infoserv/ecc_lib/essex.htm

- Knowsley Metropolitan Borough Council, Library Service[103]
  http://www.knowsley.gov.uk
- Leeds Library and Information Service
  http://www.leeds.gov/library/library.html
- South Ayrshire Library and Information Service
  http://www.south-ayrshire.gov.uk

Another network of cultural resources and local studies materials on the Internet is to be found at the Scottish Cultural Resources Access Network (SCRAN) (*http://www.scran.ac.uk*). This project began in 1996 to create a website embracing 1·5 million digitized records of Scottish artefacts, buildings and sites. The National Museum of Scotland was one of the founding partners, so the scheme is largely museum-oriented, but a number of Scottish local studies libraries have contributed images from their collections. An important feature of SCRAN is the discipline it imposes on the provision of adequate descriptive text to support the digitized image. This reinforces the local studies *Guidelines'* emphasis on the quality of the accompanying metadata. In Northern Ireland there are many references to local history and further Internet links to be found from the web pages of the Public Record Office of Northern Ireland (*http://www.proni.gov.uk*). In Wales perhaps the most innovative site is that put together by Powys for their Digital History Project (*http://history.powys.org.uk*). This project links together early documents, old photographs and material from local people to show aspects of local history from six communities in mid-Wales.

The year 1999 saw an important new development on the Internet when the Church of Jesus Christ of the Latter Day Saints put 400,000 records on the web onto its Family Search page (*http://www.familysearch.org*). When this site first went live it was inundated by people trying to access the information, as it is an extremely valuable resource for people wanting to research family history.

PROBLEMS WITH NEW TECHNOLOGY

Digitization of local studies collections has some problem areas, one of which is copyright, since many items have been deposited in local studies libraries over a number of years and copyright implications were often not considered at the time of the original deposit. It is only now, when publishing them on the Internet or in another format, that the problem is coming to light. In order to ensure that copyright has not been infringed, the owner of the copyright of the material to be used, if known, should be contacted to obtain permission to publish. This is usually granted after payment of an appropriate fee and acknowledgment somewhere in the finished publication. There are ways of watermarking images, for example with the source's name, to enable the user to know where it has come

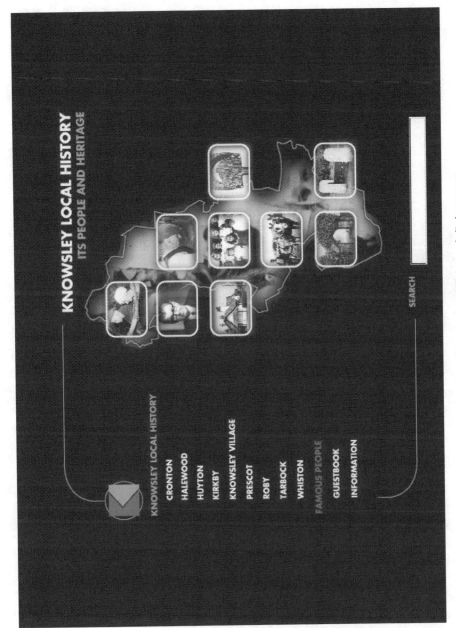

Figure 6.1 Knowsley Local History website home page

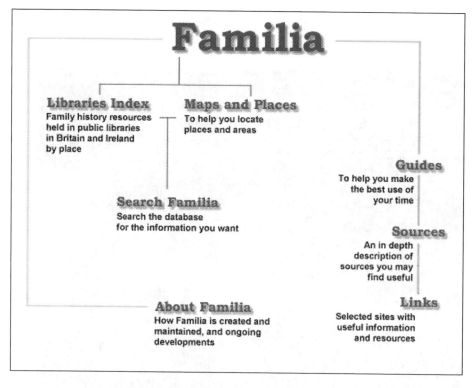

Figure 6.2 Familia home page of the EARL website

from. Images are usually published on the Internet at a low resolution (not usually above 75–100 dpi (dots per inch), and this ensures that they download faster while still presenting a readable image, although reproduction is of too poor a quality to be useful commercially. It is also possible to fingerprint images. This provides the source institution with data on subsequent use of the image. In the future however, with the advent of e-commerce (sales over the Internet), copyright will have to be considered much more fully.[104] It is, of course, always possible to remove an image if it is discovered that copyright regulations have been infringed.

The technology to protect copyright will continue to develop and mechanisms to protect the rights of content providers will improve. A recent development in this field has been in the technique of steganography, which is the art of hiding information in ways that prevents the detection of hidden messages. Steganography's role in security is to supplement cryptography, not replace it. If a hidden message is encrypted, it must also be decrypted, if discovered, which provides another layer of protection for the digitized item. Steganography goes well beyond simply embedding text in an image. It also pertains to other media, including voice and text. There can be no single mechanism, whether copyright

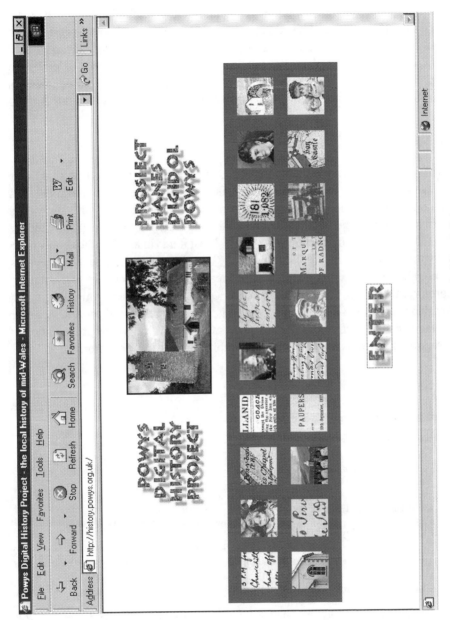

Figure 6.3 Powys Digital History Project website home page

statement, technical security or watermarks, to protect digital material, but standardization will be an essential feature for the effective implementation of future copyright protection technologies.[105]

Another problem area concerns the quality and standards that need to be adhered to when undertaking digitization of materials. A report issued by the Digital Library Federation and the Research Libraries Group (*http://www.rlg.org/ visguides/*) attempts to collate the shared knowledge and experience of leaders in this field to provide a comprehensive set of guidelines for accomplishing a digitization project. It is intended that these guidelines will be updated regularly.

CONCLUSION

Providing access to local studies materials is undergoing a transition that is far from complete. In the foreseeable future, as in the past, the role of library staff is paramount and, while specialist knowledge of the collection will always be important in the immediate future, the role of staff in creating electronic finding aids and assisting readers will be increased. Most items in local studies collections are by their very nature irreplaceable. They have been acquired over many years and hold the social record, not just of the local area but, collectively, of the nation. Therefore, their long-term preservation is crucial. At the same time, the digital copy also allows multi-user access to material, a bonus that could previously never be imagined. The technology of the future should allow the better preservation of the record of the past as well as enabling improved access to the information.

NOTES

The authors would like to thank George Maddock and Ian Maxted for their comments and advice.

1   Parry, D. (1998), *Virtually new. Creating the digital collection: a review of digitisation projects in local authority libraries and archives*, London: Library and Information Commission; Chapman, A., Kingsley, Nicholas and Dempsey, Lorcan (1999), *Full disclosure: releasing the value of library and archive collections*, London: UKOLN.
2   Parry, D. (1998), vi.
3   Chapman, A. et al (1999), 12.
4   Falk, H. (1999), 'View through the display window', *Electronic library* 17 (4), 263–7.
5   Chapman, A. et al (1999), 14.
6   Bryant, P. (1997), *Making the most of our libraries. The report of two studies on the retrospective conversion of library catalogues in the United Kingdom and the need for a national strategy*, London: Research and Innovation Centre, 16.
7   Chapman, A. et al (1999), 20.
8   Baker, N. (1994), 'Annals of scholarship: discards', *New Yorker* 4 April, 64–86; Crawford, W. (1999), 'The card catalog and other digital controversies', *American libraries* January, 52–8; Crawford, W. (1999), 'Bits is bits; pitfalls in digital reformatting', *American libraries* May, 47–9.
9   Massey-Burzio, V. (1999), 'The rush to technology: a view from the humanists', *Library trends* 47 (4), 620–39.

10   MacDonald, B. (1998), 'Stella Project: retrospective conversion at Trinity College, Dublin', *Catalogue and index* (127), 1–5.

11   Hieb, F. (1997), 'Issues in retrospective conversion for a small special collection: a case study', *North Carolina libraries* 55 (2), 86–9.

12   Parry, D. (1998), 80–81.

13   Bofta, J.M. (1995), 'I had a dream ... to computerise Malta's state libraries', *Focus* 26 (3), 146–52.

14   Nicholson, C. (1998), 'Locate GUI round the edges', *Local studies librarian* 17 (2), 2–5.

15   Bryant, P. (1997), 17.

16   Chapman, A. et al (1999), 32; Bryant, P. (1997), 3.

17   Maxted, I. (1997), 'What's new? What's cool? Surf Devon and see', *Local studies librarian* 16 (1), 10–11.

18   Gilbert, J. (1997), 'AACR2 headings for local churches and parishes in Great Britain', *Catalogue and index* (123), 1–5.

19   Library Association Rare Books Group (1999), *Guidelines for the cataloguing of rare books*, 2nd edn, London: Library Association.

20   *Bibliography of north-west England* (formerly *Lancashire Bibliography*) (1968–date), Manchester: NWRLS; *Bibliography of printed works on London history to 1939* (1994), London: Library Association; *Devon bibliography*, annually from 1989, a web-based catalogue (*http://www.devon-cc.gov.uk/library/locstudy/*); *East Anglian bibliography* (1960–date), Bury St Edmunds: East Anglian Libraries Consultative Committee; *Bibliography of Scotland* (1984–date), Edinburgh: National Library of Scotland; Dunsire, G. (1990), 'SCOTLOC – Automation for local studies', *Local studies librarian* 9 (2), 4–8.

21   *Local studies librarian* (1992), 11 (1), 26; Dyson, B. (1991), 'Humad, Hull University's online guide to archives and manuscripts', *Local studies librarian* 10 (2), 13–15.

22   Girard, A. (1993), 'Local and regional studies in French libraries', *Local studies librarian* 12 (2), 2–11.

23   Gancs, E. (1993), 'Local studies in Hungary. A case study', *Local studies librarian* 12 (2), 25–7.

24   Maxted, I. (1995), 'Hungary for more. Report of a study tour in July and August', *Local studies librarian* 14 (2), 14–18.

25   Melrose, E. (1995), 'Co-operation with Romania', *Local studies librarian* 14 (2), 22–3.

26   Juvik, L.H. (1999), 'Libraries as bridges to fellowship and belonging in the Barents region', *Library review* 48 (1 & 2), 31–5.

27   Biswas, S.C. (1994), 'Microfilming of Indian Publications Project: a narrative description of the past, present and future', *Focus* 25 (3), 125–33.

28   *New Library; the people's network* (1997), London: Library and Information Commission.

29   (*http://www.mnhs.org/library/*).

30   Chapman, A. et al (1999), 27.

31   Roberts, H. (2000), 'Our friends in the north', *Library Association record* 102 (2), 88–9; Chapman, A. et al (1999), 59.

32   Chapman, A. et al (1999), 24.

33   Beaney, S. with Bagley, S., Moore, R., Skelton, S. and Sykes, A. (1998), 'The CD Demonstrator Project – a case study in cataloguing using CD-ROMs', in Carpenter, L. et al (eds), *Towards the digital library*, London: British Library, 112–20.

34   Lewis, M.J. and Lloyd-Jones, R. (1996), *Using computers in history. A practical guide*, London: Routledge, 125.

35   *Black and Asian Studies Association newsletter* (1999), 25 September, 3–4; Chappell, C. and Wissenburg, A. (1998), 'The view from history', *New review of academic librarianship* 4, 175–7; Musgrave, S. (1997), 'Technological determinism or user demand? Current developments at the Data Archive', *New review of information networking* 3, 173–83; Condron, F. and Wise, A. 'The view from archaeology' (1998), *New review of academic librarianship* 4, 172–4.

36   Sherwood, L.E. (1998), 'Discovering buffalo story robes: a case for cross domain information strategies', *Computers and the humanities* 32, 57–64.

37   Harris, O. (1996), 'United we stand – Croydon's multi-disciplinary historical database', *ITs news* (33), 17–21; see also Batt, C., MacDonald S. and Scott, T. (1993), 'MUSLS – a multi-media, multi-discipline database: part 1, defining requirements, selecting the system and initial development', *Program*, 27 (1), 17–36; Scott, T. (1993), 'Sherlock – MUSLS' black box public user interface', *Aslib information* 21 (7/8), 286–8.

38   Sherwood, L.E. (1998), 60–61.

39   Baker, N. (1994), 82.

40   *Archives-On-line: The establishment of a United Kingdom archival network* (1998), London: National Council on Archives; Shepherd, E. and Smith, C. (2000), 'The application of ISAD (G) to the description of archival datasets', *Journal of the Society of Archivists* 21 (1), 55–86.

41   Chapman, A. et al (1999), 22.

42   An alternative to closed access is the use of glass fronted security shelving as in Zadar: see Sturges, P. (1999), 'Zadar City Library, Croatia', *Focus* 30 (1), 33–4.

43   Cook, M. (1993), *Information management and archival data*, London: Library Association Publishing, 124.

44   Langridge, D.W. (1976), *Classification and indexing in the humanities*, London: Butterworth, 119.

45   Duckett, B. (1997), 'If you can't access it, does it exist?', *Library Association record* 99 (4), 207.

46   Chandler, J. (1987), 'Indexing', in Dewe, M. (ed.), *A manual of local studies librarianship*, Aldershot: Gower, 232.

47   *National Monuments Records Thesauri* (at *http://www.rchme.gov.uk/thesaurus/newuser.htm*).

48   Garrod, P. (2000), 'Use of the UNESCO Thesaurus for archival subject indexing at UK NDAD', *Journal of the Society of Archivists* 21 (1), 37–54; Willpower Information, Information Management Consultants, *Thesaurus principles and practice* (*http://www.willpower.demon.co.uk/thesprin.htm*).

49   Flint, J. and Franklin, A. (comps) (1981), *Local studies collections: guidelines and subject headings for organizing and indexing resources* (Occasional paper no. 5), Sydney: Library Association of Australia, NSW Branch.

50   Winterbotham, D. (1983), 'Access to local studies materials', *Local studies librarian* 2 (2), 23.

51   Hume, Eileen Mitchell (1999), 'Results of local studies cataloguing questionnaire' (available from *http://www.oakedge.demon.co.uk*). It can also be found in the archives of lis-pub-libs, a mailbase discussion list (at *http://www.mailbase.ac.uk*) using the search term local studies cataloguing.

52   LSL Index (1998), *Local studies librarian* 17 (1), 7.

53   *Catalogue of the newspaper library Colindale* (1968), London: British Library (8 vols) is the most comprehensive list of newspapers; Copeman, H., Eagle, S. and Harrison, M. (1998), 'NEWSPLAN – first on the net; LASER leads – how to follow', in *NEWSPLAN, millennia and grids: The digital challenges*, London: NEWSPLAN, 73–84.

54   David, R.C. (1997), 'Reading through the American Periodical Series in search of newspapers: a Florida retrospective conversion', *Serials review* 23 (3), 11–20; Newton, E. (1998), 'Newseum – and the future of the past', in *NEWSPLAN, millennia and grids*, 51–4.

55   Kuhn, T.J. (1999), 'Classifying newspapers using Dewey Decimal Classification', *Library resources and technical services* 43 (2), 106–13.

56   *Local studies librarian* (1991), 10 (1), 10.

57   Chapman, P. (1998), 'Developing this is the North East', *Aslib proceedings* 50 (9), 264–6; Williams, P. and Nicholas, D. (1998), 'The Internet, a regional newspaper and the provision of "value added" information', *Aslib proceedings* 50 (9), 255–63.

58   Brand, S. (1999), 'Escaping the digital dark age', *Library journal* 124 (2), 46–8.

59   Neilson, K. and Willett, P. (1999), 'United Kingdom regional newspapers on the World Wide Web', *Aslib proceedings* 51 (3), 78–90.

60   Stoker, D. (1999), 'Should newspaper preservation be a lottery?', *Journal of librarianship and information science* 31 (3), 131–4.

61   Alexander, M. (1998), 'Digitising the Burney Collection', in *NEWSPLAN, millennia and grids*, 59–62; Podmore, H. (1998), 'The digitisation of microfilm', in Carpenter, L., Shaw, S. and

Prescott, A. (eds), *Towards the digital library: The British Library initiatives for access programme*, London: British Library, 68–72.

62   Hammond, H. (1998), 'Norfolk's potential newspaper database; a cautionary tale', in *NEWSPLAN, millennia and grids*, 55–8.

63   Howell, A. (1998), 'Preservation digitising of newspapers', *International preservation news* (16), 24–8.

64   Kilcullen, M. and Spohn, M. (1996), 'Indexing a local paper using dBase IV', *The Indexer* 20 (1), 16–17, 22; Kilcullen, M. (1997), 'Publishing a newspaper index on the World Wide Web using Microsoft Access 97', *The Indexer* 20 (4), 195–6; Morris, C.D. and Morris, S.R. (1995), *How to index your local newspaper using WordPerfect or Microsoft Word for Windows*, Englewood, Colorado: Libraries Unlimited.

65   This is also recommended by *Guidelines for indexing newspapers* (1997), Northern Ireland: Library and Information Services Council (Northern Ireland) Local History Panel.

66   Day, K. (1996), 'The Denver post', *Colorado libraries* 22 (3), 49–50.

67   Sule, N.N. (1996), 'Indexing of newspapers in Nigeria, The Guardian experience', *International information communication education* 15 (2), 185–94.

68   Parry, D. (1998), 67.

69   Cunnew, R. (1995), 'The analytic OPAC incorporating a journal index in an on-line catalogue using CAIRS and AACR2', *Catalogue and index* (118), 1–5.

70   For example, South West Lancashire Family History Society, St. Helens Branch, *Index to 1851 Census Returns for St. Helens, Lancashire*.

71   Drew, P. and Dewe, M. (1992), 'Welsh Ephemera Project: a progress report', *Local studies librarian* 11 (2), 16–18.

72   Atton, C. (1996), *Alternative literature: a practical guide for librarians*, Aldershot: Gower.

73   Gray, J. (1996), 'Documenting a community in conflict: The Northern Ireland political collection at the Linen Hall Library, Belfast', *Law librarian* 27 (4), 216–22.

74   Manzo, B. (1997), 'Microform management in academic libraries', *Microform and imaging review* 26 (2), 73–80.

75   Myers, F. (1998), 'Cataloging the Slavery Pamphlets Collection: An OCLC major microforms project', *Microform and imaging review* 27 (2), 43–5; David, R.C. (1997), 'Reading through the American Periodical Series in search of newspapers: a Florida retrospective conversion', *Serials review* 23 (3), 11–20.

76   *http://www.bodley.ox.ac.uk/ilej/start.htm*

77   Shiu, M. (1999), 'The Hong Kong Film Archive Library: towards information technology', *Multimedia, information and technology* 25 (1), 72–4.

78   Evans, G. and Del-Pizzo, J. (1999), 'Look, hear upon this picture: a survey of academic users of the Sound and Moving Image Collection of the National Library of Wales', *Journal of librarianship and information science* 31 (3), 152–67.

79   Batt, C. (1995), 'The Cutting Edge 26, Local History, Global Vision', *Public library journal* 10 (4), 91–3.

80   Beagrie, N. and Greenstein, D. (1998), 'Report on Creating and Preserving Digital Resources', *Managing information* 5 (5), 18; also full report (at *http://ahds.ac.uk/manage/framework.htm*).

81   Wilson, S. (1998), 'Knowsley local history, using the Internet to enhance access', *Journal of the Society of Archivists* 19 (2), 199–209.

82   Hampson, A. (1998), 'Managing a Digitisation Project', *Managing information* 5 (10), 25–32.

83   Parry, D. (1998) (available from *http://www.ukoln.ac.uk/services/lic/digitisation*).

84   Tanner, S. and Lomax-Smith, J. (1999), 'Digitisation: how much does it really cost?', paper for the Digital Resources for the Humanities 1999 Conference, held at Kings College, London: 12–15 September 1999 (full version at *http://heds.herts.ac.uk*).

85   iBase (*http://www.ibase.com*), House of Images (*http://www.homages.co.uk*); also HEDS (*http://heds.herts.ac.uk*).

86   Ostrow, S. (1998), *Digitizing historical pictorial collections for the Internet*, Washington, DC: Council on Library and Information Resources, 25.

87   Baxter, D. and Anderson, D. (1995), 'Image indexing and retrieval: some problems and proposed solutions', *New library world* 96 (1123), 4–13; Jacobs, C. (1999), 'If a picture is worth a thousand words, then...', *The indexer* 21 (3), 119–21.

88   Schroeder, K.A. (1998), 'Indexing, training and workflow on large digitisation projects', *The indexer* 21 (2), 67–9; Schroeder, K.A. (1998), 'Layered indexing of images', *The indexer* 21 (1), 11–14.

89   Nurse, B., 'Views of the past. Locating topographical drawings', *Local studies librarian* 16 (2), 10–12; Barley, M.W. (1974), *Guide to topographical collections*, London: Council for British Archaeology.

90   McGlamery, P. (1995), 'Maps and spatial information: changes in the map library', *LIBER quarterly* 5 (3), 229–34; Perkins, C.R. (1995), 'Leave it to the labs? Options for the future of map and spatial data collections', *LIBER quarterly* 5 (3), 312–29.

91   Parry, D. (1998), 29–30.

92   Perkins, C.R. (1995), 319.

93   Copeland, P. (1998), 'Project digitise', in Carpenter, L. et al, 121–9.

94   Horvat, F. (1997), 'The archives of Slovak Radio and digital technique', *IASA journal*, 9, May, 32–3.

95   *Managing information* (1998), 24 (1), 256; Holland, M. (1999), 'BBC Radio 4 Analysis Project', *Electronic library* 17 (1), 213–15.

96   *Information research news* (1999), 34 (3), 7.

97   Milano, M. (1997), 'National Film and Sound Archive (Australia)', *IASA journal* 9 May, 49–57.

98   Ward, A. (1990), *A manual of sound archive administration*, Aldershot: Gower; Ritchie, D.A. (1995), *Doing Oral History*, New York: Twayne; Bell, H.K. (1992), 'Indexing biographies and other stories of human lives', Society of Indexers occasional papers on indexing no 1, London: Society of Indexers.

99   Watson, I. (1996), 'The Durham Record', *Local studies librarian* 15 (2), 2–6.

100 Laing, K. and Mander, D. (1996), 'Where history and technology meet', *Library Association record*, 98 (8), 420–21.

101 Carnaffin, E. (1997), 'Gateshead 1900: a CDI-guide', *Local studies librarian* 16, 10–13.

102 Woodhouse, S. (1998), 'From collections to connections', *Library Association record*, 100 (5), 34–6.

103 Marchant, P. and Hume, E. (1998), 'Visiting Knowsley's past', *Library Association record* 100 (9), 468–70; also (1998), 'Best on the Web from public libraries', *Library Association record technology* 3 (1), 9.

104 'Digitisation remains a sticking point' (1998), *Library Association record* 100 (5), 227.

105 Tanner, S. (2000), 'Copyright: please look but don't touch!', paper presented at Internet Librarian International 2000, London, 21 March.

7   Marketing

Jill Barber

Marketing, with its traditional links to business, has been viewed with suspicion by many who view their role as providing a public service. Librarians have been more used to talking about the promotion or exploitation of the collection.[1] Essentially this has meant increasing public awareness, with the hope that this will lead to increased use. It is now recognized that the financial and other constraints under which the local studies library has to operate calls for a more focused approach, rather than trying to serve all potential demands equally. Initiatives such as the Annual Library Plan, Lifelong Learning and Best Value require libraries to demonstrate how they compare with others, how they operate in a market place which includes competition from other information providers,[2] and above all that they are economic, efficient and effective. Many are now asked to produce a Marketing Plan and, far from being a distraction from the perceived aim of providing a service, the positive benefits to be gained by implementing a marketing strategy are considerable.[3] Marketing is about being customer-centred (what customers actually want) rather than product-based (what the library provides without reference to customers or potential customers). Promotion may be concerned with the contents of the local studies collection and its importance, but unless attention is given, not only to what is being promoted, but to whom and why, it will not necessarily mean that staff time and energy is being expended in the most effective way to benefit both the user and the library.

DEVELOPING A MARKETING STRATEGY: THE PLANNING PROCESS

The mission statement, aims and objectives of the wider library service, and the department, will provide a starting point for developing a marketing plan. If the local studies collection has its own aims and objectives, these may need readjustment in the light of the planning process. This process will focus initially on what, to whom and why. The answers to these questions will lead on to how and when. Marketing tools and techniques can be used to carry out an assessment of marketing opportunities to decide how best to meet the needs of the market. A SWOT analysis can enable the local studies library to examine its present position, and future possibilities, by identifying its strengths, weaknesses, opportunities and threats. The planning process also involves a consideration of the marketing mix, or the four 'Ps'.

THE FOUR 'Ps'

In marketing, the four 'Ps' are product, price, place and promotion, although the mix will vary according to the particular product or service. Questions need to be asked about the nature of the service or *product* being offered, and whether it is aimed at meeting an identified demand. In considering what is to be marketed, it is important to recognize that the collection itself is only part of the 'product'. A SWOT analysis might identify the commercial potential of the illustrations collection as a strength, or an opportunity, but it will also highlight the specialist knowledge and expertise of the staff as a unique asset which local studies has to offer. An analysis of the life cycle of services or products also needs to be considered. Three stages, for example, can be identified for publications: stage one is 'rising stars' (high costs but worth promoting), stage two is 'cash cows' (income equals pure profit) and finally they become 'dead dogs' (no demand, not worth promoting). Similarly, services which were once profitable, or met a perceived need, should not continue indefinitely without question, and before embarking on any new product or service there needs to be adequate justification.

Price is becoming more of an issue for local studies libraries, facing new income generation targets, and may be included in the aims of the marketing plan. Any charges imposed must be acceptable to the target audience. Access to the local studies collection is still usually free of charge, but decisions must be made as to whether additional services such as photocopying, reproduction fees or research are intended to make a profit or cover costs. The marketing plan must take into account what resources are available, but it can also be used to justify expenditure.

Place involves making services or products accessible in the place where they can be used by actual or potential customers. This might be through local service points, including mobile libraries serving rural communities, and also through local schools and community groups. Although original, rare and unique items need proper storage, local studies provision and services should not be centred entirely on central libraries.[4]

Promotion is the element of the marketing mix that will concern libraries the most. This is about how we make the service or product accessible to potential users.

IDENTIFYING THE MARKET

Techniques of market analysis and research can be used to identify the market. Market analysis is concerned with identifying groups of people or organizations that can be the targets of services or products. Market research involves determining what their specific requirements might be. Customer surveys and visitors' books may be some of the tools used to collect evidence about existing users.[5] Family historians are often the largest group, accounting for two-thirds of the users at the Westcountry Studies Library.[6] Others include local historians, academics, and commercial and business users. Education includes teachers, students from primary schools to higher education and adult learners. Some may be taking Open University courses, or part of local groups such as the University of the Third Age (U3A). The media, including television and radio, can be demanding users, with local newspapers making good use of the illustration collection. Tourism officers may seek material to publicize the heritage or environmental features of localities. Interior designers use the collection when decorating old people's homes, or even supermarkets. When public houses are given a make-over, breweries often like to include a history of the pub and old views of the area. Economic development officers and market researchers may call on local information files and statistics. Planners and amenity groups often want maps, plans and historical information to help with new developments and conservation areas. Local government, including councillors, departments and employees, may need to refer to reports or minutes. Local societies, organizations and community groups, such as Age Concern, may also use the collection.

This pattern of use reflects a much wider spectrum than ever before, and deserves greater recognition. Local studies libraries can all too easily be thought to serve a very narrow interest group, whereas the reality is very different, being involved today with the varied needs of lively and developing communities. It has been pointed out that: 'The more that this change of emphasis is appreciated, the greater the likely prestige and status of the local studies librarian in the community.'[7]

It is useful to analyse the geographical profile of users as well as their reason for using the collection. One difficulty encountered by local studies is that, unlike the case of other libraries, the majority of users may not live in the county or borough which is providing the service.[8] Initiatives to focus on local residents may be particularly well received by the local authority, as may schemes for charging outside users for certain services. Local studies librarians know that they are providing reciprocal services as part of a national network of provision, but councillors may need to be made aware of this. If a large percentage of enquiries are shown to come from overseas users, or the housebound, requiring remote access, this may provide useful evidence to support a bid for increased funding for a website, or setting up credit card purchase of publications via the Internet. Age, gender and ethnic background are also significant. It may not be surprising to find that the majority of local studies users are over 50, but if the number of users in the 16–25 age range is low this could indicate that local schools and colleges are not fully aware of the benefits of using the collection, and staff time might usefully be deployed in concentrating on that particular market. Ethnic minority groups may be suspicious of depositing their records unless a local contact has been established. Community profiles produced by the local planning department may be useful in highlighting where there may be significant communities who could be invited to take part in an appropriate activity, such as an oral history programme. It is essential to analyse potential, as well as actual, markets. Some work has been done on creating non-user surveys. These could be distributed to local residents via libraries, or free newspapers. Community profiles can be used to discover which local areas have the greatest residential density. If these are poorly represented among current users, this might be evidence for the need to hold a promotional event in that community.

Having analysed the identity of actual and potential users, it is important to gain a better understanding of their requirements. Questionnaires and interviews need to discover, not only expressed needs, but those which remain unexpressed because people are unaware that the local studies collection might fulfil them. As with all reference enquiries, a user's initial question might bear little relation to the actual nature of their query. One of the challenges for local studies is to provide answers to questions that people do not yet know they want to ask. Through a greater understanding of the background, skills and knowledge of potential customers, the service can ensure that fewer users go away frustrated because they cannot find what they are looking for.

SETTING OBJECTIVES

To develop an action plan which will use the marketing opportunities that have been identified to meet the needs of potential customers through selective services and products, it is important to consider the benefits that can be achieved for both users and the collection. These will provide the vision for setting the objectives of the marketing plan. Revisiting the initial mission statement of the department at this stage will ensure that local studies objectives are helping to meet wider service aims. It may also be desirable to prioritize objectives (as high, medium or low), as there will inevitably be more ideas generated than there are the resources, in terms of staff time and money, to put into practice. These ideas can be incorporated into the marketing plan by including five- or ten-year projections, as well as an annual plan. A key objective may be promoting the local studies library as a source of information, highlighting its value as a major research collection. One benefit may be the opportunity to acquire new material for the collection. Don Martin has pointed out that the promotion of the local studies collection and its development are part of the same process, because the main source of new acquisitions must be the people themselves.[9] Reaching new markets, in terms both of increasing the numbers of those using the collection, and of increasing income generation through the sale of publications or other projects, may be another objective. Raising the profile of the local studies collection internally, locally, nationally and even globally could result in increased funding as well as widening access to the collection.

DEVELOPING AN ACTION PLAN

The next challenge is to 'walk the talk', translating the information that has been gleaned about markets, products and benefits into action. The services offered can now be tailored to the needs of potential customers, drawing on strengths such as specialist staff skills, and exploiting gaps in alternative provision by 'competitors'. In some cases the local studies library will be able to develop opportunities to work in partnership with other providers, such as archives, museums, WEA (Workers' Educational Association) or family history societies. The marketing plan should include some or all of the following areas.

PUBLIC RELATIONS, PUBLICITY AND NETWORKING

The most important place to begin is at home. Local studies staff are often so absorbed in their work that they assume, usually wrongly, that their colleagues know what they are doing. Formal, as well as informal, means of communication are needed to ensure that all staff are kept up-to-date and well-informed. Regular staff meetings, internally circulated memos and newsletters and a white board for daily updates are some of the ways this might be achieved. The benefits will be seen, not only in increased morale and motivation, but in a well-informed staff who are better equipped to pass their knowledge on to customers. It is equally important to disseminate information about local studies throughout the library service, as local libraries are often the first point of contact for potential customers. Surveys at Westminster show that the majority of those attending adult education courses for the first time hear about them at their local library. Many libraries run familiarization programmes which give all new staff the opportunity to visit local studies. If staff are encouraged to see for themselves what local studies has to offer they are better able to refer relevant enquiries.

Publicity within the council, including other departments such as planning, social services and housing, can lead to better networking, and raise the profile of local studies which may still be seen as a back-room, 'Cinderella' service. This image can be transformed by showing how the collection can be used to enhance the work of the rest of the council in new ways. At Westminster, social services staff not only came away from a visit to the centre with a new sense of their own role in its historical context, but were fascinated by images of workhouses and child labour, and subsequently used them in an exhibition. Good public relations is often a matter of demonstrating the reciprocal benefits that are to be gained. A press office that can rely on local studies to supply it with photographs at short notice will be more likely to help with publicising events.

Addressing local councillors should be a high priority as they set budgets and agree policy which affect the quality and level of the service that local studies can provide. Their contacts with local communities can help promote the collection if they are aware it exists. Newsletters, annual reports and copies of publications can be circulated, at least to those on the relevant committee, or for particular areas. Invitations to book launches and events keep councillors informed, even if they do not attend. Whenever possible, councillors should be encouraged to come and see for themselves. Personal guided tours can create an enthusiastic response and demonstrate the potential of the collection to act as an ambassador for the local authority in a global as well as national context. The mayor of Westminster, for example, now takes local studies publications with him on overseas visits, and uses them as gifts for visiting dignitaries.

Internal publicity and networking should also be practised within the profession. Contributing to professional journals, such as *Local studies librarian*, or regional newsletters such as London's *Metlines*; involvement in regional groups and collaborative ventures between libraries, museums and record offices are all ways of publicizing the work that is being done, so that other professionals can refer potential users.[10] Staff from other institutions, such as university libraries or specialist repositories, can also be invited to visit the local studies collection, so they can be better informed about the materials it contains.[11]

External publicity, on a national as well as local scale, can be achieved through good quality printed material. Posters in libraries and community centres, and brochures or leaflets, sent through the post or left in key venues, can help to inform people of the existence of local studies provision.[12] Many local studies libraries now produce their own newsletter, which can be circulated internally, and used more widely to promote new acquisitions, events and local information.[13] The former librarian of the Cambridge collection, Mike Petty, received an award for public relations achievement in recognition of his work. This included weekly articles in the local newspaper and weekly broadcasts on Radio Cambridgeshire.[14] Local press and radio can be particularly successful for engaging those who do not go into libraries.[15] For national coverage aimed at particular user groups, regular information about events and publications can be sent to the news section of the

Local historian, and other local and family history magazines. Staff knowledge and expertise can be exploited to write academic articles, highlighting sources in the collection and increasing their use. If time is short, local studies librarians are well placed to write 'snappy relevant pieces for hard-pressed editors'. It can be time well spent to 'invest a few minutes wisely to reach not only your regular audience but many new customers'. It might also 'enhance your image and your status with many people you had no intention of targeting'.[16]

Publicity, public relations and networking are time-consuming but they can be a powerful political tool.[17] On a national level, efforts must be made to ensure that local studies receives a higher profile in government reports, such as the Public Library Review. There is a lot to shout about: it is the only national network for non-archival information generally available, it is (in most cases) the only institution that has been collecting local information over a long period of time; the collections form significant research libraries; and use of them is growing.[18] On a local level, librarians need to take every opportunity to 'laud your efforts' often while seeking solely to inform,[19] for by taking time to establish good public relations it can raise awareness of the department's work, highlight professional expertise and provide justification and support for future initiatives.

OUTREACH

Encouraging and developing links with community groups of all kinds is emphasized by the local studies *Guidelines* as important both for the exploitation of the collection and for the acquisition of material which will help to preserve a permanent record of the locality.[20] Links with local groups can include ethnic minorities, local and family history societies and voluntary and statutory agencies.[21] Many local societies and organizations, from the Red Cross to Young Farmers' Clubs, have regular meetings to which they are keen to invite speakers, and this may reach new audiences and create useful links with local residents.[22] Taking resources out into the community can also be a good way of reaching those who find it difficult to visit, such as the elderly.[23] Reminiscence groups, in which local studies material acts as a stimulus for discussion with benefits for the participants, can encourage the deposit of new material for the collection, such as photographs and ephemera.[24] They may also generate oral history projects, or lead to a publication based on local memories. A project on Firbeck Colliery and village life in Langold, Nottinghamshire, helped raise the community's awareness of its own history. Once people are aware of their own history, and how they can help to make it and interpret it, they not only use local collections, but add to them and enhance them with their own contributions.[25]

There are many other ways in which local studies can reach out into the local community, including displays and exhibitions,[26] competitions, open days, and local and family history fairs.[27] West Lothian libraries even organized mystery bus tours.[28] In the former Strathkelvin district, outside Glasgow, a specific community is selected each year. Following a public meeting, key people are appointed as 'collecting agents', culminating in an exhibition which is an important local event.[29] Participation in national promotions, such as Adult Learners' Week, and involvement with media partnerships such as BBC History 2000, can gain wider publicity. In 1993, Darlington contributed to the European Year of Older People through an exhibition in collaboration with other agencies such as the Women's Royal Voluntary Service (WRVS), social services and local schools and businesses. Volunteers demonstrated domestic crafts, and rooms were built representing different periods. The exhibition ran for a month and attracted 7,982 visitors. It was a considerable drain on staff resources, but positive results included a surge in orders for copies of photographs, and a widened network of contacts from other agencies.[30]

Both Scotland and Northern Ireland hold Local History Weeks to provide libraries with an opportunity to exploit the resources available for local history through exhibitions, lectures and other activities. In Northern Ireland, it is organized by the Local History Panel of the Library and Information Services Council, which brings together museums, libraries, the Public Record Office and the Federation for Ulster Local Studies. In Scotland events are coordinated by the Scottish branch of the Library Association Local Studies Group (LOCSCOT), and each year a special theme is adopted: in 1999 it was Health and Welfare.

The growing trend for convergence between libraries, archives and museums can provide greater opportunities for promotion of the collection.[31] In West Sussex a Special Events Group, with representatives from a number of council departments, including the tourism and press officers, has successfully organized events centred on famous people. Activities have included pastime postcards, guided walks, talks, displays, information leaflets, plaque unveiling, literary competitions, adult education courses, a schools' poetry competition, and booklists. In 1992, to mark the bicentenary of the birth of the poet Shelley, 20 events were organized, including nine by the library service. The publicity generated 88 articles in the local press, as well as radio and television coverage. Wider networking can generate more ideas than can be put into practice, and meetings can be time-consuming, but coordination of effort saves time and money, can produce better quality publicity, and receives better media coverage.[32] In Westminster a similar group, including the youth service, education department, arts, libraries, archives and community partnerships has been formed to organize events linked to Black History Month. Such a coordinated approach seems to be a particularly effective way of marketing a local studies service, educating existing users about what is on offer, reaching people who have never heard about the collection, and developing closer links with other departments.

Enthusiastic users of the local studies collection are often its best ambassadors. Many libraries are now setting up Friends organizations. In 1997, a successful series of adult education classes at Westminster resulted in a close-knit group who became the first 'Friends'. They meet for an annual social, with a local history quiz and talks on aspects of the collection, receive copies of the quarterly newsletter and annual journal, are invited to special events, and receive discounts on courses and publications. Some act as volunteers on open days and at family history fairs, and several are actively engaged in producing name indexes to increase access to sources. Others have helped repackage illustrations and theatre programmes, and remount the slide collection. Their willingness to express support at every level has been invaluable and, above all, they spread the word about the collection to others.[33]

EDUCATION

Many local studies libraries now run an education service aimed at schools in their area, offering class visits, resource packs, exhibitions and INSET training for teachers.[34] The appointment of a member of the local studies staff to liaise with schools can help to make this work more possible and productive. They can also work closely with the Schools Library Service and, where appropriate, with local record offices and museums.[35] Some schools may want help to develop a local studies collection within their school library or learning resource centre.[36] The introduction of the National Curriculum for England and Wales in 1990 provided new opportunities for liaison with schools. Primary teachers, who may have no historical training, have often felt ill-equipped to undertake local history, and have needed the guidance of local studies librarians to direct them to appropriate sources, such as maps, photographs, directories and census returns. Since September 2000, secondary schools are required to study local history 'where appropriate' within British history from 1066 to 1900.[37]

If the potential of these changes is to be realized, local studies librarians must be proactive, showing teachers how local sources can bring national history to life. At GCSE and A level, individual projects are often based on local studies, particularly for geography, business studies and, increasingly, tourism. Liaison with the teacher, followed by a class visit to the collection, with an introduction to appropriate sources, can help to maximize use of the collection and minimize frustrations for students and staff. It is important for staff to keep up-to-date with educational developments and changes to the curriculum, to ensure that the service offered meets requirements. Recent initiatives, such as literacy and numeracy strategies, have provided opportunities for the local studies collection to respond to the needs of teachers and students in new ways. Diaries and letters can be used for literacy work, introducing pupils to different genres, and encouraging their own writing. Census returns provide an ideal base for ICT-related work. Following the MacPherson report, many schools are now including sources for black history, which are being rediscovered in the local studies collection. Citizenship, introduced into the secondary curriculum from September 2002, will provide an opportunity to look at the heritage of the local area, issues such as crime and punishment, the development of local government, and key local figures who have played a role in the emergence of democracy and human rights.

Services for schools may be only part of the education programme of the local studies library, which will also make a target of colleges of further and higher education. One of the most exciting aspects of initiatives such as lifelong learning is tapping into new groups of users, including those who did not enjoy studying at school, but for whom engaging with original sources such as maps, photographs, posters and theatre programmes can bring excitement and discovery, as history comes alive for the first time.[38] Adult education provides the opportunity to involve new groups, particularly local residents, through talks, courses and day schools, and can become the gateway to further study. Family history courses are particularly successful in the numbers they attract, as they appeal to a group that is already aware of the potential of the local studies collection. Such courses increase use of the collection, and reduce demands on staff time by making family historians more aware of the nature of sources, and how to use and interpret them. Course members can even give advice to new family historians, through special help desks or advice sessions. To ensure that an education service is not merely reacting to the demands of those who are already aware of its existence, but reaching all those who might benefit from what it has to offer, many local studies libraries are now producing an education policy. Not only is this an important tool for obtaining funds, but it may help to ensure a proactive approach.

PUBLICATIONS

Many local studies libraries, including Camden, Newcastle[39] and Birmingham now have flourishing publication programmes. The Alan Ball Local History Awards were founded in 1984 to encourage high-quality local history publishing by local authorities.[40] Although publications should aim to cover their cost, they are not primarily a profit-making venture.[41] The main criteria for local studies publications should be that they bring into print worthwhile material which would not otherwise be available.[42] Publications may include guides to the collection,[43] or guides to sources aimed at particular interest groups, such as *How to trace the history of your family, How to trace the history of your house* or *How to research black history.*[44] Facsimiles require relatively little staff time to produce, and often sell

144

well. As well as out-of-print texts, postcards are a good means of making illustrations from the collection more widely available. Maps and posters are also popular. Some libraries have produced mugs, pencils and even ties or underwear, but these are harder to justify. Calendars should normally be avoided. Libraries which have embarked on such publications, such as Camden, have found it not economically viable given the limited window of opportunity for sales. Local studies publications may need a five- to ten-year period to recover production costs.

Local histories will be an important part of a publications programme, particularly for areas where little or no published material already exists. As well as increasing access to the collection, one of Newcastle's aims is to encourage local people to look at their environment with an informed eye.[45] Town trails are an excellent way of achieving this. Partnerships with local history societies may help to share the cost, and sponsorship from local businesses is another possibility. Libraries frequently work with commercial publishers like Sutton Publishing to produce books of old photographs. Educational publications such as resource packs on topics related to the National Curriculum are welcomed by schools;[46] Hertfordshire has produced packs on child labour and cholera. Other popular subjects are Victorian schools, Tudor farmers or World War II.[47] Oral history projects can also lead to publications based on the memories of local residents.[48] Tameside used volunteers to carry out interviews and transcriptions and then produced a book in which each chapter was researched and written by a volunteer, although it still meant a lot of work for library staff.[49] The individual researcher can produce valuable original work which the local studies library can enable to reach a wider audience. In 1999, the *Westminster History Review* received the Alan Ball Local History Award, recognizing its achievement as a significant local history journal. Although the primary aim of this venture was to increase access to information about the local area, it has also helped to raise the profile of local studies, particularly among local councillors. As they are responsible for agreeing funding for the publications programme, the benefits are longstanding.

Publications will not always be in printed format. Microfiche is now a very cheap way of publishing a limited number of copies for sale. This has been used by family history societies for producing indexes to local sources, and is increasingly being taken up by local studies libraries to create greater access to the collection. There is great demand for indexes in this format from users who need remote access, either because they are housebound or because they live at a distance. Income can also be generated through requests for photocopies of the original records. Some libraries have produced videos, such as Newcastle's *Shops and shopping*,[50] and others, including the Royal Bank of Scotland, have produced their own CD-ROMs. Gateshead produced a fascinating interactive resource based on the stories of three families and individual members within them (largely fictitious to show particular local places and occupations), using a number of routes, which provides an excellent model. It was produced in response to a need for illustrative material outside the library, for use in homes for the elderly, schools and local groups. The limitations are that it relies on users having access to a particular piece of equipment.[51]

The success of a publications programme will largely depend on marketing. The product may be suitable (there is a potential market) and the price right (it is worth noting that customers expect library publications to be less expensive than those by commercial publishers) but attention needs to be paid to place – retail outlets – and promotion. Libraries may provide useful sales points, and the local studies library might have its own 'local history shop'. At Newcastle, the tourist information service is based in the city library which has been a factor in its success. However, it has been estimated that 70 per cent of sales can be achieved outside the public sector, so it can be important to identify external outlets.[52] In some areas there may be opportunities for cooperative marketing and distribution with other publishers.[53] Local bookshops are an obvious target, but may only take publications on sale or return, which is time-consuming to manage. Mail order is important given that many interest groups live at a distance. Many libraries produce a 'publications for sale' leaflet, which can be enclosed in replies to enquiries. Opportunities for selling publications on the Internet are increasing rapidly, and there is already a collaborative site for the sale of family history material. In terms of promotion, the local press and media can be exploited, particularly if a book launch is held with a talk and book signing providing photo opportunities. Review copies can be sent to specialist journals, such as the *Local historian* or *Family tree magazine*. Advance publicity can include posters and flyers, which can be produced cheaply in-house and either delivered door-to-door, distributed through a local newspaper or included in council mailings. The success of Camden's publishing programme has been largely due to time invested in making personal contacts with potential retail outlets.

INCOME GENERATION

Income generation may be viewed with suspicion, as librarians are afraid that it will detract from the service offered. However, it is an aspect that local studies collections can no longer afford to ignore, and are increasingly expected to include when setting targets. There are many ways in which libraries are already exploiting the economic potential of the collection, through local history shops for the sale of in-house and externally produced local history publications, photocopying and microprint charges, reproduction fees and, in some cases, use of the Internet.[54] It has been suggested that, if admission is charged for events, customers value them more highly. The new demands posed by e-mail enquiries have meant that many libraries can no longer cope with the level of research demanded of them. Some limit the time spent on enquiries, others are introducing a research service, charging an hourly fee. This makes it possible in some cases to employ part-time researchers to ease the pressure on staff time. Use by legal firms and business companies, many of which pass charges on to their customers, has led some libraries to introduce a commercial rate. By offering a paid, professional service, local studies can meet a real need, particularly for those unable to visit the collection, while helping to increase resources. The lucrative potential of the illustrations collection is considerable, and television companies, book publishers and picture agencies should all be asked to pay realistic reproduction and copyright fees. The use of scanners can also help to provide a better service for individual customers as, instead of using a photographer to supply copies of individual illustrations, library staff can supply high-quality scanned copies on demand, at less cost to the customer.[55]

USE OF THE INTERNET

Marketing opportunities have been transformed since technological developments brought the Internet into schools, libraries, businesses and, increasingly, the majority of homes in the late 1990s.[56] The Internet can now be accessed from cars, mobile phones and televisions. Local, national and global markets can be reached with ease, local information updated regularly, publications purchased and copies of items from the collection ordered. Most libraries now have their own web pages, usually under the council's site, and many have developed exciting local history resources on-line. The exploitation of this new market is one of the major challenges facing local studies libraries today, with the pace of change in the 21st century bringing ever-expanding opportunities. First of all, it requires new skills. It is not appropriate to put existing brochures and leaflets onto a website to publicize the local studies collection. A different medium requires a different, often more informal, style. Leaflets look very dull when transferred as they stand to a website. Text should not be too dense or the font too small. Illustrations are essential, but care needs to be taken that they do not take too much time to download. The Internet is three-dimensional, which means that judicious use of a few key words can lead to multi-levels of information, enabling the visitor to select according to their needs rather than confronting an indigestible mass. The best way to learn is to look at a variety of sites, and compare them for readability, interest and usefulness. As well as having its own web pages, the local studies collection should ensure adequate links to and from relevant sites. This means that the user does not need prior knowledge of the collection, but can be led to it through other sites. Family historians, for example, can discover what lies in local studies collections in Britain and Ireland through EARL's *Familia*.[57]

As well as having a website giving information about the collection and how to access it, funding may be available to develop more ambitious learning resources.[58] The Public Record Office's Learning Curve is a good example of what can be achieved with specialist education staff and a good ICT department,[59] and the Scottish Cultural Resources Access Network (SCRAN), a joint libraries, museums and archives project, has had a major impact in Scotland. The National Grid for Learning has produced a demand for content creation and on-line resources for schools, to which local studies can respond. In Westminster, a local grid for learning has been set up, and the local studies collection asked to create a site which uses sources such as maps, photographs and census returns, for teachers and pupils to access on the Internet.[60] The New Opportunities Fund is making money available to a number of consortia, many of which have exciting ideas for local studies projects, which should come to fruition over the next few years. In 1997 the Public Libraries Challenge Fund was established to enhance access to reference material. A total of 30 local history projects shared a £3,000,000 award. One of these, produced by Knowsley library service, won a best-on-the-web award in 1998, with special mention for best information content, taking just three months to complete. It uses over 400 photographs from the local studies collection, with maps, artefacts and audio interviews. Although it was aimed primarily at creating access for local people, in the first six months it attracted 75,000 visits from all over the world.[61]

EVALUATION AND REVIEW

Having developed a marketing strategy and put it into action, it is vital to know whether the objectives have been, or are being, achieved. To do this a plan needs to include targets. These should be SMART (Specific, Measurable, Achievable, Realistic and Time-related). These performance indicators monitor progress and highlight areas of success and underachievement.[62] This will provide feedback to inform the next stage of the planning cycle. There is always the danger that performance indicators will become meaningless number-crunching exercises. Although statistics gathering is an important part of the process, evaluation should always be qualitative, not just quantitative. It is important to know, not just that an event attracted 50 newcomers, but whether they enjoyed the event and would come again. This might be achieved through the use of evaluation forms, by recording verbal comments or by encouraging written comments. Similarly, if the aim of an event is to attract new items for the collection, it is useful to know, not just how many new acquisitions have been generated, but whether they will meet the needs of users. Some libraries find this is best achieved by setting up user panels, and Friends organizations can provide a useful forum for consultation.

CONCLUSION

If local studies collections are to maintain their position at a time of shrinking resources, greater accountability and increased competition, it is essential to demonstrate a professional approach. A well-developed marketing plan can

- help secure resources and act as a tool to obtain future funding,
- clarify aims and objectives,
- ensure a service that meets the real needs of users rather than reflecting the preconceptions of staff,
- maximize successful promotion to selected groups and individuals,
- increase use of and access to the collection,
- ensure a higher profile for local studies within the council,
- lead to the attraction and retention of good staff,
- raise the status and influence of local studies as a national network of specialist research libraries.

Digitization projects, new funding opportunities and the global influence of the Internet make this an exciting time for local studies libraries as they rise to the challenge of developing an effective marketing strategy.

NOTES

1   Melrose, E. (1999), 'Marketing the local studies collection: some observations', *Local studies librarian* 18 (2), 11–15.

2   For examples of competition, see Melrose, E. (1999), 13.

3   Discussed in Smith, R. (1987), 'Marketing the library', *Aslib proceedings* 39 (9), 231–3.

4   Library Association Local Studies Group (2002), *Local studies libraries: Library Association guidelines for local studies provision in public libraries*, London: Library Association, para B6.2.1.

5   Social audit techniques can also be used; *Local studies libraries: Library Association guidelines ...* (2002), para A4.4.

6   Nurse, B. (1987), 'Services to users and extension activities', in *Local studies collections: a manual*, vol. 1, edited by M. Dewe, Aldershot: Gower, 249. In Hungary, too, family historians form a high proportion of local studies users: Melrose, E. (1994), 'Köszönöm a Meghivast – and the bus was very comfortable', *Local studies librarian* 13 (2), 5.

7   (1988), *Library Association record* 90 (12), 718.

8   Nurse, B. (1987), 249.

9   Martin, D. (1994), 'Local studies at the new Kirkintilloch library', *Local studies librarian* 13 (2), 3.

10   In Cambridgeshire a heritage officers' group brought together archivists, librarians, a museum officer, building conservation and an education adviser; Petty, M. (1996), 'Networking local studies', *Local studies librarian* 15 (1), 5. The setting up of Re:Source, bringing together museums, libraries and archives on a regional basis, is in recognition of the work that has been going on at local level and provides a new framework for collaboration.

11   Familiarization visits have been made to Westminster by staff from the British Library, University of Westminster, the Crown Estates Office and the Royal Institute of British Architects.

12   Leaflets are discussed in Nurse, B. (1987), 261–3; Batstone, M. (1991), 'Publicity, exhibition and display work', in *Local studies collections: a manual*, vol. 2, edited by M. Dewe, Aldershot: Gower, 236–7.

13   For example, the *Salopian recorder*, the newspaper of the friends of Shropshire Records and Research, and *New at COWAC*, produced by the City of Westminster Archives Centre. See Batstone, M. (1991), 237; *Local studies libraries: Library Association guidelines* ... (2002), para A4.3.4.

14   'News' (1990), *Local studies librarian* 9 (2), 14; *Local studies libraries: Library Association guidelines* ... (2002), para A4.3.6.

15   For use of the media, see Batstone, M. (1991), 232–5. For press releases, see Phillips, F. (1995), *Local history collections in libraries*, Englewood, Colorado: Libraries Unlimited, 101–3; *Local studies libraries: Library Association guidelines* ... (2002), para A4.3.5.

16   Cooke, S. (1991), 'With the eclat of a proverb: or, blow your own trumpet', *Local studies librarian* 10 (1), 3–4.

17   See Batstone, M. (1991), 225–42.

18   Jamieson, I. (1994), 'Editorial', *Local studies librarian*, 13 (2), 1.

19   Cooke, S. (1991), 3–4.

20   *Local studies libraries: Library Association guidelines* ... (2002), para A3.9.

21   For cooperation with local societies, see Batstone, M. (1991), 238–9.

22   *Local studies libraries: Library Association guidelines* ... (2002), para A4.3.1.

23   *Local studies libraries: Library Association guidelines* ... (2002), para A2.3.11.

24   Armstrong, N. (1991), 'Reminiscence work with local studies material', in *Local studies collections: a manual*, vol. 2, edited by M. Dewe, Aldershot: Gower, 194–224.

25   Corcoran, N. (1990), 'Living history in the making: the promotion and use of an oral history project', *Local studies librarian* 9 (1), 6–8.

26   See also Phillips, F. (1995), 106–10; *Local studies libraries: Library Association guidelines* ... (2002), para A4.3.2.

27   See Batstone, M. (1991), 235–6; *Local studies libraries: Library Association guidelines* ... (2002), paras A4.3.3 and A4.3.8.

28   Calderwood, M.S. (1991), 'Mystery tours in West Lothian', *Local studies librarian* 10 (1), 11–12.

29   Martin, D. (1994), 2–3; *Local studies libraries: Library Association guidelines* ... (2002), para A4.1.

30   White, P. (1994), 'All our yesterdays: the making of an exhibition', *Local studies librarian* 13 (2), 7–10.

31   *Local studies libraries: Library Association guidelines* ... (2002), para A3.1.

32   Hayes, M. (1995), 'His sins were scarlet but his books were read: the work of West Sussex county council's special events group', *Local studies librarian* 14 (2), 4–9; *Local studies libraries: Library Association guidelines* ... (2002), para A4.3.

33   For the experience of Friends groups in the USA, see Phillips, F. (1995), 111.

34   See Blizzard, A. (1987), 'Local studies and education', in *Local studies collections: a manual*, vol. 1, edited by M. Dewe, Aldershot: Gower, 271–308.

35   In Barnstaple, the library, record office and museum set up a Joint Educational Development Initiative (JEDI), producing a joint booklet which was circulated to schools. See Lawrence, M. (1991), 'North Devon Local Studies Centre, Barnstaple', *Local studies librarian* 10 (2), 3–7.

36   See Blizzard, A. (1991), *A sense of place: local studies and the school library*, Swindon: School Library Association.

37   Full details of the National Curriculum can be found at: *http//www.nc.uk.net*; another useful site is *http://www.dfee.gov.uk/nc*. Scotland has its own curriculum.

38   *Local studies libraries: Library Association guidelines* ... (2002), para A4.1.

39   Flowers, A. (1999), 'Local history publishing at Newcastle libraries and information service', *Local studies librarian* 18 (1), 7–9.

40   Barnes, M. (1991), 'The Alan Ball local history awards', *Local studies librarian* 10 (2), 10–11. See Field, R. (1987), 'Publications and products', in *Local studies collections: a manual*, vol. 1, edited by M. Dewe, Aldershot: Gower, 376–90.

41   For a list of stages in the process and questions which should be asked, see Pyle, J. (1990), *Publishing programmes in libraries*, Nottingham: Library Association Public Libraries Group. A checklist of points for consideration and action is given in Reid, A. (1996), 'Publish and be damned', *Scottish libraries* 10 (2), 20–21.

42   The market may be too small to attract a commercial publisher; *Local studies libraries: Library Association guidelines* ... (2002), paras A4.3.4 and 6.6.

43   Many guides to collections are now being published on the Internet as this is easily updated.

44   The City of Westminster, for example, has produced its own version of the first two and the third is in progress.

45   Flowers, A. (1999), 7–9.

46   *Local studies libraries: Library Association guidelines* ... (2002), para B6.6.7.

47   France, which has a highly centralized education system, has produced impressive study packs. In the past Britain was hampered by not knowing what topics teachers would set, but this is no longer an excuse. See Stevens, P. (1991), 'Entente cordiale in Hampshire', *Local studies librarian* 10 (1), 9.

48   Adams, P.M. (1999), 'Library publishing on a shoestring', *Local studies librarian* 18 (1), 10–12.

49   Lock, A. (1994), 'Living memories of Hyde: using volunteers in an oral history project', *Local studies librarian* 13 (2), 11–15.

50   Airey, J. (1990), 'Newcastle past and present: shops and shopping (the video)', *Local studies librarian* 9 (2), 12.

51   Camaffin, E. (1995), 'Gateshead 1900: a CD-I guide', *Local studies librarian* 14 (2), 10–13.

52   Field, R. (1987), 387.

53   Parry, D. (1989), *A feasibility study in joint co-operative marketing and distribution of material published by local authorities and independent publishers in the Northern Region*. [Newcastle upon Tyne]: Information North.

54   *Local studies libraries: Library Association guidelines* ... (2002), para B6.5.

55   Petty, M. (1996), 'Networking local studies', *Local studies librarian* 15 (1), 5.

56   *Local studies libraries: Library Association guidelines* ... (2002), para A4.3.7.

57   *http://www.earl.org.uk/familia*.

58   *Local studies libraries: Library Association guidelines* ... (2002), para B6.4.

59   *http://learningcurve.pro.gov.uk*

60   The Foley Street Story was produced as a case study of the sources available for local history at Key Stage 2, based on the street in which one local primary school is situated. It can be seen at *http://wgfl.westminster.gov.uk/foley*. This provided a good opportunity to inform teachers about the collection, and how they can use it.

61   *http://history.knowsley.gov.uk*; Marchant, P. and Hume, E. (1998), 'Visiting Knowsley's past', *Library Association record* 100 (9), 468–9.

62   Melrose, E. (1999), 15.

8 Enquiries

Nicola Smith

ENQUIRERS AND THEIR ENQUIRIES

ENQUIRER GROUPS

Local studies staff receive enquiries on a huge range of topics, not always connected with the locality in which they are situated. They can find themselves answering general historical queries also, as other library and council staff perceive them as the people to ask about the past in general.

The most common enquiries from the public relate to family history, the history of a house, or an institution or the life of a famous or infamous person within the particular area. Students of all ages account for a significant proportion of enquiries and can be interested in families or buildings, but tend to have wider queries. Primary school children can be engaged in a study of their street, or trying to find out what it was like to be a Victorian child at school, or living in the workhouse. Older children will be studying to GCSE level work on a range of projects including both the world wars, suffragettes and the influence of particular groups on an area.

In recent years, university students have become regular users of local studies collections as universities set projects related to their town. Here the range extends beyond history and geography into tourism and business studies. Any area which has had extensive redevelopment can expect geographers wanting to study changing townscapes and industries. Students working for research degrees are rarer but most collections will have one or two; their work can be very important when completed, but while being researched such enquirers can be very demanding. As pointed out in previous chapters, family and local history studies are particularly popular with older or retired people, who have the time available to pursue their researches.

Outside of these main groups there are other common enquirers. Organizations moving into new offices or opening new shops are often looking for suitable illustrations with which to decorate their new premises, or interesting historical anecdotes to put in their publicity material. Archaeologists who have a short time to carry out an excavation before redevelopment begins want to research a site and are particularly interested in maps and plans. People considering buying a new house want to check rights of ways, boundaries or the previous uses of the site. Property owners who want to change the use of their property from business to residential, or to change the type of business, want to look through the rate books or directories for evidence that this has been done before. Residents groups or tenants associations want to check through council minutes, reports and agendas to see if the council has kept its word over redevelopment or repairs. Researchers for television and film look for visual references to get set design right or want to research a story or check facts, and picture researchers look for the 'right' image for their book.

ENQUIRY RESPONSE

Enquiries arrive in person, by telephone, by letter and now by e-mail, and libraries have to decide how much time to devote to each category of enquiry. Enquiry work is at the heart of the role and most librarians will want to give people who visit the library as much help as possible. However, steadily increasing visitor numbers mean that there is a limit to the time which can be spent on an individual enquirer. Letter enquiries can provide a particular challenge for libraries who find themselves attempting to meet local authority targets for response times, which are often set without considering the volume of correspondence received by local collections. Libraries need to analyse both the nature and means of receipt of all enquiries and the time taken each week to answer them. The growth of e-mail has seen a rise in the number of enquiries received, as it is very easy to send an e-mail, and libraries report that they range from the very simple to the most complex, and new strategies need to be developed to deal with them. One way is to adopt the Frequently Asked Questions (FAQs) as used in many mailing lists. Visitors to the website can be reminded to check the FAQs before they send in an enquiry. Hackney Archives[1] report that they received 791 letter and e-mail enquiries in 1999/2000, compared with 543 in 1998/99, and that the increase was almost entirely due to e-mail. Southwark report six to twelve e-mail enquiries a week, which are treated in the same way as letter enquiries.

Local studies libraries also have to consider how much work they are prepared to do on behalf of a letter or e-mail enquirer and whether to charge for that work. Most collections will respond to requests for information on holdings and opening hours, but the amount of actual research that might be undertaken on behalf of an enquirer varies. Libraries find themselves in a dilemma: they are a local authority service funded out of the rates, and yet many of the written enquiries received will come from people who live outside the authority area, and possibly in another country. It is unlikely that many of the enquirers will ever visit the library, and if all research enquiries received were answered fully staff would have little time for anything else. Libraries and librarians have to strike a balance between answering queries themselves, putting enquirers in touch with those who can undertake research for a fee or on a reciprocal basis, and encouraging those who have made written enquiries to visit if at all possible.

There are various approaches to the need to give enquirers who cannot visit the library a way of pursuing their research. Some libraries limit the time they will spend on an enquiry and others will only undertake specific searches for a fee. Libraries will, for example, supply a photocopy of a specified census entry, but will not search through the census looking for a named individual. It is sometimes possible to work with the local family or local history society. In Southwark enquirers are provided with a list of AGRA (Association of Genealogists and Record Agents) researchers and the address of the Surrey Family History Society who, like many societies, have a page in their journal where members can advertise their interests and seek to exchange searching. An enquirer to a northern family history society who is able to reach London libraries and record offices may be able to reach an accommodation with a northern-based member to do each other's research locally. Close links between the family history society and the library are enhanced by the society holding meetings in the library's meeting room.

Some libraries will have a list of researchers. It is difficult, however, for offices to recommend researchers without taking some responsibility for the quality of the work. One solution is to only list searchers who are members of AGRA. Hackney Archives have a self-employed searcher based in the library. The enquiry process is managed by the Archives staff, which allows them to check the quality of the work and handle any problems. The archives receive a percentage of the fee charged to the public. A similar service is offered by Guildhall Library, where the basic charge to the public is £50 per hour with a minimum of charge of £25.[2]

STAFF TRAINING

Local studies staff, like all library staff, should be trained to be sensitive to user needs and to appear to be willing to help. Staff who appear 'busy' or uninterested can intimidate a user. The reference interview is particularly important in local studies work. Enquirers will often begin by asking a very general question.

'Do you have any information on railways?'
'Yes, what sort of railways are you interested in?'

'Do you have anything on old railways?'
'Yes, was there a particular railway that you wanted to know about?'
'Do you have anything on London Bridge Station?'
'Yes, what period are you interested in?'
'Do you have any illustrations of the first London Bridge Station?'

The public may be afraid of appearing stupid, or not realize the range of materials available, or may have met an off-putting librarian on their last visit. Staff need to be taught to ask open-ended questions, to reflect back the enquirer's question, and above all to be patient. All of which becomes more difficult if there is a queue of people, letters to be answered and the telephone is ringing. A useful guide to reference techniques is *Success at the enquiry desk*.[3]

Local studies staff should be curious and interested in their locality and want to share their knowledge with all their users. All collections have their 'regulars', the reader that comes in every week and is an expert in their field. They get to know the staff and how the collection works and staff will often discuss their latest findings. Such people can become a valuable resource by offering advice to other readers interested in their speciality, but there is also a danger that the library can begin to appear like a private club to the outsider or new reader, who may feel intimidated and excluded. Staff should always be alert to the opportunity to explain their service to new or potentially new readers. Local studies staff frequently get asked to give talks on their locality, and this is a chance to explain to the audience the role of the local studies library and to solicit new material for the collection.

Local studies material is sometimes housed in a public library where lending library staff are expected to answer queries in the absence of specialist staff. In these situations it is particularly important that these staff receive the appropriate training and are able to locate the items listed in the catalogue or other finding aids. Sometimes branch libraries may be able to cooperate with the local historical society who may even provide volunteers to provide advice from time to time. It is important that members of staff in branch libraries which house satellite collections view the collection as an important part of the resources of their library, worth promoting and developing.

Although much training will be done on the job, it can be helpful for new members to attend courses. This not only helps in training but it demonstrates that there are other people with similar concerns. A number of organizations run training courses: the Local Studies Group of the Library Association through its branches runs training days and visits; the Greater London Archives Network (GLAN) runs courses for its members in the London area dealing with topics relating to holdings such as maps and more general subjects such as customer care, and the Society of Genealogists organizes a variety of courses on various aspects of family history.

Staff in local studies libraries can also be encouraged to study for courses in local history which are run by various universities and by the Open University. The OU course DA301, Studying Family and Community History: 19th and 20th Centuries, would provide a solid basis for work in local studies libraries. A number of universities, including Birmingham, Leicester and Sussex, offer certificates or masters degrees in local history, usually concentrating on the history of their area.

SELF-HELP

Librarians are accustomed to dealing with enquiries, but what makes local studies enquiries more challenging is that a single user can spend a day in a library during which time they will have a variety of queries, some of which might be avoided given better general guidance. Often family or local historians visit a range of local collections, where they may be under time pressure and anxious to achieve as much as possible on their visit. Although they may be relatively expert users of collections, they may be new to a particular collection. Libraries need to help their users make the best use of their time with the collection. There should be an easily available simple guide to the collection, which includes a plan of the library, instructions on how to use the catalogue, how to order material, and explanations of any indexes, and which introduces the services provided by the library. The same information should be available on the library's web pages and should be sent to anyone writing to the library with the intention of visiting later.

The library itself should be well laid out and clearly signed; the library staff and the enquiry point should be easily identifiable. New users of the collection should know where to go and who to ask for advice. Local collections are often overcrowded and understaffed and the first-time visitor can find it hard to know who to ask for advice, particularly if the member of staff on the enquiry desk appears occupied with another task.

Another difficulty in local studies work is that of fitting the resource to the enquiry. A ten-year-old child doing a project on workhouses will not be helped by the production of a volume of workhouse minutes, but they would be essential to the PhD researcher. Libraries usually become aware of school projects and can help themselves by consulting teachers and pre-selecting some items which will be suitable for the age group concerned. Universities which set projects can also be contacted and are often very pleased if the librarian will give a short talk to the students on the most likely sources of information.

Another source of help can be members of local societies; most areas will have a local history society, a family history society as well as amenity and ecological groups. Their publications often contain articles of interest researched by members. If such groups can be encouraged to meet in the library they may even be able to provide volunteers to answer queries. Meetings provide local studies staff with the opportunity of training members of the society in using the collections and making best use of the available material.

Local studies collections need to maintain good links with neighbouring collections so that users can be advised where else to look for sources not available locally. Staff also need to be aware of the main national collections and their holdings. Encouraging staff to join the Local Studies Group of the Library Association can help staff and information networking.

RESOURCES FOR ENQUIRIES

Good indexes are often the key to local studies enquiry work and a user of collections will always look for the indexes (they are often still on cards), which are invaluable. Creating indexes is very labour-intensive and some collections have abandoned newspaper indexes in favour of cuttings file, but for picking up the minutiae of local life indexes are hard to beat. There are different types; for example, family historians want name indexes of parish registers, poor law records, wills and similar sources. The local index is often a mixture of references to local people found in a variety of sources, such as local newspapers or periodicals, and also to entries for the short articles found in local directories. Dudley local collection has an excellent index to people and places within the borough. Family history groups will sometimes provide volunteers who will work on indexing genealogical sources.

A good catalogue will also make answering enquiries easier. It is often preferable for local studies material to be catalogued and indexed by staff within the collection rather than relying on the more general cataloguing likely to be undertaken by centralized bibliographical services staff. Guildhall Library in London includes in its catalogue analytical entries for London periodicals. The periodicals found in local collections are unlikely to be covered by the large indexing and abstracting services, which local collections are in any case unlikely to subscribe to, and important material in local periodicals is 'lost' unless picked up by the local studies library catalogue. This can mean that the local collection must adopt different cataloguing and indexing standards from the remainder of the library service. It is important that the library management software selected be able to cope with the special needs of the local collection. Local studies staff will have to explain their needs to colleagues in bibliographic services, and expect to do the extra indexing or more detailed cataloguing themselves. It is the people who are most familiar with the collection and the nature of the enquiries who make the best indexers.

THE WORLD WIDE WEB

The World Wide Web (WWW) has now become a major resource for family historians and other researchers. Bibliographic checking is made much easier by recourse to the British Library OPAC97[4] or to COPAC[5] (Consortium of University Research Libraries, OPAC). As already mentioned in earlier chapters, family historians can now access the International Genealogical Index through *http://www.familysearch.org/*, a site made available by the Church of Jesus Christ of the Latter Day Saints. The Commonwealth War Graves Commission has made available electronically its indexes under the title, the Debt of Honour Register, at *http://yard.ccta.gov.uk/ cwgc/register.nsf.*

EARL, the Consortium for Public Library Networking, has created pages specifically for family history at *http://www.earl.org.uk/familia/main.html.*[6] They describe their pages thus: 'Familia is a web-based directory of family history resources held in public libraries in the UK and Ireland. Updated and maintained by the Family History Task Group of the EARL Consortium, Familia is the on-line starting-place to find information about materials in public libraries, which will help you trace your family history.' The Familia pages make planning visits to libraries and checking collections for availability of sources very straightforward. If the EARL Family History Task Group[7] succeeds in their bid for New Opportunities Fund support they hope to develop their pages into a family history portal which will increase their value to local studies staff.

It is to be hoped that in time other local studies collections will be able to follow the example of Devon,[8] and put their catalogues on to the Web. The catalogue is just part of a comprehensive website which includes guides to holding and lists of sources.

Genuki (UK and Ireland genealogy) is an invaluable resource for family historians. It describes itself as a 'virtual reference library of genealogical information that is of particular relevance to the UK and Ireland. It is a non-commercial service, provided by an ever-growing group of volunteers in co-operation with the Federation of Family History Societies and a number of its member societies'.[9] The information is divided by county and contains surnames lists and other links relating to family history in each area.

Libraries are now expected to be able to evaluate all areas of their service and routinely conduct customer satisfaction surveys. Local studies readers are likely to be more varied and generally to include fewer regular readers, and so it can be hard to gauge the level of customer satisfaction. Local studies librarians may need to press for specially composed questionnaires for local collections. Some libraries, such as Southwark, contain a suggestions box or a comments book where users can put their views forward. Libraries may have to state how many written enquiries are answered within the council's standard for response.

CASE STUDY

As has been seen, amongst the most common enquiries are those relating to family history and the history of a building. Imagine a little scenario...

Someone enters library looking uneasy. The friendly librarian on the desk enquires if she can help. The person explains that he has just received the birth certificate of his grandfather and it refers to an address he cannot find on the current *A–Z*. He is only in this part of the world for a day and was hoping to find out where the house was so that he could take a photograph of it. He hoped to find out more about his grandfather.

The first step would be to find out the date of birth, and then to look at a commercial directory or electoral register to locate the street. Some towns have published a list of streets and when they were first named, which provides a short cut.

Depending on the date and availability, an index to the streets in the census can also be used to identify a particular street. Failing directories, it is necessary to consult any available street maps or Ordnance Survey maps. The 25 inch or 60 inch plans available for towns are the best. Some local authorities used the 60 inch plans for council purposes and these may have house numbers and changes of street name added to the maps. It should be possible to show the enquirer where his grandfather's street used to be.

Once the street has been identified, the user might be advised to look at the census for the nearest year. Many local collections will have extensive files of photographs of streets and the enquirer may be lucky and find one of his street or at least it should be possible to supply the enquirer with a view of a similar street. The census should give an occupation for his great-grandfather and it may be possible to follow that up in the collection with additional information on the industries and trades common to that area.

Experienced local studies librarians will realize that not all enquiries are that easily solved. The street address may turn out to correspond to an institution of some sort, perhaps a home for unmarried mothers, and the address will not help our enquirer in his quest for his family history. The address may be partial and difficult to trace. The enquirer may not have brought the certificate with him and the address may have been copied badly. All of these scenarios may be compounded by lack of time on the enquirer's part and a busy library. A comparatively simple enquiry such as the one detailed above can occupy a considerable amount of staff time and, for a one-off visit, it is often easiest for the staff to help the enquirer rather than trying to explain how to search for the answers.

SERVICES TO ENQUIRERS

Librarians are trained to help users find the information they require. Local studies librarians also have a responsibility to the sources that contain the information. Local studies material may be rare or even unique and it requires careful storage and handling. Users of the collection may be unaware of its value and fragility and it is important that staff abide by simple rules concerning its use.

If possible, lockers should be provided so that users only take into the local studies area material that they need. Increasingly, users will want to use laptops while researching and provision should be made with circuit breakers and power points available at some desks. Lincoln local collection housed in the central reference library has study carrels that can be booked by readers and locked, which are ideal for laptop users. Users should be visible to staff at all times so that a watch may be kept. Staff should not leave the local studies area without a member of library staff present. Users should be warned not to lean on material, not to stack open books on top of each other; not to trace items without a protective sheet on top of the original, and preferably should use pencils rather than pens. Rules concerning eating and drinking should be strictly enforced. If possible, libraries should provide an area where users can eat and drink. Some collections, such as Dudley, have vending machines for selling hot drinks.

Most collections will have a photocopier, but staff need to think carefully about how copies are to be made. Practice in this area varies quite widely; Dudley Archives does not allow any photocopying by members of the public, all the copying is done promptly, by a member of staff. Lincoln allows public copying of a range of printed materials, as does Southwark; in both cases the photocopier is adjacent to the enquiry desk. Collections need to strike a balance between conserving delicate resources and providing a user-oriented service. Some collections, as is the case at Guildhall Library, limit by date the material that may be copied by the public and have a separate service provided by staff for older and more delicate materials. It is possible to purchase photocopiers that are kinder to delicate materials, but these are expensive. Few collections will allow the copying of bound volumes of manuscripts or newspapers. Many collections will have microfilms of newspapers and commonly requested sources such as parish registers, and photocopies can be made from the films.

Photography is sometimes an alternative means of copying and again some libraries help users by supplying copy stands, which can be hired at a small fee as in Southwark. Libraries should also have an arrangement with a commercial photographer who can provide good quality copies for a fee. A number of collections – Hackney Archives is a notable example – have begun to digitize images and can provide prints from the digital version without endangering the original.

Copying, by whatever means, raises questions of copyright and the protection of a collection's rights to material. For example, libraries will often allow users to copy photographs and other material which is out of copyright for purposes of private study, but would charge a fee if the same material was to be reproduced and sold for commercial advantage. Unfortunately, the identity of the copyright holder for some local studies material, such as photographs, can be unclear, and libraries should be very cautious about allowing such material to be copied. Sandy Norman's guide, *Copyright in public libraries*,[10] suggests that the key questions local studies collections need to ask about copyright are 'Is it in copyright? Is it in the public domain? Has it been published? Who owns the copyright? If it is unpublished, has permission been given to copy it? Is it subject to any publication right?' She offers some sensible guidance on how libraries can avoid potentially embarrassing mistakes.

Copyright in photographs created after 1 August 1989 lies with the photographer and subsists for 70 years after the end of the calendar year of the photographer's death. If the photographer is unknown, copyright is 70 years from date of creation or, if the work is made available to the public, 70 years from when it is first made available.

The position for earlier works is that the copyright on all photographs taken before 1912 is now expired. Photographs taken between 1 July 1912 and 1 June 1957 are in copyright until 50 years after the photograph was taken, those taken between June 1957 and 1 August 1989 are in copyright for 70 years from the date of the negative.

Local collections often find users wanting to photocopy from Ordnance Survey (OS) maps and must be careful to enforce the law as the OS are vigilant protectors of copyright. The copyright for OS maps runs for 50 years from the end of the year in which the map was published. Norman says[11] that requests must be accompanied by a copyright declaration form and that the maximum amount that may be copied from an in-copyright map is four copies of a single extract which does not exceed 625 sq. cm, or A4 size.

PUBLICATIONS

Many local studies collections have developed a range of leaflets and publications to help users make the best use of the collection. There are various approaches to guides to the collection. Some offices have simple guides to the various sources available and how to use them. These guides are sometimes made available to potential users via the World Wide Web. The Public Record Office's extensive guides to its collections are perhaps the best example of this approach. It is tempting to charge for even the simplest leaflet, but librarians need to be aware that even small charges may be too much for some users, and the time saved in giving users a guide is well worth the cost of photocopying. Leeds Local Studies library has produced a series of guides to various sources, such as the census and electoral registers.

However, it is possible to produce more detailed guides to tracing family history or the history of a building and charge for these. Here users can be taken through the entire research process, with links being made between sources, and the opportunity can be taken to point users to other useful sources such as the county record office or archives and local museums.

CONCLUSIONS: FUTURE OF ENQUIRIES, ELECTRONIC DEVELOPMENTS

The spread of e-mail has affected the nature and number of enquiries received by local collections. Government interest in community identity and the role of public libraries as guardians of community memory was highlighted in *New library: the people's network*,[12] and more recently the Wolfson awards have been awarding money to public libraries to promote British history. Local studies collections are becoming more visible and more popular; the challenge for local studies librarians is to develop electronic techniques to answer electronic enquiries, while still maintaining the traditional service to those who can visit the library in person. Hackney Archives allow visitors to their website to post messages and requests for help with their research, which is a good use of web technology.[13]

However, the most important ingredient of a successful enquiry service remains a well trained and enthusiastic staff, working in a well organized and welcoming library. Local studies librarians need to take basic library skills and apply them within the local studies collection.

NOTES

1   My thanks go to David Mander for this and other facts concerning Hackney Archives.
2   The costs quoted are correct as at January 2001.
3   Owen, T. (1998), *Success at the enquiry desk: successful enquiry answering every time*, 2nd rev. edn, London: Library Association Publishing.
4   *http://opac97.bl.uk/*.
5   *http://copac.ac.uk/copac/*.
6   'About Familia' at *http://www.earl.org.uk/familia/about.html* (accessed 20 July 2000).
7   'EARL's content themes. Family history', *http://www.earl.org.uk/ideabank/earl.html* (accessed 20 July 2000).
8   *http://www.devon-cc.gov.uk/library/locstudy/search.html*.
9   *http://www.genuki.org.uk/*.
10 Norman, Sandy (1999), *Copyright in public libraries*, 4th edn, London: Library Association Publishing, 63.

11   Ibid., 37.
12   Library and Information Commission (1997), *New library: the people's network*, London: LIC (downloaded from *http://www.ukoln.ac.uk/services/lic/newlibrary/full.html*).
13   *http://www.hackney.gov.uk/history/index.html.*

9 The international context and the future in the UK

Michael Dewe

Any forecast about the future direction of local studies libraries and librarianship in the UK must be largely based on an evaluation of current trends both here (as outlined in Chapter 1) and abroad, as described below. Such a forecast may be misleading, based as it is on a limited number of examples instanced in the professional literature, and the future could also be severely distorted by unexpected events and developments. Predictions cannot, in any case, be put in an orderly timeframe. Nevertheless, it is the duty of a chapter such as this not only to look to the future, by monitoring trends abroad and at home and their likely implications, but to seek to influence that future by suggesting appropriate changes and developments in local studies provision in UK libraries and within the broader local studies scene.

RESOURCE PROVIDERS

Writing about the international local studies scene at the end of the 1980s, Sturges and Bapty commented: 'The concept and import of specialized local collections does now seem to be widely recognized throughout the world'[1] – although South America, unlike North America, much of Europe, Australasia and parts of Africa and Asia, seems particularly absent from the professional literature. However, the task of discerning international and national trends is difficult because the professional literature reports few general surveys of the local studies situation in any one country set in the wider library or other context. Although there are, for example, two such accounts for Australia and one for Hungary, these by no means provide a full picture.

Based largely on visits to New South Wales and Victoria in 1992, and concerned mainly with public libraries, one description of the local studies situation in Australia, set in the context of the wider national and state scene, shows the extent of professional planning for the then coming millennium.[2] A more recent account looks at local history libraries in that country, their role in supporting cultural heritage, and current issues that need resolution, such as the need for a better understanding of users, and for assistance with the developments in information technology.[3] In Hungary, the impact of political and economic change on local studies collections (a prime responsibility of county libraries) has been described, as well as the problems and challenges faced, such as increased demand and difficulties in acquiring books and periodicals.[4]

Sturges and Bapty demonstrated the importance of libraries of all kinds for local studies, although their roles and activities, and therefore the significance of particular institutions, may vary from country to country, and this continues to be the case today, as the following examples show.

NATIONAL LIBRARIES

As part of its role in preserving its country's documentary heritage, the National Library of Australia is involved in the collection of local ephemera.[5]

STATE LIBRARIES

The State Library of Victoria, Australia provides an on-line cultural history record called 'First Families 2001'. This is a database about the people of Australia, accessible to all Australians via the Internet, which welcomes contributions from all. A 'first family' is the earliest person in a family known to have lived in Australia and information can be submitted on the earliest generation of each branch of a family.[6]

PUBLIC LIBRARIES

'Public libraries, large and small are everywhere an important element in local studies provision'[7] and recent descriptions of their activities are to be found, for example, in the USA, as instanced by an account of the genealogical and historical resources at the Queens Borough Public Library.[8] In Canada, a survey of local history collections in Southern Ontario public libraries found there were challenges in a time of financial austerity and that there were common problems, seemingly similar to those in the UK. These problems stemmed from the labour-intensive nature of local collections, combined with lack of staff time and expertise, insufficient space and inadequate funds.[9]

Descriptions of resources and surveys, other issues, such as on-line catalogues, libraries with archives and promotional activities, as well as fundamental discussions about the local studies role of public libraries, are evidenced by the professional literature. Hilversum Public Library in The Netherlands, for example, has had its local collection available via the library's on-line catalogue since 1993,[10] while in Spain the collection and services of the Alhambra Library and Archive are based in the Granada administrative headquarters.[11] The Warsaw Public Library, Poland, has used its specialist collections and associated activities, such as exhibitions, publications, meetings and conventions, to spread knowledge about the capital.[12]

A recent article from Taiwan considers the role of public libraries, seeing it as their duty to collect, organize and preserve local documents for the use of patrons.[13] In Ireland there has been some discussion of its 'collective memory', as represented by public libraries, and suggestions have been made as to how to increase awareness and usage through an on-line network, digitization, preservation and publications in print and electronic form.[14]

REGIONAL LIBRARIES

In France a number of developments have been carried out by certain cities and regions in connection with local and regional studies; these include developments in cataloguing and indexing, regional bibliographies, and preservation and restoration. Niort Municipal Library, for example, which has a Centre for Cultural Action housing the collections of over 70 local associations, also had a project in hand in 1993 to set up a Centre for Research and Study on Regional Identity, based on a multimedia database covering all the collections in the region.[15]

ACADEMIC AND RESEARCH LIBRARIES

A survey in Nigeria of local history collections in this type of institution was carried out in the late 1990s, and offered suggestions for improving collection development and bibliographic control, staff recruitment and the library school curriculum.[16] In the USA, the Historic New Orleans Collection, a privately-endowed, independent organization, opened its Williams Research Centre in 1996, bringing together varied types of material (previously housed in separate locations) which documents the history of New Orleans, Louisiana and the colonial Gulf South.[17] The Joyo Archive in Mito City, Japan, established to commemorate 60 years of the Joyo Bank, is an important focus for local information. It includes an exhibition hall, art gallery and library, which has material on both local and banking history.[18] For various reasons, some research libraries may hold material related to places elsewhere in the world. For example, the University of Illinois houses the Cavagna collection, covering the local history of Italian cities, institutions, families and so on, primarily in Lombardy and Piedmont.[19]

HISTORICAL SOCIETIES

The importance of American historical societies for local studies – the Chicago Historical Society, for example – has been emphasized by Sturges and Bapty,[20] and they may make significant contributions elsewhere. In Germany, the value of diocesan archives for research and the importance of collaboration with associations for the study of diocesan history have been noted,[21] while, in South Africa, the Simon's Town Historical Society, Cape Province, has been creating an oral and documentary history collection (which is now housed in the town's museum) since 1966, covering aspects of town life and its long association with the Royal Navy.[22]

What this diversity of resource provision, both here and abroad, would seem to indicate is the lack in most instances of a national strategy, which would identify, in the developed world, the local studies responsibilities of libraries at the various tiers of provision, from national to public libraries and, in the developing world, how existing structures can take responsibility for local studies, where public (or other) libraries, if available, are unable to do so. However, such a strategy does not necessarily concern only libraries but could, indeed should, involve other institutions with a view, perhaps, of promoting not only cooperation but, where appropriate, convergence or, more fundamentally, integration.

CONVERGENCE AND INTEGRATION

Arrangements for local archives and their relationship to local studies libraries in public libraries vary around the world, but with some examples of convergence and integration outside the UK in countries such as Germany and Denmark.[23] This trend towards convergence or integration in the UK, exemplified by local studies centres, has been noted in earlier chapters, and is an issue that has evoked debate elsewhere. In Australia, for example, a study concluded (after visits to the Canada and the UK) that an integrated approach to local resource management 'emphasising cooperation between librarians, archivists and record managers is desirable and possible'.[24] In France it has been recognized that there are many overlapping areas (and the potential for competition) between archives, libraries and museums, and that information technology offers new ways of cooperating without renouncing the methods of the three professions.[25]

As noted in Chapter 1, there is a danger that such convergence or integration emphasizes the historical dimension to local studies and may therefore give insufficient attention to other aspects of a locality, such as its contemporary life, environmental issues, modern governance and community information provision. The use of terms such as, 'heritage', 'history archive', or 'record and research' centre, applied to situations of integration or convergence, also suggests a historical approach to community life. Thus, in the absence of a suitable alternative description, a local studies centre has to be shown by its collection, services and activities to mean just that. The inclusion of local museums, with their collections that go beyond the mainly historical, would probably help achieve this end.

PROFESSIONAL EDUCATION

Integration (more so than convergence, where professions may more easily remain distinct) suggests the need for a new kind of professional who can operate in a service with mixed formats, where until now (as separate bodies) there have been differing priorities, and who has more varied knowledge and skills. Leaving aside specialisms, it can be argued that the three professions of librarian, archivist and museum curator have much in common. They have many similar core concerns and challenges, and share skills that differ largely in their application. A unified education programme could be considered, therefore, in order to create a new kind of information professional who can operate in this more unified and complex local studies environment. It is argued that local collections 'should be managed by people who are not only librarians but also have some knowledge of archival and museum sciences'.[26]

Some efforts along these lines, although apparently not especially concerned with the education of local studies staff, have been recorded, particularly in Germany.[27] In Leipzig, three institutions have been replaced by a book and museum science college, which covers museum science, librarianship and bookselling. Since 1998, also in Germany, technical staff can benefit from a unified training programme for archives, information centres, picture agencies and libraries, the qualification replacing the 'library technician' designation. However, whatever their professional description or institutional location, all local studies resource providers must respond to a growing number and variety of users.[28]

A Slovak commentator on the characteristics of local studies staff sees them already as multi-skilled individuals – collecting, processing and delivering documents and information – as well as researchers, publicists and exhibition organizers, and this multi-skilled, flexible approach could be developed further.[29] Continuing education is also an issue of concern and, for volunteers and professional staff alike, has been taken up in the USA by the Ohio Association of Historical Societies and Museums. It offers to teach the professional procedures for collecting, preserving and interpreting history, as well as historical agency administration.[30]

Change, it would seem, is also in the air for associated professions, for in Scandinavia it is reported that in the five Nordic archive services there is a trend towards fewer but more specialist cross-disciplinary staff in restoration work.[31]

There is no doubt that professional education, for curators and archivists, as well as librarians wishing to work in the local studies field, needs to be re-examined to take account of the changes caused by financial constraints, the increasing volume and nature of use, the impact of information technology and the trend towards convergence and integration of the three types of provision. As noted earlier, this may mean creating a new type of professional who is competent to work in this converged or integrated local studies environment. Whether such an individual comes to replace the archivist, curator or local studies librarian or is an additional professional specialist for particular circumstances remains to be debated.

COOPERATION

If convergence or integration in local studies, in terms of both organizations and professional education and training, does not happen on a large scale in the UK, or elsewhere in the world, cooperation between libraries, archives and museums, and with other bodies and organizations (as in the UK NEWSPLAN example), will continue to be of major importance. As some of the following examples show, the potential for cooperation is considerable, and can include work with genealogical societies, and with day centres for the elderly. Grasse, in France, has a municipal library rich in historical and modern collections and has had some joint activities, such as exhibitions and work with schools, with its three local museums. It is recognized that further cooperation between the library and museums could include computerization and joint cataloguing, cultural services to schools and the development of information networks.[32]

A report of a mid-1990s survey of over 100 genealogical societies in Ohio, USA, conducted to determine (amongst other things) their degree of cooperation with libraries, suggested that this was possible: for instance, over collection development, genealogical societies acting as referral sources and, if facilities were shared, for meetings and programmes.[33]

Hasseris branch library in Denmark has been involved in a project to collect, register and present one hundred years' development of the locality. In cooperation with Aalborg's local history archives and a day centre, the project group arranged an exhibition and interviewed the elderly.[34]

Even if convergence and integration occur on any scale to create local studies centres, this is only likely to occur within the local tier of a nation's provision of libraries, archives and museums. There will still be a need, however, for local studies centres to cooperate with other types of local library or museum (academic libraries and independent museums, for example), as well as with bodies such as historical societies. It seems likely also that there will always be a need for cooperation between the tiers of resource provision, especially in the absence of a national strategy that might formalize such cooperation. Networks facilitate cooperation, especially if they are more than just information-sharing. The Canadian Archival Information Network (CAIN) initiative, for example, aims to facilitate access to archives and the documentary heritage of Canada and will include provincial and territorial networks; it has considerable implications for coordination, development and standardization.[35]

CATALOGUING

Cooperation, or the potential for cooperation, is a theme that is also explored in relation to retrospective cataloguing, joint cataloguing (between libraries and museums) and the compilation of union lists. In France, a national library project has seen the catalogues of the heritage and local collections of 26 municipal libraries retrospectively converted, and the catalogues of 30 more libraries began to be added in 1996. Retroconversion demonstrated the need for a radically different approach to accessing these materials.[36] Also cooperation between libraries and museums in France in creating joint catalogues of document collections, using library rules, has also been explored. It is considered technically feasible but, it is suggested, their divergent approaches to bibliographical description create problems. It is proposed that, by libraries moving closer to museum cataloguing practice, cooperation would be facilitated.[37]

In Lower Normandy, France, a cooperative initiative was undertaken in the 1990s to create a union catalogue of regional collections of heritage material in public libraries. The subsequent computerization of the catalogue and its distribution on CD-ROM has been seen to meet the needs of professionals and users alike. An earlier example of this cooperative approach comes from Northern Ireland, where a union list of Irish periodicals was produced by the Local Studies Panel some ten years ago.[38]

Libraries may also benefit from the work carried out by other institutions on the cataloguing of different types of material, such as ephemera in museums, even though the museum's interpretative role, in addition to its access role, means that it requires different cataloguing criteria from those used in libraries. At the Strong Room Museum, Rochester, New York State, a museum classification scheme is used for naming ephemera, a computer software package for description, and authority lists of themes and subjects for interpretation.[39]

These few examples seem to suggest that, in working out new approaches to cataloguing local studies material, whether retrospectively or currently, there may be much to be gained by libraries working with each other and with other institutions.

COLLECTIONS

Considerations of cataloguing lead on to issues related to the materials of the local studies collection and, in particular, the vogue for digitization as a way of improving access and contributing to preservation. The concept of collection management, as described in Chapter 5, is not one that has been embraced by UK public libraries generally, or by their local collections in particular. Such a policy should also be compiled for each local studies collection and staff trained in its implementation.

Taken as a whole, public library local collections form a unique national network that is an important part of a distributed national collection (DNC), although such a DNC is not yet formally recognized in the UK. This approach employs the Australian concept of a DNC, to which local studies collections make a contribution as a cohesive unit, especially as public libraries hold material which the state libraries and national library may not acquire.[40] However, it was recognized in the early 1990s in Australia that intellectual access to the full variety of formats held is generally inadequate and that most collections were not represented on national databases – a National Bibliographic Database (NBD) is the corollary of the DNC. Ryde Library and Information Service, New South Wales, used a hardware and software upgrade of its library management system, however, to automate the description of all its local studies formats using international standards to create shareable records.[41]

This Australian approach is echoed in the more recently formulated British concept of the British National Archive noted in Chapter 1. However, public library local collections are only part of that unique national network of historical and other collections in a wide variety of institutions that, as shown in Chapter 2, can have relevance for local studies. A national strategy, which recognizes and furthers this network of collections, as regards the contribution each institution makes towards a total national collection for local studies, cannot therefore be solely concerned with libraries and could include the provision of records for archives and artefacts in its NBD. A strategy for public and other library local collections must therefore be set in the wider cultural heritage context.

Another approach to collection development, that also involves recognition of the importance of local libraries, is the Library of Congress-sponsored Local Legacies project to document unique traditions for the American Folklore Center. For space reasons, only a selection of the material produced will be acquired by the Library of Congress; the rest, it is hoped, will be housed by local libraries for users and residents.[42]

Alongside such broad national and local collection policy issues, libraries continue to take an interest in oral history material. In Australia, for example, the Rockhampton Biographical Register on the citizens of that Queensland town records background information on the place, as well as carrying out oral history interviews for deposit in the library's collection. The wider purposes of the project are to foster the community's interest in its heritage and to raise awareness of the Central Queensland Collection of local studies material.[43]

A group scheme of guided autobiography for older people operates in the public library in Franklin Lakes, New Jersey, USA, motivated by the desire to expand the library's local history section with the reminiscences of local people.[44] Librarians also need to know about accessing local newspapers on-line and to understand the various models of service, as evidenced by the American experience, that can emerge – from the on-line edition to the special interest guide.[45]

The digitization of photographs,[46] archives,[47] maps[48] and other local material has been reported in a number of European countries, such as Denmark, France, Portugal, Norway and Spain (in addition to UK projects noted in earlier chapters), as well as in the USA.[49] Some American libraries – such as the Carnegie Library, Pittsburgh, Charleston County Library, South Carolina, the State Library of Virginia and Palos Verdes Library District, Southern California – are also mounting images and documents on their websites, creating 'virtual files' of local history. A collaborative collection digitization project in Colorado provides access to its libraries, archives and museums through a website.[50]

Another account of a collaborative library project, to digitize the heritage images of north-east France, includes a report of users' behaviour, analysed in order to measure the improvements brought about by digitization.[51] One public library in Vigo County, Indiana, however, chose to create indexes, such as the Wabash Valley Obituary Index, to its archival resources, and make these available on the Web, rather than digitize materials. Though this approach is not considered ideal, the indexes assist in the searching for and retrieving of documents.[52] The public library of Charlotte and Mecklenburg County, North Carolina also took a different approach when it premiered a CD-ROM history of the area's African–American community: an electronic photograph album from the 1940s to the 1990s.[53]

As in the UK, there is a worldwide interest in the preservation of collections, which digitization assists, but, recognizing in particular the problems of archiving electronic information, there has been a call in Canada for a national strategy, together with a recognition of the importance of training.[54] A preservation initiative in Western Australia by the library and information service has led to a 'Save Our Century Fund' aimed at local history.[55] While Belgium and Canada have plans for preserving cultural materials in times of disaster, this is not the case in the UK or Ireland and so a steering committee has been set up under the auspices of the National Preservation Office.[56]

INFORMATION AND COMMUNICATIONS TECHNOLOGY

Cataloguing and digitization both make use of modern technology, with all the technical and other challenges that this involves. Fortunately, small public libraries in the USA can turn to various organizations, such as the Library of Congress or the Northeast Document Conservation Center, for information and advice on whether to hold their local history collections in print or in digitized formats.[57] Other information technology initiatives include a concern in Australia, through its national library's Pandora Project, for the archiving and preserving of electronic publishing. While not specifically about local studies material, it is nevertheless an issue that local studies staff will need to take into account.[58]

In the USA, as in the UK, the Internet has been used to provide a home page for local history and genealogy (at St Charles City County Library District, Missouri, for example),[59] for making genealogical resources available,[60] and for promoting a sense of community with its multicultural character.[61] Although recognizing the benefits of the World Wide Web, one commentator has raised concerns about the problem of text alteration, the emphasis on secondary sources, and questions of accuracy and legitimacy faced in historical research through its use.[62]

USE AND PROMOTION

A number of case studies cited under other headings have shown a concern for users and the promotion of local studies materials and services. Additional examples can be drawn from the USA, Japan, Australia, Iceland and Poland. A 1994 user study in Saratoga Springs (NY) Public Library, to determine the patterns of use of the local history collection, showed, amongst other things, that users were general patrons looking for personal histories.[63]

The importance of local studies for lifelong learning and its promotion is exemplified in Japan, where study programmes have been developed at the Oita Prefectural Library relating to local social and natural history, with further programmes being considered.[64] Clearly, family history and lifelong learning are important, but on a broader front the government at all levels in Australia is working to create community spirit (considered eroded in recent years), through cultural heritage projects, although the documentary heritage has been neglected in comparison to the built and natural environment.[65] On Iceland's Vestmanna Islands, the museum and regional archives set up a permanent exhibition on the volcanic eruption of 1973. The archive is digitizing its collection of microfilmed parish records, diaries of former residents from Denmark and Canada, and other documents.[66] The county and city public libraries in Kalisz, Poland, in conjunction with a local cable television company, organized a competition which demonstrated the great interest shown by young people in the local history of their area.[67]

TEN YEARS ON

A decade after Sturges and Bapty's description of the international scene, this brief international survey of local studies librarianship continues to confirm the importance of local studies provision in many parts of the world and in particular the significance of public library collections, whether as a local focus or as a wider, regional one. However, it is clear that in many countries, as in the UK, public library collections are only part of a wider national network of library and other resource providers that interested enquirers are able to draw on. Yet, in spite of this national framework of resource providers, local studies collections continue to be viewed perhaps from a local, even parochial aspect, rather than a national or even international one, although there are signs of this changing given the influence of information technology.

This absence of a wider view is perhaps best illustrated by the concerns of UK local studies librarians in the late 1980s and the first half of the 1990s, regarding issues such as cutbacks and increasing demands; guidelines for local studies libraries; researching for enquiries and charging; local government reorganization; local studies centres; specialist staff in smaller authorities; and the too few library schools teaching the subject;[68] and some of these issues, as indicated below, are still live.

THE FUTURE

Given that the public library local studies collection is a special collection, because of the nature of its contents, its staffing and use, it can be argued that, as a research collection, its presence in the public library service is a historical accident. If not located within the public library service, it is suggested that the proper future of the local studies collection lies in a closer association with archive and museums – 'three integral parts of a greater whole'.[69] In the UK, the local studies centre concept, as implied by the foregoing, is well developed but by no means universal, with local studies collections coming together with archival ones under one roof being the most common solution. The inclusion of local museums, which can be the responsibility of a different local authority or an independent institution, is less usual.

Whatever the administrative, professional or other difficulties, the way to provide a coherent, economic, efficient and effective local studies service, however described, would seem to be through convergence of these three elements or, even more radically, integration. As suggested in Chapter 1, the further encouragement of this approach at the local level is one that might be expected from the recently established Re:source, combining as it does now a common concern for museums, libraries and archives. Such a development, if fostered as convergence, where certain benefits are enjoyed but the professions operate 'independently' within the local studies centre, is a possible outcome, and less problematical as far as the professions involved are concerned. More fundamental, and therefore more challenging, is integration, which seeks to minimize the barriers to bringing together archive, museum and library materials. This would require a category of staff, both professional and in support, who would be at ease in such an integrated environment, and would necessitate innovative qualifications to reflect these requirements.

Whether convergence or integration of the library local collections and those of museums and archives takes place on a greater scale than hitherto, cooperation will continue to be of importance in this field. Such cooperation might involve the collection of materials, union catalogues and bibliographies, for example, or the development of working methods, such as guidelines, standards, manuals of practice, databases, research projects, publications and exhibitions.

However, if cooperation takes place which favours, for example, newspapers over ephemera and digitization over integrated database development, some kind of plan and structure is needed to deal with the nation's many 'collective memories' housed locally throughout the UK. Similarly, if externally funded one-off or group local studies projects are not to result in uneven, haphazard and uncoordinated development, whose achievements may be difficult to sustain in the coming years, a more planned, structured and prioritized approach to the subject of such funding needs considering.

Information technology provides a major tool for increased cooperation between libraries and other institutions, as well as a way of helping to bring about the convergence and integration of local studies, archive and museum services. No one can be in any doubt about its potential ability to create the virtual local studies collection, which may rarely necessitate a visit to the site where the originals are stored, or its potential to make the resources of other relevant providers – national libraries, museums and archives, for example – equally accessible. However, note must be taken of the questions raised about the limited life and integrity of electronic information made available in this way.

Unlike other public library collections, local studies materials are, with few exceptions, acquired and preserved for posterity. Thus any contribution on a continuing basis to create electronic finding aids and to digitize local information, photographs, for example, is a cumulative investment in the electronic future of local studies provision. Regrettably, the UK approach to digitization, mainly supported by lottery funding, is an unstructured and wasteful one. Some libraries have expended much valuable time on unsuccessful bids, while others have received funding to enhance electronic access. The end result is uneven development of the application of information technology to local collections and the probable duplication of much developmental work.

The potential of local studies to contribute to lifelong learning, social inclusion and creating a sense of community must be brought into play alongside the more traditional roles of study and research. This involves knowing more about the users of local studies collections, concentrating on particular groups and developing ways of attracting users generally to the collection and its services. Marketing, promotion and publicity are vital tools in these efforts.

The future development of local studies provision, in its broadest sense, as outlined earlier by a discussion of such topics as integrated professional education and the use of information technology, is, in some instances, already under way. But, as with digitization and professional education, there seems to be no overall national plan for these issues, or for the local studies context of which they are part.

The elements of a national plan for local studies and the relevant local institutions must clearly be part of a national plan for the country's cultural heritage, patrimony, collective memory, or whatever it might be called – a plan that recognizes the unique qualities and national importance of each library local studies collection and the contribution that each makes to local, national and international understanding. As with national libraries, archives, museums and galleries, such important local cultural provision should be underpinned by appropriate legislation and funding if collections are to do more than just survive the future and the demands made upon them.

A national plan that would do more than tinker with the existing situation would require a legal framework that codifies the status of local studies collections which, although held locally, must be seen as of national significance; places a duty on local authorities to provide a local studies service, including archive, museums, archaeology and so on, for the use of present and future local people and others; and gives appropriate central government oversight and funding for such collections. Legislation would also be required to devolve, with necessary safeguards, certain copyright privileges (which in the future could cover a range of formats), from national libraries to local studies collections, thus creating a distributed national collection of local information and material in which the collection privileges, duties and responsibilities of individual contributors can be spelt out.

Arising out of the legislation, or dealt with as separate considerations, are further issues such as the following:

- the encouragement of the convergence and, in the long term, the integration of local studies and local archive and museum collections;
- the establishment of new cross-disciplinary qualifications for those who work with library, archive and museum materials;
- the development of local cooperation with family and local history societies, as well as, for example, with branches of national societies concerned with historical and environmental matters;
- the creation of a national strategy for the best use of information and communications technology in the local context, exploring issues such as integrated databases, digitization and the use of the Web, thus helping to make the virtual local studies collection a universal reality;
- a statement as to the core and other services that might be provided related to appropriate guidelines, model policies, standards of staffing, accommodation and so on.

In designing such a plan and the strategy for its implementation, there would clearly be much work to do, involving central government, professional associations and other bodies. The Library Association Local Studies Group, the Society of Archivists and the Museums Association, for example, would need to have a significant input. In a sense this more holistic approach gets back to an earlier concept of museum, archive and library that saw all such materials brought together, whatever the title of the institution responsible for them.

A focus for this work, and one that could exercise a degree of leadership, as well as offer advice and guidance on a variety of policy, practical and technical issues, would seem to be essential. A recasting of the role, duties and services of an upgraded National Preservation Office could provide such a focus.

While the foregoing and the earlier chapters of this work provide some indication of a growing concept of a national UK strategy for local studies libraries, framed to take into account the role and work of museums and archives, no such complete plan has been formulated, although regional and local heritage strategies exist of which local studies provision is a part. While a heritage 'label' would no doubt help the legislative process and future funding of such a plan, it might not be seen as an entirely helpful description, given the aims of local studies provision in libraries. Unfortunately, it may be the only label there is; but, however described, local studies must be about understanding (as much as memory or nostalgia), concerned with the environment (as much as history) and about today's issues as much as with those of yesteryear.

Local studies provision in the UK, it has been suggested, needs to be considered from the local, regional and national viewpoints and contexts. Benefits are also to be gained from an international approach, as many of the issues raised in this chapter would seem to have a relevance elsewhere round the globe. As an

Australian commentator has written: 'it is worthwhile developing international standards and policies to strengthen the local history librarian in the field.'[70] And, one might add, the user and local studies provision as a whole.

NOTES

1   Sturges, P. and Bapty, R. (1991), 'An international view of local studies librarianship', in *Local studies collections: a manual*, vol. 2, edited by M. Dewe, Aldershot: Gower, 16.

2   Dewe, M. (1993), 'Local studies librarianship and libraries in Australia', *Local studies librarian* 12 (1), 2–7.

3   Partridge, J. (2000), 'Local history in Australia: supporting cultural heritage', *Inspel* 34 (1), 31–9.

4   Kappel, J. (1995), 'Local history collections in Hungary: problems and solutions of the current collection development', *Focus on international and comparative librarianship* 26 (3), 153–6.

5   Dewe, M. and Drew, P.R. (1993), 'The collection of printed ephemera in Australia at national, state and local levels', *International information & library review* 25 (2), 123–40.

6   Van De Velde, J. (1999), 'First families 2000: creating and preserving Australian cultural history online', *LASIE* 30 (2), 5–11.

7   Sturges, P. and Bapty, R. (1991), 17.

8   Chao, S.J. (1994), 'The Long Island Division: the genealogical and historical resources at the Queens Borough Public Library', *Urban academic librarian* 9 (1), 46–50.

9   Palmer, J.W. (1997), 'Local history resources in Southern Ontario public libraries: results of a survey', *Feliciter* 43 (1), 32–6.

10 Doek, A. (1993), 'Special collections: the Gooi collection at Hilversum Public Library', (in Dutch), *Bibliotheek en samenleving* 21 (4) April, 140–41; v.d. Walt, J.H. (1993), 'The public library and local history', (in Dutch), *Mousaion* 11 (2), 100–109.

11 Rafales, M.C.M. (1995), 'The Alhambra library and archive', (in Spanish), *Boletin de la Asociacion Andaluza de Bibliotecarios* 11 (40) September, 47–54; Lopez, S.P. and Pardo, J.V. (1992), 'The local collection', (in Spanish), *Boletin de la Asociacion Andaluza de Bibliotecarios* 8 (28), 23–36.

12 Blaszczyk, J. (1997), 'A centre of knowledge about Warsaw – the Varsaviana section', (in Polish), *Bibliotekarz* (5), 25–7.

13 Chen, c.-Y. (1998), 'Public libraries and local documents collections services', *Journal of library and information science* (USA/Taiwan) 24 (1), 94–109.

14 Ronayne, L. (1998), 'The collective memory: local studies resources in the public libraries of the Republic of Ireland', *An leabharlann* 14 (3/4), 120–29.

15 Girard, A. (1993), 'Local and regional studies in French libraries', *Local studies librarian* 12 (2), 2–11; Surget, E. (1993), 'Regional collective memory: the example of Niort', (in French), *Bulletin d'informations de l'Association des Bibliothécaires Français* 160 (3rd quarter), 27–31.

16 Akintunde, S.A. and Adelusi, J.O. (1997), 'A survey of local history collections in Nigerian academic and research libraries', *African journal of library, archives and information science* 7 (2), 151–62.

17 Travis, J. (1996), 'Adaptive reuse of a French Quarter building: a change of address for the Historic New Orleans Collection', *LLA bulletin* 58 (4), 181–5; Arceneaux, P.D. (1997), 'The Historic New Orleans Collection', *College & research libraries news* 58 (11), 766–8.

18 Sakuyama, A. (1995), 'The Joyo archive', (in Japanese), *Toshokan zasshi/Library journal* 89 (11), 922–3.

19 Cardman, E.R. (2000), 'The Cavagna collection: a case study in special collections', *Libraries and culture* 35 (1), 244–50.

20 Sturges and Bapty (1991), 17–18.

21 Ammerich, H. (1998), 'The relationship between associations of diocesan history and diocesan archives' (in German), *Archivar* 5 (1), 71–80.

22   Dilley, C. (1995), 'Building up a history collection: oral and documentary', *Cape librarian* 39 (9) October, 11.

23   Sturges and Bapty (1991), 18–19.

24   Wyatt, M. (1991), 'The management of local studies resources: a total archives approach', *Australasian public libraries and information services* 4 (3), 159–66.

25   René-Bazin, P. (1994), 'Archivists and their partners: specific fields, converging paths', (in French), *Bulletin des bibliothèques de France* 39 (5), 33–9.

26   Goropeusek, B. (1995), 'Local collections, yesterday, today, tomorrow: the development of local studies and collections in Slovenian libraries' (in Slovak), *Knjiznica* 39 (3), 61–79.

27   Plassmann, E. and Seela, T. (1994), 'Library education in Leipzig' (in German), *Zeitschrift für bibliothekswesen und bibliographie* 41 (2) March/April, 229–32; Holste-Flinspach, K. (1998), 'Technical staff for media and information services: a new profession for the entire information sector and its past history from a library science perspective' (in German), *Bibliothek forschung und praxis* 22 (3), 313–24.

28   René-Bazin (1994).

29   Zupanic, S.K., Praznik, V. and Staubar, V. (1997), 'Typical characteristics of the staff in the local studies service', (in Slovak), *Knjiznica* 41 (2/3), 103–21.

30   Britton, J.D. (1996), 'Conduit to history education', *Ohio libraries* 9 (1), 42–3.

31   Fornas, A. (1999), 'Restoration in the Nordic archive services' (in Norwegian), *Nordisk arkivnyt* 44 (1), 25–7.

32   Grasse, M.-C. and Guibert, F. (1999), 'The municipal library of Grasse, what partnership with the museums?' (in French), *Bulletin d'informations de l'Association des Bibliothécaires Français* 182 (1st quarter), 87–91.

33   Litzer, D.S. (1997), 'Library and genealogical society cooperation in developing local genealogical services and collections', *Reference and user services quarterly* 37 (1), 37–51.

34   Larsen, P.D. (1994), 'From village to suburb' (in Danish), *B70 (Bibliotek 70)* (19), 566–7.

35   Houde, M. (1998–9), 'The Canadian Archival Information Network' (in French), *Archives* (Quebec) 20 (1), 45–61.

36   Perrin, G. (1996), 'The retroconversion of the catalogues of municipal libraries: a chronicle of modernization and an outline of an assessment' (in French), *Bulletin des bibliothèques de France* 41 (3), 15–18.

37   Lersche, F. (1999), 'Libraries and museums: are joint catalogues possible?' (in French), *Bulletin d'informations de l'Association des Bibliothécaires Français* 182 (1st quarter), 100–103.

38   Desgranges, S. (1996), 'The old and local stocks of the libraries in Lower Normandy: a union catalogue on CD-ROM' (in French), *Bulletin des bibliothèques de France* 41 (3), 50–53; McAllister, K. (1990), 'Producing a union list – step by step', *Local studies librarian* 9 (2), 8–9.

39   Smith, D.A. (1996), 'Intellectual control of ephemera: a museum's perspective', *Popular culture in libraries* 4 (1), 63–70.

40   Wyatt, M. (1993), 'Accessing Australia's heritage of local resources: distribution or division', *Australian library review* 10 (4), 423–31.

41   Martin, M. and Heath, A. (1994), 'Mainstreaming local studies: integrating and automating access and collection management of local studies material', *Australian public libraries and information services* 7 (1), 29–44.

42   Lamolinara, G. (1999), 'Lauding local legacies', *American libraries* 30 (6), 95–6, 98.

43   Tom, N. (1997), 'Collecting a community's oral history', *Link-up* March, 13–14.

44   Cooke, G.W. (1994), 'Building local history collections through guided autobiography', *American libraries* 25 (9), 825–8. For a South African experience of building collections through oral history, see Dilley (1995).

45   Conhaim, W.W. (1998), 'Linking up to a global network', *Link-up* (USA) 15 (1), 5, 11–12.

46   Bach, M. (1993), 'Electronic storage of photographic picture collection' (in Danish), *B70 (Bibliotek 70)* (21), 697–8; Pavao, L. (1998), 'The photographic archives of the city hall in Lisbon', *International preservation news* (17), 17–19.

47   Herstad, J. (1998), 'A 24 hour archive' (in Norwegian), *Nordisk arkivnyt* 43 (1), 19; Gonzalez, P. (1999), 'Computerization of the Archivo General de Indias: strategies and results, part II', *Microform and imaging review* 28 (1), 13–31.

48   Crotts, J. and Besnard, D. (1994), 'Developing an historical cartographic database for accessing local history', *Western Association of Map Libraries information bulletin* 25 (3), 129–37.

49   Chad, B. (1995), 'Bridging the urban landscape', *Ohio libraries* 8 (3), 13–16; Beagle, D. (1996), 'The virtual city: putting Charleston on the World Wide Web', *Microcomputers for information management* 13 (1), 3–19; Hattery, M. (1997), 'Library of Virginia: old records in new skins', *Information retrieval and library automation* 32 (8), 1–3; Roderick, E., Somaiya, S. and Taylor, J.M. (1997), 'The Library of Virginia digital initiative', *Microform & imaging review* 26 (2), 59–66; Theyer, H. (1999), 'Planning the future of history: making a digital historical resource', *Computers in libraries* 19 (9), 16–18.

50   Allen, N. and Bishoff, L.J. (1999), 'The Colorado Digitization Project', *Colorado libraries* 25 (1), 32–5.

51   Despres-Lonnet, M., Aubry, M. and Briatte, K. (1998), 'The LIB.R.I.S. project: from heritage conservation to user-oriented concerns', *Vine* (107), 8–15.

52   Puacz, J.H. (2000), 'Bringing archives to life on the Web', *Computers in libraries* 20 (2), 32–6.

53   Johnston, S. (1999), 'An African-American album: preserving local history on CD-ROM', *American libraries* 30 (3), 54–6.

54   Turko, K. (1996), 'Preservation activities in Canada: a unifying theme in a decentralised country', *European research libraries cooperation* 6 (2), 117–47.

55   Behrnan, S.T. (1999), 'Australian preservation effort aims $5 million at local history', *American libraries* 30 (3), 26.

56   'Disaster plan' (2000), *Library Association record* 102 (1), 6.

57   Balas, J.L. (2000), 'Original vs. digital', *Computers in libraries* 20 (2), 51–2, 54.

58   Smith, W. (1997), 'The National Library of Australia's Pandora Project', *Libri* 47 (3), 169–79.

59   King, A. (1996), 'Using a homepage to promote a local history and genealogical collection', *Missouri library world* 1 (3), 6–7.

60   Jobe, M.M. (1998), 'What's in a name: from birth to death and in between. Genealogy resources on the Internet', *Colorado libraries* 24 (2), 19–21.

61   Glogoff, L.G. and Glogoff, S. (1998), 'Using the World Wide Web for community outreach: enriching library service to the community', *Internet reference services quarterly* 3 (1), 15–26.

62   Perkins, J.M. (1998), 'Technology and the brave new world of research', *Missouri library world* 3 (3), 8–9.

63   Burns, C.J. (1994), 'User study of the local history collection at the Saratoga Springs (NY) Public Library', *Acquisitions librarian* (11), 111–23.

64   Watanabe, Z. (1996), 'In search of the ideal library: in the age of lifelong learning', (in Japanese), *Toshokan zasshi/Library journal* 90 (9), 711–13.

65   Partridge, J. (2000).

66   Gudmundsdottir, J.B. (1998), 'Permanent exhibition and other activities in the regional archives in Vestmanna Islands, Iceland' (in Danish), *Nordisk arkivnyt* 43 (1), 14–15.

67   Schlender, G. (1997), 'A regional competition – a new route to cooperation with young people' (in Polish), *Poradnik bibliotekarza* (12), 7–9.

68   Jamieson, I. (1992), 'Local studies', in *British librarianship and information work 1986–1990*, vol. 1, edited by D.W. Bromley and A.M. Allott, London: Library Association, 117–31; 'The sharp end before lunch' (1994), *Local studies librarian* 13 (1) 34–7; Jones, A.F. (1995), 'Local studies – the future', *Locscot* 3 (5), 18–21.

69   Fisher, J. (1985), 'Local studies, what art thou?', *SLA news* (186), 5.

70   Partridge, J. (2000), 39.

Index